Pen to Print

A Beginner's Guide to Self-Publishing

E. J. Kitchens

Brier Road Press

Cover design by Megan McCullough

Edited by J.J. Fischer @ www.jjfischer.com

Pen to Print: A Beginner's Guide to Self-Publishing / E.J. Kitchens—1st ed.

Ebook ISBN: 978-1-958167-04-5

Paperback ISBN: 978-1-958167-01-4

To all those who've helped me in my writing journey—thank you

Contents

Part Eight
Getting the Book Ready

Part Nine
Getting the Word Out: The Launch and Beyond

Part Ten
Getting the Book Published and Stocked

Part Eleven
Beyond Ebook and Print

Part Twelve
The End

Part One

Introduction to Self-Publishing

Chapter 1

Introduction

If there are two words that typically come to mind when writers consider self-publishing, they are *freedom* and *overwhelming*. You can publish what you want, when you want, how you want, but there are so many choices to make and details to be thought through that it can feel overwhelming. This guide walks you through the process of self-publishing (also called indie publishing), taking away the fear and uncertainty about what to do and, hopefully, preventing many novice mistakes along the way. This isn't a book about writing a book (especially not writing one in thirty days with the expectation that you can then retire on the profits). It's a book on how to get from a finished manuscript to a professional quality book published on common retailers, including Amazon's Kindle Direct Publishing platform (KDP), Apple Books, Kobo, and others, and how to go about getting into bookstores and libraries.

You may have noticed that this is a pretty hefty guide. It covers a lot of information. Feel free to skim or skip as you wish, as your background and author goals demand. Not everyone needs all of this, and I'll point out the essentials for all authors versus the aspects geared toward those who wish to make a career of self-publishing. If you can, though, read (or skim) it in sequence. There is a method to my madness, and I hope you'll trust me to lead you wisely. Yes, we don't get to formatting your book and uploading files to retailers until deep into this guide, for instance, but there's a reason for that: you do those things late in the publishing process. There's a lot to think about beforehand! Often, I will need to introduce a topic but save the details for later so we don't get bogged down with rabbit trails. Hang in there, we'll get to it. I also provide references for more information at the end of each chapter, and for your convenience, I've prepared a complete list of references and extra resources on my website: https://www.ejkitchens.com/author-resources.

Whether you simply want to publish your memoir and be done or make your living or a side-job out of writing, this guide will help you get started as an indie author. I've been studying the craft of writing, publishing, and marketing for over ten years, have self-published (as of early 2022) seven novels and multiple short stories, earned a certificate in copyediting, been a Book of the Month author four times in an online book club (Fellowship of Fantasy Indie Book Club), and had a book in a subscription book box (Phoenix Crate). My experience is mostly in fantasy fiction, but the essentials of the publishing process are the same as for other genres. I hope my research and experience are of help to you!

———

Before we begin, I want to make an essential clarification about what indie publishing is and isn't. Let's talk a minute about small presses, indie publishing, and vanity or hybrid publishers. These are sometimes all lumped together, in opposition to traditional publishing, but there are important distinctions to be aware of. True indie publishing is where the author finances and is responsible for the edits, cover, formatting, and other expenses related to getting the book published. He or she uploads the book to a retailer, such as Amazon Kindle Direct Publishing or Apple Books, and is paid directly by them. There are no middlemen between store and author. The author is responsible for all marketing and receives all the royalties from the retailers (which might be up to 70% of the retail price, depending on the retailer). Because the author takes care of everything in getting the book out, the author is the publisher. Importantly, they hold all the rights to the book.

With a small press, the press usually handles the cover, editing, and other expenses, and uploads the book to the retailers. They have some rights to the book, including the right to publish it, but which rights they have and for how long those rights are held are determined by the contract. Depending on the publisher, they might also pay the author an advance and do some marketing (the author is still expected to do a lot of this). Once the advance is earned out, then the author gets royalties, as with a larger traditional publisher. An *advance* is an early payment on expected royalties, so the author doesn't get royalties until the amount of royalties exceeds what they've already been given. So small presses are small versions of traditional publishers (like Penguin-Random House): they pay you for the right to publish your book and pay all the expenses of producing said book.

This is a great way to go for some authors; however, not all small presses are the same. Contracts should be looked at carefully and other authors who have published with the press spoken to before a decision is made. Some small presses are just indie authors who've decided to publish others' books along with their own and so may not be professional in their approach. Some fold quickly, and some don't do any long-term marketing of the book and won't fix errors or update the manuscript later. Careful research is essential. You may or may not need an agent to submit to a small press, and you'll certainly want help with the contract, either from a respected literary agent or a lawyer familiar with intellectual property. Many authors publish with small presses or larger traditional publishers in addition to self-publishing and are considered hybrid authors.

Vanity or hybrid presses help authors with edits, the cover, and so on for a fee. The author is paying someone to publish their book for them, or at the least, get it ready to publish. These companies are notorious for scams, bad contracts, and high costs. They often prey upon the author's pride in their work by seeming to want to publish the work for itself rather than purely as a means to get the author to pay them. Be careful of flatterers. Writers Beware, the Alliance of Independent Authors' watchdog page, and similar websites were created to help authors remain aware of scams and bad businesses. Legitimate, high quality publishers are beset with authors trying to get them to publish their books; they are not seeking out books to publish—not unless they are written by huge celebrities—and they do not charge the author anything (or require them to purchase copies of the published book). Publishers pay authors for the rights to publish their books.

There are companies, however, that simply help indie authors get their books ready that are legitimate; Reedsy, Lulu, and BookBaby are three such service companies. I haven't used them, but they seem to check out okay.

———

Now that the necessary clarification of indie publishing is done, let's get started. As you go through this guide, remember that the most important elements of your book's launch into the world—and your entire author career—are a great book, great packaging, a waiting audience, and a next book. Remembering this will help you keep your focus. There are a lot of details, but remembering the goal of them (that is, how they play into those essential elements), and the goal of your writing itself, will light your way.

Toward that end, we'll talk about getting yourself ready to be a published author (you have a lot of decisions to make); how to get your finished manuscript ready to publish (editing); how to schedule your release; marketing; getting the book itself ready (with cover, price, ISBN, and so on); and handling the release itself. We'll talk a bit as well about post-release marketing, scheduling and budgeting, and organization (it's really important to keep track of all your expenses and earnings!).

We'll start with introducing Amazon's Kindle Direct Publishing and going over some important terms, then we'll take a look at an Amazon book page—to see the end goal, so to speak—and what you need to achieve it.

There are no guarantees to riches and fame in indie publishing, or of changing the world with your words, but the writing world is a great place to be, and I hope you find this guide helpful in starting you on your publishing journey.

References and Resources

Alliance of Independent Authors. "The Best Self-Publishing Services. (And the Worst). Rated by ALLi." Accessed March 3, 2022. https://selfpublishingadvice.org/best-self-publishing-services/.

"Book Publishers to Avoid (and Other Shady Author Scams)." August 21, 2019. https://blog.reedsy.com/guide/publishing-companies-to-avoid/.

SFWA. "Writers Beware." Accessed March 3, 2022. https://www.sfwa.org/other-resources/for-authors/writer-beware/.

Strauss, Victoria. "Vanity/Subsidy Publishers." *SFWA*. Accessed March 3, 2022. https://www.sfwa.org/other-resources/for-authors/writer-beware/vanity/.

Chapter 2

Introduction to Amazon and important terms

Indie publishing, like any industry, has its own vocabulary. Many terms are introduced and used throughout this guide, so for ease of use, here is a list of important terms as well as a brief introduction to the biggest player in indie publishing, Amazon.

Amazon is familiar to most of us as an online store that carries just about anything we could possibly want. A number of other companies are associated with it, including Kindle Direct Publishing, Audible, ACX, and Amazon Web Services. Through the development of the e-reader Kindle device and the self-publishing platform Kindle Direct Publishing, Amazon has caused a huge shift in the book industry, making self-publishing relatively easy and profitable.

Amazon uses data from customer searches and purchases to recommend products to customers and place ads. It uses the sales history of products to rank them in its best seller lists. **Amazon algorithms** are the data-driven processes by which Amazon makes these determinations (to recommend and rank products). Amazon generally doesn't reveal the specifics of its algorithms, which aren't static. Given the importance of product placement in searches and ads, understanding the algorithms and how to use them to one's advantage are common subjects of speculation and concern among authors.

Kindle Direct Publishing (KDP)—Amazon's self-publishing platform. It is the means by which indie authors get their books into Amazon's store. Authors often just refer to this platform as Amazon.

Kindle Unlimited (KU)—Amazon's subscription program that allows readers unlimited reading of books enrolled in the program. The author gets books enrolled in KU through the Kindle Select program, but authors generally refer to the program as KU. KU/Kindle Select requires that the author's ebooks be exclusive to Amazon.

Kindle Select—The program by which authors get their books into the reader subscription program. Kindle Unlimited requires ebook exclusivity to Amazon and is usually referred to as KU.

Wide—To sell ebooks or audiobooks in many stores rather than exclusively through Amazon's KU or Audible/ACX platforms is to go wide. So ebooks would be available through retailers such as Apple Books and Kobo.

Audible—An audiobook store associated with Amazon. Authors can get their narrated audiobooks into Audible through distributors ACX and Findaway Voices.

ACX—A marketplace for professional narrators, authors, publishers, and rights holders to connect and create audiobooks. It's an Amazon company and can distribute completed audiobooks to Amazon, Audible, and iTunes.

Findaway Voices—An audiobook distributor connected to Findaway Voices Marketplace, an audiobook creation platform. It can distribute audiobooks to Audible and many other retailers and libraries and is considered the wide alternative to ACX.

IngramSpark—A self-publishing platform known for producing paperbacks and hardbacks. It can get books listed in the catalogues that bookstores and libraries prefer to order from.

Draft2Digital (D2D)—An aggregator, D2D can distribute your ebooks for sale to many retailers, saving you from having to create accounts with each platform. It is used by many wide authors. It is associated with the universal links generator Books2Read.

Universal link—A link to a page that contains links to all the stores a book is available in and which sets the stores to the searcher's country.

Smashwords—An aggregator, it can distribute your ebooks for sale to many retailers, saving you from having to create accounts with each platform. It is used by many wide authors. It has its own storefront.

Pre-order—Your book is listed for sale and can be ordered before the release date, though it won't be delivered until the release date.

Beta-reader—A reader or another author who reads a rough draft of a manuscript to provide big-picture feedback. The book may or may not change much between the beta-read and the final, published draft.

Advance Reader Copy (ARC)—A pre-release copy of a book that is very similar to the finished version. It is given out for review purposes. This is not a beta-reader copy.

Book promotion service—A company that sends out email newsletters to its subscribers to alert them to books that are on sale or free. BookBub is one such service.

Reader magnet—A short work given away for free to encourage readers to subscribe to your email newsletter.

Trim size—The dimensions of a print book. Common trim sizes include 6 x 9 and 5.5 x 8.5 inches.

Chapter 3

Retail book page overview

When you're working a puzzle, you always start by finding the border pieces, don't you? Okay, that was something of a trick question, because I imagine the first thing you really do is look at the box lid to study the image you're going to make by putting all the puzzle pieces together. That's what we're doing in this section. We're looking at an Amazon Product Detail Page because it will show us the final product (from the potential buyer's point of view) and will allow me to point out some things you may not have thought about.

So take a moment to go to Amazon or your favorite online book retailer and study a few book pages. Choose famous books and books by indie authors in your target market, both with and without lots of reviews. Try looking at some of the recommended books or sponsored books. The latter are book ads that authors have set up through Amazon Ads. They will show up in search results and in the recommended books and are easily recognized by the "Sponsored" tag above them.

If you have an ad blocker, you might want to turn it off briefly for Amazon to allow you to see the ads/sponsored books. Ads are targeted to certain reader search terms or books based on keywords set by the authors who create the sponsored product ads. Amazon uses these keywords to decide what sponsored books to place in which search results and on which product pages. Seeing the ads helps you get a feel for the authors Amazon thinks you might like based on your buying and browsing habits. These authors might be ones with books that are comparable to yours or authors your fans might be reading, though not all advertising is on-target. Understanding the market, the books like yours, and the books your fans read, is essential for successful marketing. And it might help you find more books you'd enjoy!

So take a look at a few retail book pages and notice these things:

- Cover
- Look Inside Feature
- Book title, subtitle (if applicable), series (if applicable)
- Price
- Available on Kindle Unlimited or not
- Formats (ebook, print, audiobook)
- Follow the Author: Author name and bio and option to follow the author
- Book description (back cover copy)
- Reviews
- Age range
- Length of the books
- Books in the series
- Publication date
- Product details, including ISBN or ASIN, publisher and publication date, and language
- Best Sellers Rank in various categories
- Editorial Reviews (optional—an author must add this information through Amazon Author Central)
- A+ Content (optional, not common among authors)
- Sponsored Ads
- Recommended for You
- Products Related to This Product (Sponsored Products)
- Customer Reviews

Amazon periodically changes the name of the carousels of books on its product pages, from Also Bought to Recommended for You, and so on. These may not match what's mentioned here.

A note about Editorial Reviews and A+ Content. These are optional and are added through your Author Central account (explained later) and your author dashboard, respectively.

Editorial reviews are for professional reviews (Library Journal, Kirkus, other authors, or book bloggers). These are not for "normal" readers, whose reviews go into the customer review section.

A+ Content, which is separate from the Editorial Reviews, is a new feature for book pages (it's been on other product pages for a while). It can hold images, text, and tables. You don't have to use this section, but if the idea appeals to you, look around at book pages and see what's there that you like, don't like, and find helpful or not. You don't want to distract the reader, so remember to consider them when deciding on this section.

————

Now that we have an idea of the finished product, which goes beyond just a book and cover, let's talk about getting yourself ready to be a published author. You'll be making several decisions in this section that will show up in your book's product page, including author name, imprint, and formats.

Part Two

Getting Yourself Ready

Chapter 4

Getting yourself ready

There are many decisions to make before you publish your book, including your author name, which retailers you will use, what formats you will be creating, how much money you will spend, and how long the process will take. We'll talk briefly about some of the major decisions and how to organize yourself to make things easier before we move on to getting your manuscript ready.

The most important decision to make, though, is what you expect to get out of indie publishing. Is this a onetime thing to get your memoirs published for your kids? A fun hobby, where you'll publish a few books at a leisurely pace, not caring about cost and profit? Or is this something you intend to pursue as a major, or perhaps sole, source of income?

There's a certain expectation that indie publishing is an easy way to get money and retire in style. This is often promoted by the rare breakout author and especially by those who earn money training authors. Most authors do not make a living on their writing or make much, if any, profit over their expenses. So even if you can name ten high-earning indie authors, there are thousands who aren't high-earning and whom you can't name. For a good grounding, go to a bookstore and look around or note the number of books on the Kindle store. How many of those books have you read? How many authors can you name? How many of those authors that you can name would also be named by five of your friends? Authors are part of a large team of entertainers and educators, and we need to be okay with that instead of assuming we'll somehow become a household name and be wealthy if we publish a book.

Take it from someone who's been in the indie publishing world for over ten years and has met or followed dozens of authors—it's not a guarantee of easy money or fame. It takes money to produce quality books, and there is no guarantee the book or books will sell enough to pay you back for your expenses, much less buy that condo you've been wishing for, or allow you to quit your day job and write full time. Some authors really do make six figures. They are marketing savvy, write fast, and have a team helping them. Some of these also suffer major burnout and have to quit, slow down, or simply lose their love for their work.

Know going in that writing, like any business, is hard work and brings a lot of uncertainty and challenges. But it also brings opportunities, so if it's your passion, don't get discouraged. I just want you to have a clear view of what you're getting into.

And as a sidenote, I recently heard some full-time authors and an author coach lamenting the idea that if you want to be an author, you must be a full-time author. This is great for some, but for others, it's actually bad for them and their writing careers. Some personality types need the structure and social interactions of a full- or part-time job. They write better and more consistently when life only allows them an hour a day to devote to writing. Others write better when not under the pressure to pay all the bills from their writing income (and I mean *all* the bills, because if you're full-time, you're responsible for self-employment taxes, retirement, and insurance). That pressure and the uncertain nature of the industry—your earnings might tank for seemingly no reason at all or because a change in policy ruined the advertising you were relying on etc.—might ruin your love of writing and make writing a chore. So don't rush into writing as a full-time career until you know it fits your personality and can supply your financial needs.

Writing, as is often stated, is a business, and successful authors treat it as such. This means dedication to learning the craft, marketing, and a disciplined approach to your time and resources. It means creating goals and strategies and changing them as needed. So as you read through this guide, think about what you want from your writing. Jot down your goals, a time by which you want to achieve them, and then add in actionable steps to help you do so. Also, create another sheet with all the decisions you'll be making throughout the book, beginning with your author name.

Chapter 5

Author name

Have you ever dreamed of having a pen name? A sobriquet you keep secret so no one will know about those scandalous romance novels or inflammatory exposés you've been writing? No? Well, maybe that's only a useful plot device in movies. You may think using a pseudonym is a form of lying. You may have never thought about it. Either way, using your full name, initials, or a pen name for your books is an important decision you will want to take a little while to consider and research.

Whether you value the privacy of a pen name or the transparency of using your real name, there are several factors to consider before making that decision. We'll discuss four here: privacy, branding, uniqueness and ease of remembering, and complications of using a pen name.

Privacy

Using your whole name or first and last name will bring a certain amount of exposure to you and your family. I originally used my full name (first, middle, and last), but when I began getting "I love you" comments from strangers on my Facebook author page profile photo, I changed to my initials. The comments stopped.

Depending on how unique your name is and how much information you put in your biography or newsletter, it could be easy to find personal information on you. That doesn't mean anything bad will happen, but it's something to consider. You should also consider how your writing will affect other aspects of your life. Will the views expressed in your books cause issues at your work? Or will using your name help with your business, as it might establish you as an expert in your field?

If you want to use your name but desire greater privacy, consider following in the tradition of many great authors and use your initials.

If you fear using a pseudonym is lying, know that using a pen name is an established and legal way of publishing, so it is not lying. It is for privacy or branding. Many actors use stage names for branding purposes or to escape a difficult-to-spell name. Beloved actor Cary Grant's real name was Archibald Leach, which didn't fit his onscreen persona at all. So there are reasons to use a pen name beyond privacy. Know that when you set up your author account with booksellers, you generally use your real name; it's only the readers who see the pen name. You're not creating a whole fake persona. Retailers, book promotion services, registration at conferences: they all ask for your real name and your pen name, if they're different.

Branding

Like it or not, most of your earnings are likely to come from ebooks and online retailers. Consequently, you want your books to be easily found online. Thus, what shows up when someone searches for your name online is a major consideration. Is it easily searchable? Does it come with a certain expectation? (Like kitchen products for a last name like Kitchens?) Does the name fit a different genre than the one you write in, like a romance or military science fiction? Your author name is part of your branding. A name like "Kitty Hearts" may be great for contemporary romance, but it doesn't have the right ring for epic fantasy. Is your name similar to another author's or a famous individual? You might think that's a good thing, but in reality, it creates confusion and will make you (as the lesser known of the two) harder to find in the search results.

Using professional degrees is another issue. That doctorate may be useful for certain genres—nonfiction on a particular topic, medical romance, hard sci-fi, or suspense—but harmful in others. Ascribing Dr. So-and-so to your fantasy novel or historical romance probably isn't going to help and may turn readers off, as they might be afraid it will be too technical or may consider you a show-off.

Be honest, of course, if you choose a pen name. Don't use fake degrees or falsify other credentials. And think twice about doing a gender swap because you think it will increase the chances of your book being bought. A man who writes romance under a feminine name and is found out might get in trouble with readers who thought they were reading books by a woman. They now feel deceived. They may or may not have a problem reading romances written by a man, but they don't want to be lied to. A woman writing fantasy under a man's name will face the same issue. Using initials is likely a better choice in such a circumstance.

Two people writing under one pen name is a different issue and is well-established (Alexandre Dumas of *The Count of Monte Cristo* fame had an unnamed writing partner). However, if the partnership breaks up, or if there's a swap in authors, there could be conflict about what happens to that name and the fans of those books. This issue would need to be addressed along with the other details of the partnership.

What about using both a pen name and a real name? Many authors write in different genres and use both their real name and a pen name, or multiple pen names, to keep their audiences separate. One author might write fantasy under her real name and write contemporary romance under a pen name. Separate newsletters and marketing strategies are employed. The different names are helpful to the author and to the readers, who may not care about the other genre. They don't want to be disappointed when their favorite fantasy author releases a new book and it turns out to be a romance.

Regarding writing in multiple genres, another thing to consider is the Amazon algorithms. Their book retail pages have a "Recommended for You" section to let potential customers know what other customers interested in this product also purchased, or what the store thinks they'd be interested in based on their own browsing history. If you publish both romance and fantasy under the same name, people who come to your fantasy book pages and who aren't into romance may be shown a lot of romances, because the people who bought your romance novel went and bought other romance books instead of other fantasy books. Your fantasy readers may assume there's a lot more romance in the story than the blurb indicates and go look for other books with fantasy stories in the "Recommended for You" section. (This was discussed on the *Six Figure Authors Podcast* a few times as it happened to one of the hosts.)

Uniqueness and ease of remembering

Will readers remember your name or be able to spell it? When you meet someone and they find out you are an author and want to look up your books, how easy will it be for them to remember or spell your name? Or for a reader to share it with another reader?

Are there other authors or celebrity individuals with your name with whom you might be confused? You might think it a good thing to share a name, or have a similar name, to a celebrity, but it's not where search engines are concerned: when someone searches your name, the books or websites for the celebrity will show, and you will be lost on page 10. You also do not want to share a name with an author who writes in a genre your readers might find offensive. If you write clean romance, but there is an erotica author with your same name, this might cause some confusion for your readers!

Sharing a name with a celebrity or another author isn't ideal, but sometimes it can't be avoided: someone might become famous or start writing after you've been published. If that happens, don't panic. For ungainly names or too-similar names, remember that people can still search for your book titles. And for in-person interactions, a bookmark with your book, title, author name, and website will help.

Complications of using a pen name

Managing a pen name adds complications, as you will have author connections and personal connections who know you by your real name whom you must inform that your books are under another name. If you publish under more than one name (multiple pen names), things get more even complicated because you have multiple email addresses, fan bases, and newsletters to keep up with. Also, consider whether you'll be comfortable signing books using the pen name or being called by that name at events.

If you use a pen name, as with your real name, it's recommended that you buy the domain name for that name. You might also want to file a Fictitious Business Name Statement (FBN statement) if you are planning to get payments to that name. However, if you have your author account for your book retailers (that is, Amazon, Apple Books, and so on) set up in your real name, you can simply list your pen name in the author box on the book setup page and not have to worry about this, as the payments are going to your real name.

Your copyright notice should be in your pen name or both pen name and real name. Register your copyright under both pen name and real name for extra protection, as it might be difficult to prove the pen name is you in case of a lawsuit if you only registered with your pen name. We'll talk more about copyright later.

———

When considering your author name, consider privacy, the benefit of using your own name versus a pen name, and the uniqueness yet ease-of-remembering of your author name. Do some internet research on your name and any potential pen names to get an idea of what will come up in a search. You need your author website and books to be easily found.

References and Resources

Sedwick, Helen. *Self-Publisher's Legal Handbook*, 2nd edition. Ten Gallon Press, 2017.

Six Figure Authors Podcast. Episode 122, "When Pen Names Make Sense and How to Rock Them." March 3, 2022. https://6figureauthors.com/podcast/all-things-pen-names/.

Chapter 6

Imprint name

As an indie author, you are responsible for the editing, cover, formatting, marketing, etc. of your story. You hold the copyright and can put it up for sale on retailers. In other words, you are acting like a publisher, just only for your own books.

In the Product Details section of a KDP book page, you see the publisher listed. When you set up your book page, you can provide the publisher name for your book. If you leave this blank, nothing will show there. Do not list Kindle Direct Publishing or Amazon. They are not a publisher. They are a self-publishing platform, and they make this very clear in their terms. You are the publisher. You can make up a name for your publishing company and provide that if you want, and many of us do, or leave this blank. For indie publishing, this publisher name is generally considered your imprint and vice versa. As a sidenote, Amazon does act as a publisher with multiple imprints but in a more traditional publishing way—this is completely separate from KDP.

It would be good to do a little internet research on your publisher name before you choose it. You don't want to use a traditional publisher's name or a name that might be confused with a famous brand (such as Starbucks), a trademarked name, or a name used by someone in your county. Also, don't use *corp.*, *corporation*, or *inc.* unless you actually set up a corporation.

You can, but don't have to, get a publishing logo designed to put on your book's title page and spine. It's a matter of budget, time, and preference. You can also come back and do this later, if you want. This is probably the best course of action, as it gives you time to decide on your brand. Many authors end up discovering they write best in a different genre than they first thought.

Also, you don't have to set up a business in order to publish or use your own publishing name. Once you publish, you are in business and have a sole proprietorship (depending on your state, you might then need a business license or a fictitious business name statement, but you don't have to get permission from the government to be a sole proprietor). Helen Sedwick, in her book *Self-Publisher's Legal Handbook*, recommends you name your author business. This will be your company name and your publishing imprint name. She writes Westerns and uses "Ten Gallon Press" as her company name. This is her imprint and is listed as her publisher. My imprint name is Brier Road Press.

References and Resources

Amazon KDP. "Metadata Guidelines for Books." Accessed April 6, 2022. https://kdp.amazon.com/en_US/help/topic/ G201097560#publisher.

Fishman, Stephen J.D. *Working for Yourself: Law and Taxes for Independent Contractors, Freelancers & Gig Workers of All Types,* 12th edition. NOLO, 2022.

Sedwick, Helen. *Self-Publisher's Legal Handbook,* 2nd edition. Ten Gallon Press, 2017.

TurboTax. "Tax Tips for Freelance Writers and Self-Published Authors." Accessed March 21, 2022. https://turbotax.intuit.com/tax-tips/self-employment-taxes/tax-tips-for-freelance-writers-and-self-published-authors/L1v0lGVru.

U.S. Small Business Administration. "Choose a Business Structure." Accessed March 21, 2022. https://www.sba.gov/business-guide/launch-your-business/choose-business-structure.

U.S. Small Business Administration. "Find Local Assistance." Accessed March 21, 2022. https://www.sba.gov/local-assistance/find.

Chapter 7

Writing as a business

You'll hear a lot that writing is a business (you heard it here too!) and that if you want to be successful, you must treat it as such. Part of this mindset is keeping a close record of all your expenses for tax purposes, and so you can determine if what you're spending money on is worth it or not. Ask yourself if you're turning a profit. Also like a proper business, you'll have to resist the urge to spend all the money you have coming in, remembering that some of it will need to be put aside for taxes and some for the writing business itself—for edits, covers, marketing, etc. This is just like any business. You need to develop a plan for how much to spend to get the business started and how much of the earnings to reinvest in the business, to save, to put aside for taxes (about a third is a common estimate), and to pay yourself with. You need to regularly evaluate and see what marketing strategies are working to sell your books and what books or series are earning the most. There are no guarantees on a profit, so look carefully at your budget. Do the same with your time.

Whoa, what? I only wanna publish my memoirs! you say. I only want to tell great stories!

Right. But you're still a business; a very small one, but still a business. If you don't publish a lot and don't earn a lot, things are still fairly simple for you. Don't worry. If you achieve great success, things get more complicated. But it will be worth it!

This area of the writing life—business and taxes and such—is an area where I'm going to send you off to do research and soul-searching on your own, as your location and circumstances affect what your plan will look like. I'll only mention a few points, then share some resources and references. I am not a tax professional or a business expert; I am just sharing what I have learned and heard and read.

1. If you're in the US, you'll get a 1099-MISC each year from retailers showing your earnings. You'll need to include these in your tax reporting. You'll also need your expense records, other sales, and print stock (inventory) information *if* you're planning to take deductions. You don't have claims deductions, so don't worry if that sounds like too much of a hassle. Before you try to take deductions, make sure you can.

2. Once you start selling things—that is, you go into business—you have a sole proprietorship. Depending on your state, you might need to get a business license or file a fictitious business name statement. You can, if you choose, set up a company, such as a Limited Liability Company (LLC). Some recommend this; others say it's generally not worth the hassle and expense and that it doesn't really protect your personal property in case of a lawsuit. You can purchase insurance instead. Look into what is best for you.

3. If you plan to sell books direct either in person or through your website, you'll need to find out about the tax laws for your city, county, and state. You may need to collect and remit sales taxes. You may need a license.

4. Talk to a tax professional about whether you will need to pay self-employment taxes on your writing income.

5. If you pay someone, such as a cover designer or editor, more than $600 over the course of a year *by check, direct deposit to his or her bank, or cash,* you should file a Form 1099-NEC for them by February 1 of the

following your with the IRS, the state tax office (if the state has income tax), and send it to him or her. However, if you paid *by credit card, debit card, or by using a third-party settlement organization (like PayPal or Stripe)*, you do *not* need to file a 1099-NEC. The same is true for those hired through online platforms like Upwork and Fiverr. Most editors and cover designers request payment through PayPal, meaning you do not need to file a Form 1099-NEC for them.

––––––

Curious about sales taxes and selling direct, I spoke with an accountant who works for my state (Alabama) about it. Here is a summary of what he said regarding me collecting sales tax for online and in-person sales.

> I live in Alabama and so I charge Alabama sales tax on other people living in Alabama. I'd have to go over a minimum economic threshold to charge tax on out-of-state purchasers. So no tax on Georgia folks unless I sell a ton of books in Georgia.

> If I sell to someone in the same city or county as the one I am in residence in, I would have to charge them city or county tax too. If I travel, I charge taxes for wherever I travel.

> If I lived in the City of Birmingham in Jefferson County in the State of Alabama, I would need to set up state, city, and county tax licenses and file each monthly, regardless of sales.

> If I went to Montgomery or another city for a live event, I would need to collect city, county, and state taxes and file using a One Time form. There is no fee in Alabama to set up a license. It just takes time each month to file returns. Shipping carriers and physical delivery of products adds another dimension.

> *But what about selling non-physical products, such as audiobooks or ebooks? No actual shipping or physical product?*

It may vary by state, but in Alabama, the State looks at the digital items as if the person "owns" them and can download them, print them or put them on CDs etc. and so they are taxable. However, they don't consider a subscription to an online portal to view specific items, such as a course, as taxable. Customers have no digital rights to the course, so no sales taxes are collected.

———

Ready to give up yet? Don't. You can work through all the hoops and learn everything you need to know. It just takes time. Retailers like Amazon handle sales tax for you, so this is only for direct sales, which we'll talk about more in its own section later. If you have questions about taxes, contact the tax people for your location; they'd love to help you. You can also talk to your accountant or consider some of the various apps built to help, such as TaxJar.

———

In conclusion, writing is a business, so making a plan and figuring out now how much to spend on it and how to handle your revenues is essential. There's no guarantee of any return on your investment, much less a good one or a fast one. Don't go into debt to publish or market. That said, there are plenty of people who do make money from self-publishing. It may be $100 a year or $100 a day, but work hard and work smart and don't give up, because it's possible to have a fulfilling and profitable indie author hobby or career.

References and Resources

Amazon KDP. "Tax Information." Accessed March 24, 2022. https://kdp.amazon.com/en_US/help/topic/G201723290.

Fishman, Stephen J.D. *Working for Yourself: Law and Taxes for Inde-*

pendent Contractors, Freelancers & Gig Workers of All Types, 12th edition. NOLO, 2022.

Penn, Joanna. *Business for Authors. How to be an Author Entrepreneur* (Books for Writers Book 5). Curl Up Press, 2014.

Penn, Joanna. *How to Make a Living with Your Writing: Turn Your Words into Multiple Streams of Income* (Books for Writers Book 3). Curl Up Press, 2021.

Penn, Joanna. *Your Author Business Plan: Take Your Author Career to the Next Level* (Books for Writers Book 12). Curl Up Press, 2020.

Sedwick, Helen. *Self-Publisher's Legal Handbook,* 2nd edition. Ten Gallon Press, 2017.

TaxJar. https://www.taxjar.com.

If you live in Alabama, these might be helpful: https://www.myalabamataxes.alabama.gov/_/; https://www.alabamainteractive.org/ador_taxrate_lookup/welcome.action; https://revenue.alabama.gov/taxpayer-advocacy/b-e-s-t-seminars/.

Chapter 8

Copyright, intellectual property, and piracy

Please note, I am not a lawyer. This information is drawn from a study of several sources, but particularly from author and lawyer Helen Sedwick's *Self-Publisher's Legal Handbook,* which I highly recommend. I am not giving legal advice. Now that the disclaimer has been given, let's continue.

Copyright and intellectual property

Copyright is a type of intellectual property (IP), which is property not fashioned by the skill of the hands but through the creative abilities of the mind. Because it is a form of property, it can be sold, assigned, licensed, given away, and left to heirs. And because you are the owner of that property—the copyright holder—you have the right over making "copies" of it. You have the exclusive right to reproduce it (as in, make copies of it in books) and reproduce it in other formats (ebook and audio, for instance). You can sell it, distribute it, and use it for commercial purposes. You can make derivative works (translations, sequels, courses, plays, apps, and video games, for instance). You can earn money by granting others the right to perform, translate, turn into a movie, etc. your work.

Earning money from your intellectual property beyond simply selling the original book is a big focus of some authorpreneurs, and if you're interested, check out the references below from Joanna Penn, an author and entrepreneur known for encouraging authors to fully utilize their IP and diversify their income.

Understand, though, that your right is to the content, the intellectual property, not to any physical products. Someone who buys a copy of your book owns the physical copy and can mark it up, sell it, burn it, or give it away. What they don't have the right to do is to reprint the work, make a translation, make it into a film, and so on.

That means you can't type up someone else's book, slap it up on Amazon, and make money from it. Unless it's out of copyright, of course, and more books are aging out of copyright every year. Note that I said *aging out* of copyright. I didn't say "didn't have 'copyrighted by [author name]' on every page."

You don't need "copyrighted by" or the copyright symbol on every page of your work. Do this and you'll look paranoid, and it won't stop criminals. Since 1977, copyright attaches to your work automatically. You don't have to mark it with the copyright symbol, publish it, or register it to get a copyright. Simply by putting your original creation into a fixed form, be it napkin or notebook or computer file, you own the copyright.

Book titles, however, are not protected by copyright, so someone else may use the same book title as yours (likely unknowingly). However, some titles or series are trademarked, so do your research. Don't write a "For Dummies" book, for instance, as that is trademarked (don't mimic their cover design either). Famous titles may also be trademarked. So scrap that "Harry Potter and the Barber of Seville" idea.

Ideas, plot lines, and themes are also not copyrighted. As Solomon said, "There is nothing new under the sun" (Ecclesiastes 1:9). Just because someone else has a similar novel to yours doesn't mean they stole your idea; they have probably never heard of you and simply had the same idea. It's much more likely they read the same books and watched the same movies, thus getting the same inspiration.

Note that lyrics are covered by copyright law (they are creative content), so you have to be careful about using lyrics in your books (unless you wrote the lyrics, of course, and haven't sold the rights). You can obtain permission to use lyrics, but this may cost money.

The copyright of characters and settings, and fanfiction, gets complicated, but know that the characters and settings you create are copyrighted to you as part of your intellectual property. That means the characters and worlds of other creators are theirs, and you can't use them willy-nilly.

If you write nonfiction, or nonfiction thinly veiled as fiction, and include information that the people being written about might object to or consider slanderous, for instance, you need to do more research about the legal issues involved and consider liability insurance. If you're concerned about any of this, or any copyright issues, please do more research. I'm mainly trying to help you figure out the "what you don't know, you don't know" side of self-publishing.

Back to the copyright of your book. You can register your copyright with the United States Copyright Office, but you don't have to. It's additional time and money, but it is still considered a good idea, and should be done within three months of publication. Having a registered copyright increases what you get for damages in an infringement action (when you sue someone for infringing on your copyright) and makes you look more professional.

To register a copyright, go to the appropriate copyright office website. For the US, that's the United States Copyright Office website: https://www.copyright.gov. The page for registering literary works is: https://www.copyright.gov/registration/literary-works/. You will need to create an account, register the work, pay a filing fee, and submit a copy of the work. There are many tutorials on their site to walk you through the process. Fees vary, but the standard fee for electronic filing for one author and a single work is $45.

Piracy

Let's take a moment to take about piracy, which is when someone takes your work and puts it up for free or for sale without your permission. These free copies would be "bootleg" copies. This is an infringement on your copyright since someone is publishing (making copies available) of your work without your permission. Some authors say piracy is inevitable and not to worry about it, that it actually serves as free marketing: some who read the pirated version may buy your other works or tell friends who employ legal methods to access their entertainment. That while it's violation of your rights, at least people are reading your work. Other authors tell horror stories of having their Amazon account shut down because overzealous Amazon bots found their book on pirate websites in violation of their Kindle Select terms (the author side of the Kindle Unlimited program), which state they must be exclusive to Amazon for ebooks. Others say Amazon sends them a warning, giving them time to take down the illegal copies. This usually only requires a little time and a few emails; no lawyers required.

How do you know if your book has been pirated (before Amazon tells you)? How do you protect yourself from piracy, and what do you do about a pirated book?

As for spotting pirates, you'd do what any captain of old would: post a lookout. In these times, that means setting up an alert with a free service like Google Alerts (https://www.google.com/alerts). Provide them with a couple of unique lines from your book, and they will notify you if the text appears online. Just make sure the alert is for a pirated book and not a review before jumping into action. But even if it appears that your book has been pirated, be careful about searching it out on pirate websites. Websites offering cheap or free PDFs or other ebook files are often scams downloading malware to visitors' computers or stealing their credit card numbers. People who use those sites are unlikely to buy books anyway (so you're not losing a customer here), and it might not be a good idea for you to go hunting for your book there and end up with malware yourself. The sites may not actually have your book, but may only be using the title as bait for their own nefarious plan against the sort of people who seek out bootleg copies.

As for protecting yourself, there is no surefire way to do this. Worrying about it or refusing to publish because of it are not the way to go. If your book is not worth the risk of piracy, then it's not worth publishing. What you can do, however, is deal with the issue if, or when, it arises. To do this, it's best if you've registered your book's copyright. If you send Advance Reader Copies (discussed later) as ebooks, consider using a service like BookFunnel to deliver them. They can include a digital watermark in the ebook and track who downloads it. Since the watermark can be traced back to the downloader, it might prevent someone from uploading it on a pirate site, or allow the offender to be traced and blocked from receiving further ARC copies.

If you discover your work has been pirated, email the pirate site and ask that the material be taken down. You don't have to threaten. Just state that you are the copyright holder and that the material is posted illegally and must be taken down. Some will comply. If they don't, then you can send a DMCA takedown notice (DMCA refers to the Digital Millennium Copyright Act). If that doesn't work, there are other steps you can take, including using WhoIs (http://www.whois.com/whois/) to find out who their website host and domain registrar is and report the piracy website to them (if they're legitimate companies, they don't want to be associated with piracy sites). You can also report the site to search engines and request they not show the offending sites in search results.

If material is posted on, or being advertised through, social media sites, or even on a retailer (say someone put your book for sale on Apple Books), you can contact those sites for help. They have online forms for reporting infringement and sending takedown notices.

Before you take any action, however, be sure that this is actual piracy, and ask whether it is worth your time to deal with. Justice is justice, but time cannot be regained. Are a few sales worth it? If you're in KU and Amazon finds pirated copies, then you definitely need to take action.

If you want to do something to prevent piracy for the sake of yourself and all creatives, educate your family (especially any teens and college kids), friends, and readers about it. Some don't understand what it means when they are downloading those free or cheap books off pirate sites rather than buying from legitimate retailers. Others think this is only a "small" thing and shouldn't matter (they really want it, after all!). I suspect this blasé about the theft of creative works (be it books, art, movies, or music) is due in part to the false idea that movie stars, artists, and authors are all filthy rich. Even if this were the case, that doesn't justify the act, nor does it take into account all the people involved in the process (the booksellers, the cameramen, and so on) who are paid through those products. The library is always an option for those who want free.

———

That's all about copyright until we reach the chapter on your book's copyright page. I do want to reiterate that your intellectual property is property that can be left to heirs, so be sure to consider that in your estate planning, as well as to leave details regarding the location of your retailer account information and final book files.

Now, we're off to talk about book formats: ebook, paperback, hardback, and audiobook.

REFERENCES AND RESOURCES

Chesson, Dave. "Ebook Piracy [2022] – What to Do If Someone Steals Your Book." *Kindlepreneur.* Accessed March 24, 2022. https://kindlepreneur.com/ebook-piracy/.

DMCA. "What Is a DMCA Takedown?" Accessed March 30, 2022. https://www.dmca.com/FAQ/What-is-a-DMCA-Takedown.

Penn, Joanna. "3 Reasons Authors Shouldn't Worry about Piracy but How to Protect Yourself Anyway." *Jerry Jenkins.* Accessed March 30, 2022. https://jerryjenkins.com/3-reasons-authors-shouldnt-worry-piracy-protect-anyway/.

Penn, Joanna. "Intellectual Property Rights." *The Creative Penn.* https://www.thecreativepenn.com/tag/intellectual-property-rights/.

Sedwick, Helen. "A Step-by-Step Guide to Dealing with Content Theft." *The Book Designer.* February 27, 2015. https://www.thebookdesigner.com/a-step-by-step-guide-to-dealing-with-content-theft/.

Sedwick, Helen. *Self-Publisher's Legal Handbook,* 2nd edition. Ten Gallon Press, 2017.

Six Figure Authors Podcast. "SFA 081 - Selling Foreign Rights and Pitching at Book Fairs with Judith Anderle." March 11, 2021. https://6figureauthors.com/podcast/selling-foreign-rights-and-pitching-at-book-fairs/.

US Copyright Office. https://www.copyright.gov.

US Copyright Office. "Registration of literary works." https://www.copyright.gov/registration/literary-works/.

US Copyright Office. "Fees." https://www.copyright.gov/about/fees.html.

Chapter 9

Deciding on book formats

The format of your book refers to how the story is consumed: ebook, serial, paperback, hardback, or audiobook. Book *formatting* refers to the layout of your book's interior, and we will discuss that later. Let's briefly look at each of the book formats here. I've given each one their own section so as to discuss important issues you'll need to be aware of.

Ebook

Ebooks are electronic versions of your book that can be read on mobile devices, tablets, computers, and dedicated ebook devices. Unless you speak at events or travel to conventions and other venues where print books are easily sold, most of your earnings will come from ebooks. Some authors only sell ebooks, eschewing the added expense and trouble of formatting and covering a print book.

We'll discuss ebook distribution more in the next section. Let's move on to the other formats for now.

Serial

A *serial* is a story released in short chunks (such as 600-5,000 words) at a time rather than as a completed unit. Sites and apps such as Wattpad and Radish have long specialized in this type of fiction, and Amazon's introduction of its own platform for serials, Kindle Vella, is bringing this format to the attention of a much greater number of authors and readers. We'll save discussion of Kindle Vella for its own chapter at the end of the book.

Print formats: Paperback and hardback

Personally, I like print books and choose to publish them as well as ebooks. There are a few things to consider when thinking about print: paperback and hardback; print-on-demand and offset printing; Amazon's Kindle Direct Publishing (KDP), KDP Expanded Distribution, and IngramSpark (IS).

Paperback or hardback or both is a matter of personal desire. These are different formats, and so require separate ISBNs. They also require different size covers and, possibly, a dust jacket for the hardback, which increases cover design costs. Hardbacks cost more to print, so the earnings may be less, depending on your pricing. Bottom line, hardbacks cost more. But many readers prefer hardbacks, as do libraries. Previously, it was harder for indie authors to produce hardback copies, as they had to go through a company such as IngramSpark (discussed later), so few did. Things are changing now as KDP has a hardback version in beta. I suspect many more authors will be producing hardbacks in the future.

Many authors create a paperback version, whether they do hardbacks or not. It's fairly easy to add, and they are nice to have for your own personal library, to give away to family, and to sell at events. You can also give them away as part of online marketing giveaways and events. Print books are generally not a huge seller online, but I do sell some, and I know hard-core fans or print-only readers prefer them.

I will go into more depth on what you need to know for this in a later chapter.

Audiobook

Audiobooks are the new books-on-tape. These digital, narrated recordings of your book can easily be listened to on your phone or computer through dedicated apps, including the audiobook store Audible's Audible app. Other stores have their own apps for audiobooks, as they do for ebooks. Indie authors can get their books into Audible, iTunes, and other retailers through ACX (owned by Amazon, like Audible), Findaway Voices, and other distributors. These companies can also connect you with narrators to produce your audiobooks.

There's been a buzz the last few years about the rise of audiobooks, and authors have been encouraged to get into this "gold rush." Like anything, it works well for some and not for others. Marketing is more complicated and not as well established for audiobooks, and the royalties and payments are confusing. There's also been an issue with customers listening to audiobooks and then returning them—as if they hadn't finished them—so they can use that credit for another audiobook. (You can look up "Audiblegate" for more information on audiobook issues and what's been done about it.)

As for royalties, you may see that you get 40% royalties on your audiobooks, know that some are priced at $20 or more, and think how great that is! In truth, that 40% may not be a percentage of the retail value, and there are so many different ways to purchase audiobooks— buy it outright, use a credit, etc.—that few listeners seem to pay full price, and you're seeing sales on your dashboard where you only make $1, if that. If you paid hundreds or thousands of dollars to produce your audiobook, or consider how much time and effort your Royalty Share narrator (a narrator you split royalties with rather than paying them upfront for their work) put into it that they're not getting much in return for, it hurts. There's no guarantee you'll ever pay yourself back for that audiobook you were told was sure money. That said, audiobooks are beloved because of their accessibility. Or, they may just be a person's preferred format. Many love the freedom of listening to audiobooks while traveling, walking, or cleaning their house. Others find print and ebooks difficult to read and rely on audiobooks. Should you produce audiobooks to release with your ebook and print versions and risk taking a loss for those people? Or wait until the books have earned the money to pay for the audiobooks? That's a decision only you can make. As for how to produce an audiobook, I'll cover that in its own chapter at the end of the guide. Do be aware that audiobooks are digital files and are not physical products, so you won't be getting CDs of your narrated book.

———

As a sidenote, this dichotomy of the very successful and the not-so-successful is normal for the indie world. You may publish quality books that your readers love; you may eschew certain high-selling content because you find it morally objectionable; you may try your best to market and be a professional, and still not have the sales or reviews you want. Yet you see authors whose books are not that great, or authors writing morally objectionable content, who are making six figures and getting hundreds or thousands of reviews. Envy, bitterness, and loser syndrome are real struggles in indie publishing, and you'll have to learn to deal with them to succeed and be happy. Success is different for everyone, and you don't have to be a full-time, six- or seven-figure author and have more reviews than Famous Author A to be successful. You don't have to publish a book a month like Author B. Publishing fast might be your talent, or your talent might be creating books that stick with readers but which take longer to write. Creating a definition of success that suits your time, talents, and financial needs, and not getting sidetracked by envy or comparison, is an important step to being happy and truly successful as an author. Remember that each of your fans (even if you only have a few) is valuable, and that using your writing gift is worthwhile, even if it only results in one book every five years.

———

Authorpreneur Joanna Penn is well-known for encouraging authors to diversify their income—to not put all their eggs in one basket, so to speak. Creating different formats of your books, selling wide, using those foreign rights, creating products related to the book to sell (such as courses for nonfiction), editing and book coaching, public speaking, and so on are all ways to safeguard your income from being vulnerable to a single blow—such as Amazon suddenly lowering royalty rates or KU payments or suffering some catastrophe. Developing other streams of income isn't easy, but it is something to consider.

And speaking of considering, let's look at each format in greater depth now, beginning with ebooks. The biggest topic of debate is whether to sell exclusively with Amazon or to sell "wide" through many stores.

Chapter 10

Ebook distribution and KU versus Wide

One of the perennial discussions in the indie world is "KU versus wide," the question of where you will sell your ebook. In short, it refers to selling your ebook exclusively through Amazon by enrolling it in their KU/Kindle Select program (a subscription program) or selling through many retailers, including Apple Books and Kobo. The latter would mean you are not in the KU/Kindle Select program, but you can still sell your ebook through Amazon. Let's talk more about the KU/Kindle Select program and its pros and cons, then we'll discuss the other retailers, the international market, and libraries.

KU/KINDLE SELECT

In case you're not familiar with this discussion, "KU" refers to Amazon's Kindle Unlimited program for readers, where they get access to "Unlimited Reading. Unlimited Listening. Any Device" for a monthly fee. (This program is called Kindle Select on the author end, but most of us still refer to it as KU for simplicity, and I usually call it KU.) The earnings from this subscription program are collected each month into the KDP Select Global Fund, and authors are paid a certain amount per page read from that fund (last I heard, the estimate was $0.004 per page read). The number of pages in your ebook isn't the same as your print page count. You can find the number of pages recognized for your ebook (called Kindle Edition Normalized Page Count—KENPC) in your author dashboard, on the Promote and Advertise page. You only get paid for the first time your book is read.

The KDP Help Center says this about payments and page numbers:

"A customer can read your ebook as many times as they like, but we will only pay you for the number of pages read the first time the customer reads them. It may take months for customers to read pages in your ebook, but no matter how long it takes, we'll still pay you once it happens. This is true even if your KDP Select enrollment period has expired, and you choose not to re-enroll. . . .

"We review the size of the KDP Select Global Fund each month in order to make it compelling for authors to enroll their ebooks in KDP Select. We announce the fund monthly in our community forum. The share of fund allocated to each country varies based on a number of factors, such as exchange rates, customer reading behavior, and local subscription pricing. Author earnings are then determined by their share of total pages read, up to a total of 3,000 pages per customer per title. . . . " (As a reference for that last number, my 550 printed page, 160,000-word novel *Wrought of Serpent and Snow* is only 809 KENPC.)

"To determine an ebook's page count in a way that works across genres, devices, and display settings, we developed the Kindle Edition Normalized Page Count (KENPC). KENPC is calculated using standard formatting settings (font, line height, line spacing, etc.). We use KENPC to measure the number of pages customers read in your ebook, starting with the Start Reading Location (SRL) to the end of your ebook. Amazon typically sets SRL at chapter 1 so readers can start reading the core content of your ebook as soon as they open it. Non-text elements within ebooks including images, charts and graphs will count toward an ebook's KENPC." (Source: https://kdp.amazon.com/en_US/help/topic/G201541130)

You will likely get less money per book through KU than for a purchase at the 70% royalty rate. However, many, many people are in the KU program, and many authors make more money through KU page reads than through sales. KU authors also get a bit of marketing help. You are allowed to run your book for free for five days or have it on sale for up to seven days each 90-day KU period, and for the sale days, you still get a 70% royalty instead of the 35% rate you'd get if you priced your book below $2.99.

One of the biggest—probably *the* biggest—quarrel with the KU/Kindle Select Program is that it requires exclusivity. When you set up your novel in the KDP dashboard, you will have the option of putting it in Kindle Select. If you choose this, your book will be in the program for 90 days, and you cannot sell the ebook anywhere else, or give it away extensively, during that time. Your book will be automatically re-enrolled at the end of those 90 days unless you uncheck the re-enroll box.

This means you cannot sell your ebook through Apple Books or Kobo or any other distribution channels so long as your book is in the Kindle Select program.

(Just to clarify, this exclusivity does not affect print. You can also give a few copies of the ebook away for marketing purposes, but not too many. Please see the Kindle Select terms for specifics.)

The decision to go wide or KU is a personal one as well as a financial one. Many people do not like Amazon as a company, do not like market dominance, want to have their books available as widely as possible, and so go wide. Others feel the same way but don't know how to reach the wide market and so stick with KDP for financial reasons. Some don't care for anything but the ease and earnings of KU.

Aside from your personal feelings about Amazon, what things should be considered before deciding on wide or KU?

KU requires exclusivity (in 90-day terms). If your audience isn't willing or able to purchase from Amazon, then you're losing readers. Amazon is not the biggest player in the international market, so if Europe is your target, for instance, KU is not your best bet.

KU and wide readers aren't exactly the same. Some genres are more suited to KU than others (voracious romance readers are more likely to be in KU since the monthly subscription saves them money), so going wide in some instances is actually losing a lot of readers. Some readers will only read books in KU since they pay for the subscription. They simply won't *buy* books. Some readers aren't on Amazon, and so won't buy books not available elsewhere. If you're looking to get your ebooks into the library ebook market, you'll need to go wide.

Marketing for KU books and marketing for wide books varies greatly. Most authors find that marketing wide books is more difficult than marketing KU books. There are growing ways to market on the non-Amazon platforms, however, and some tactics that aren't available to books in KU. Some promotion services, such as BookBub, give preference to wide authors. Wide stores tend to be less algorithm-dependent. Rapid release doesn't give the same bump in sales and ensuing plummet as on Amazon (which is good news to authors who don't release frequently).

It's harder (for most of us anyway) to gain a following wide, but many authors are very successful despite not being in KU. As mentioned, international markets are not dominated by Amazon (Kobo is much bigger in Canada, for instance), and that is one area where going wide instead of exclusive helps. Diversification of your income is also something to take into account. Having all your eggs in one basket, so to speak, by only selling through Amazon could create a problem if something goes south there—you are locked out of your account for some reason (it happens occasionally), you're accused of violating your KU terms, or something changes in marketing or the algorithms that drastically affects your book sales.

If time and simplicity are essential to your author career, KU might be your best bet, as only managing books for one retailer will save time.

That's a few things to consider in the wide vs KU dilemma. The good news is that whatever you decide doesn't have to be *the* strategy for your entire career. You can put your book in KU for however many terms you like, then take it out and put it wide, or you can sell it wide for a time and then take it down from all the stores but Amazon and enroll it in Kindle Select. Taking books in and out of wide stores isn't a good plan, though, so it might be better to start in KU and then, at a certain point, go wide. You can also have some books wide and some exclusive to KU.

A couple of other things to note: You must have exclusive rights to your book to put it in KU (no public domain works can go in KU or books in multi-author box sets). You're allowed (to the best of my knowledge) to have a series of books in KU as individual titles and in a box set: Book 1, 2, 3, 4, 5, 6 and Books 1-3, Books 4-6.

In summary, you will need to decide if you want your book available only through Amazon and their Kindle Unlimited (Kindle Select) program or through other retailers as well. Here's a brief recap of the pros and cons of KU and wide.

Pros to KU/Cons to going wide:

- KU has many, many readers.
- Some readers—including many voracious ones—only read through KU.
- Borrows are easier to get than sales.
- There's only one retailer to manage if all books are in KU, saving you time and effort.
- The KU program offers some marketing help.
- Many authors make most of their money through KU page reads.

Cons to KU/Pros to going wide:

- KU requires exclusivity; there's no exclusivity in going wide.
- Many readers do not buy from Amazon at all or use the KU program, especially in the international market, so you are losing some readers if in the KU program.
- You earn less per book borrow in KU than for a sale.
- If in KU, you are reliant on one retailer and so at a greater risk financially.
- You miss some promotional opportunities available to wide books.

- There's less chance of hitting the *New York Times* or *USA Today* Best Seller List if exclusive.
- Pricing outside of the $2.99 to $9.99 range gets a 35% royalty rate on KDP. You are not effectively penalized for books (individual or box sets) priced over $9.99 in wide stores.
- Amazon's algorithms favor authors who release frequently while wide retailers aren't as algorithm driven.
- You can't set the price on KDP to free directly but must price match; Apple and other stores allow the price to be set to free.

SELLING EBOOKS WIDE AND THE INTERNATIONAL MARKET

Who are the other retailers? What about libraries? How do I get my books into libraries and into the international market? Let's briefly look at these topics.

Where can you publish your ebook?

In addition to Amazon, you can sell your ebook through your website (called "selling direct") and in a vast number of online retailers, some of whom supply ebooks to libraries. You can set up your ebooks with the stores one by one, or all at once by using an aggregator, such as Draft2Digital (D2D) or Smashwords. Here's a list of the major retailers you can send to through the aggregator D2D. There are more stores than this, but most sales come from a few stores, so for simplicity's sake, I'm only going to list the ones D2D lists.

Amazon
Apple Books
Barnes & Noble
Kobo (including Kobo Plus)

Tolino
OverDrive
Bibliotheca
Scribd
Baker & Taylor
Hoopla
Vivlio
BorrowBox

You can find out more about each retailer on D2D's partner page: https://www.draft2digital.com/partners/. However, I will mention that Kobo (Rakuten-Kobo) is a big player in the Canadian market and has a subscription service, Kobo Plus. OverDrive, Bibliotheca, and Hoopla, among others, serve libraries (mine uses Hoopla), and Tolino is focused on the European market. Not mentioned in the list above is Google Play. You would have to upload your books there yourself.

So setting up on each platform individually or through an aggregator can get you into library ebook catalogues and the international market beyond Amazon's international stores. "What," you might ask, "I can get my books into the international market through Amazon?" Yes. (We talk about translations and foreign rights more in a later chapter.)

International market and translated works

If you put your book for sale through Kindle Direct Publishing, you will be asked if you have the rights to sell it through all of Amazon's marketplaces across the world. This means in the United Kingdom's Amazon store (amazon.co.uk), the Canadian store, German store, Mexican store, Japanese store, and so on. KDP will even help you determine prices, so you can reach English-speaking readers in those countries with no extra trouble beyond checking a box.

If you're interested in uploading books in a foreign language, you can do that too, for those languages that are supported. Here's a link to the list of languages supported for KDP: https://kdp.amazon.com/en_US/help/topic/G200673300.

As previously mentioned, some wide stores are focused more on certain international locations, and thus there is an advantage to going wide in order to reach those audiences.

Setting up your book with retailers

It's simple to set up an ebook on Amazon and other platforms, but it does take time if you upload to all the numerous ebook platforms individually. We'll talk about actually doing this later, but for now, we're considering whether you want to and the best way to do so.

Most of your sales will come through a few major retailers (currently, Amazon, Apple Books, and Kobo), so it makes more sense to set up directly with those few stores and use an aggregator for the rest, and this is what many authors do. An aggregator sends out your book for you, collects the earnings, takes a small cut, and sends you the rest. It costs a little but saves a lot of time.

Draft2Digital, Smashwords (soon to be partnered with its former "competitor" Draft2Digital), and Publish Drive (a newbie with other features), are popular aggregators.

To use an aggregator, you create an account, give them your tax and bank information, upload your books, and select the stores you want them to send your books to. You upload once; they send it out to all the retailers. When you sell books, the retailers pay the aggregator, who takes a small percentage for their work and sends you the rest.

This saves a lot of time for the initial uploading of your books, for re-uploading to correct typos or update back matter, and to check your sales (in one spot as opposed to many). You do lose a little money, so you must weigh that against your time and trouble. You can use more than one aggregator if you like (since they might reach different, smaller stores and have other features of value), but make sure you are not selling to the same retailers through both. Don't sell to Kobo through both, in other words.

Do know that changes to your book's metadata, such as price, or publishing status, take time to change on these platforms, and often longer than they take to change on Amazon. If you're planning to unpublish on D2D and move to KU, and you selected all the available retailers on D2D, know that some of them might take weeks to unpublish your book. Those partners with a slow response time are listed as such, so take that into account if you're not planning to stay wide for a long time.

Note that it's free to set up your book on Smashwords and D2D; they only take a percentage of your earnings (10% of the retail price for Draft2Digital). You do not pay them. They earn money when you earn money. However, Publish Drive operates a bit differently, and if you use it to distribute more than one book, you must pay for their subscription service. You, however, keep 100% royalties. So instead of paying a small percentage of your royalties, you pay a monthly subscription. The cost of the subscription is based on how many books you are distributing through them.

Check out the aggregators yourself, since they offer more than the aggregator service. Smashwords (the old guy here) offers coupons and a storefront; D2D offers free formatting and universal book links through Books2Read (https://books2read.com).

———

In conclusion, before you publish your ebook, you will need to decide whether your ebook will be exclusive (at least for a time) to Amazon or if you will go wide. If you're looking for ease of publishing and have a focus on a US audience, you might want to start in the KU program. Later, if you're willing to put in some marketing effort, you can remove your books from KU and put them wide. You can be successful in either KU or wide.

REFERENCES AND RESOURCES

Amazon. "Kindle Unlimited." https://www.amazon.com/kindle-dbs/hz/subscribe/ku.

Amazon. "KDP Select." https://kdp.amazon.com/en_US/help/topic/G200798990.

Amazon. "Royalties in Kindle Unlimited." Accessed April 6, 2022. https://kdp.amazon.com/en_US/help/topic/G201541130.

Apple Books for Authors. https://authors.apple.com.

Chesson, Dave. "Draft2Digital vs PublishDrive Review." *Kindlepreneur.* February 23, 2022. https://kindlepreneur.com/smashwords-vs-draft2digital/.

Chesson, Dave. "Publish Drive Review (Is It Worth It?) + Promo Code!" *Kindlepreneur.* August 16, 2021. https://kindlepreneur.com/publish-drive-review/.

Draft2Digital. "How to Publish with Draft2Digital." Accessed April 6, 2022. https://www.draft2digital.com/steps/.

Google Play. https://play.google.com/books/publish.

Kobo. https://www.kobo.com/ca/en/p/writinglife.

Lefebvre, Mark Leslie. *Wide for the Win: Strategies to Sell Globally via Multiple Platforms and Forge Your Own Path to Success.* Stark Publishing Solutions, 2021.

Publish Drive. https://publishdrive.com.

Smashwords. https://www.smashwords.com.

Six Figure Authors Podcast. "SFA 080 - Kindle Unlimited vs Wide (i.e. Amazon Exclusivity vs. Not)." March 4, 2021. https://6figureauthors.com/podcast/kindle-unlimited-vs-wide-i-e-amazon-exclusivity-vs-not/.

Six Figure Authors Podcast. "SFA 119 - Myths About Success in Self-Publishing." February 10, 2022. https://6figureauthors.com/podcast/myths-about-success-in-self-publishing/.

Chapter 11

Introduction to print books

"Just how do I get my books printed? Do I need a garage full of boxes of books? What about Amazon—will they print my book for me? I've heard of IngramSpark, but what is it?"

How do I get my books printed? Will Amazon print my book for me?

Does Amazon [fill in the blank]? If the question involves indie publishing, then the answer is *probably*. Amazon's Kindle Direct Publishing will act as a printer for your book in addition to a retailer. Using KDP is the easiest and most common way indie authors get print books. There are other options, including IngramSpark, which we will discuss.

Do I need a garage full of boxes of books?

Probably not. See the discussion below about print-on-demand versus offset printing.

Print-on-demand versus offset printing

If you print through Amazon's Kindle Direct Publishing, you are getting a print-on-demand (POD) book. Print-on-demand books are printed only when ordered, and only as many copies as are ordered are printed. Like e-readers, this is a fairly new technology, at least in an economically viable form. Because of the way these books are printed, print-on-demand books cost more per unit to produce than large print run books but are still a quality product. As a POD printer, KDP only prints the book when someone orders it from their storefront or you order copies for yourself.

If you only want a few copies of your book and don't intend to sell it through Amazon, consider a local print shop or a company such as BookBaby or Lulu. If you want a particularly fancy special edition hardback, you'll need to look elsewhere as well, as IngramSpark and KDP create nice, but simple POD books.

You may have heard of authors ordering a large run of books and storing them in the garage until they sell them. When doing this, they are using the same method as traditional publishers: a large print run, or offset printing.

Offset printing, as mentioned, requires a large order of books (1,000 or more). Books are cheaper per unit printed this way, but this requires a large upfront payment, a place to store the books, and involves a considerable risk that the books will not sell.

Consequently, most indie authors use print-on-demand, going through Amazon's KDP to print, or through publishing platform IngramSpark. Draft2Digital has a print option in beta, so be on the lookout for that. (To be in *beta* means to be in a trial phase. Kinks are still being worked out before it releases "for real." The product may only be available to a limited number of people as well.)

If someone recommends CreateSpace to you, know that KDP *is* the former CreateSpace. Amazon's printing arm is now conveniently accessible through the same dashboard as the ebook platform.

So what's the difference between IngramSpark and KDP?

Simplicity and reach. But mostly simplicity.

That's a cheat answer, but it's true. If you're looking for ease, stick to KDP. Setting up to print through KDP is simple and is accomplished through the same dashboard as for setting up your ebook.

However, if you don't mind getting more into the business side of things and want more of a chance getting your book into libraries and bookstores, then you'll want to combine KDP and IngramSpark.

But first, what is IngramSpark? IngramSpark (IS) is an independent publishing platform. They say this about themselves on their website: "Ingram is a major book distributor in the United States, distributing to 40,000+ retailers (including Barnes & Noble and your local independent bookstore), libraries, schools, and universities." They distribute both ebooks and print books. (I've only heard one person mention using the ebook option, though.) (Source: https://www.ingramspark.com/blog/book-distribution-with-ingramspark)

Unlike Amazon, IngramSpark does not act as a storefront for your book. Customers cannot order through IngramSpark (that is, customers like Aunt Susie, unless Aunt Susie owns a bookstore). They put your book in a catalog that businesses order from. In other words, Amazon —> storefront for everyday customers and some businesses, publishing platform, and printer. Ingram —> publishing platform, catalog for businesses, and printer.

Let's dig into IngramSpark and KDP a bit more.

IngramSpark versus KDP

Print book type: Print-on-demand for both. Paperback and hardback, though KDP's hardback is only in beta.

Title setup: IngramSpark requires a bit more expertise, money, and time to set up than KDP. Amazon's setup for ebook and print titles is free, as is file revision. IngramSpark charges $49 for title setup and $25 to revise files. This is because it's a professional company originally associated with traditional publishing, not because it's a scam. You can get coupons for these fees through certain memberships, including Alliance of Independent Authors (ALLi), such that setup or revision is free up to a certain number of title setups and revisions. As a sidenote, IS's and

Amazon's book cover requirements are slightly different, so you might need to pay a bit more to get a different version of your cover made for IS. It usually doesn't cost much to make the adjustments for IS, though.

Print book quality: I don't know of a quality difference between IngramSpark and Amazon print books. Some authors claim Ingram is better, others that they are the same.

Pre-orders: Print pre-order is available through IS but not Amazon. Customers cannot pre-order a KDP print book (like they can pre-order an ebook).

Wholesale print price: KDP is slightly less expensive per book than IngramSpark.

For only selling books through Amazon's storefront or ordering for yourself to sell at events, you might as well go with KDP for ease.

But what about getting books into other places than Amazon? Say, bookstores and libraries?

This is where IngramSpark becomes an important player. Amazon technically *can* reach other places, but not as well as IS. First, let's discuss how Amazon provides a way to reach other distribution channels besides its own storefront. This is accomplished through Amazon's *Expanded Distribution* feature.

Expanded Distribution is basically a box you click in your KDP dashboard that allows KDP to offer your book to a wider audience, including sites such as Book Depository (ships free and internationally) and libraries. It's not a guarantee books will be sold.

It's simple to set up, but it does affect your pricing. If you check the Expanded Distribution box, the minimum price allowed for your book goes up. You'll also note that the estimated earnings for your expanded distribution books is very small, usually less than a dollar.

Now for IngramSpark. Setting up an account with IngramSpark gets you into the Baker & Taylor catalogue. This is the catalogue that libraries and bookstores prefer to order through. Some bookstores will not order through Amazon, for a variety of reasons (competition and extra paperwork included) but will order through the IngramSpark channels. If you want to get into bookstores and libraries, it's best to set up with IngramSpark. It's generally recommended to set up with both KDP (for Amazon) and IngramSpark for everything else; just don't check the Expanded Distribution box in KDP.

If you already have your book in Amazon's Expanded Distribution but want to move it over to IngramSpark, you can uncheck Amazon's Expanded Distribution box, then email IngramSpark and they will send you a form to fill out. This involves the form and a couple of emails with Amazon customer service and IngramSpark, but it is easy to do and doesn't require a separate cover for IngramSpark (not in my experience, anyway).

Setting up with IngramSpark

I mentioned earlier that setting up with IngramSpark costs a bit more and requires more expertise. IngramSpark treats the process from a more bookstore, business-y angle than Amazon's ease-of-use angle. Let's talk about this now instead of in the section on uploading your books to retailers because everything that goes into setup for IS might influence whether or not you choose to use them.

When you set up with KDP, you get a 60% royalty rate and have few decisions to make beyond retail book pricing and paper type. Your book goes to Amazon's storefront and is presented to customers, who pay a retail price.

With IS, books are sold not to customers but to businesses. Businesses buy at wholesale and set their own retail price and sometimes return unsold products. Consequently, when you set up with IS, you will be asked about a suggested retail price, wholesale discount, and return/destroy options.

For the wholesale discount, books are usually sold at a discount of 35-55% off your recommended retail price. The 55% discount is preferred by stores and may make your book more enticing to them.

You choose the discount for your book. Hold that thought; we'll come back to it.

In addition to the wholesale discount, you need to choose a return option: Yes - Deliver; Yes - Destroy; No.

If stores order multiple copies of your book, and they don't sell, the store may want to get their money back by "returning" the books (which might mean destroying them or pulping them). What happens then depends on the settings you chose. Returning books costs money for shipping, so if you choose Yes - Deliver, you will be charged for shipping in addition to the wholesale cost of the book. The shipping and handling fees (at the time of this writing) are $2 per book for US returns to a US address and $20 per book for US returns to an international address. I think you can actually get these books delivered to you, but the condition of them is not guaranteed. For Yes - Destroy, the books are returned to Ingram and are destroyed.

The upshot of this is that you might see a spike in IS sales, then a while later, get a big bill for returned books. You may think that's outrageous, but this happens to publishers all the time, and since you're an indie author, you're a publisher now too, with all the benefits and drawbacks.

Choosing the no-return option means that stores can't return the book. This may make buyers less likely to take a chance on your work.

The Alliance of Independent Authors recommends that if you aren't as invested in bookstore sales, that you actually discourage bookstores from big purchases by setting the wholesale discount at the lower end (so maybe 35% instead of 55%) and choosing no return. If a customer asks for your book, or the buyer is fairly certain your book will sell in their store, they will still order it. You will just be less likely to get a large order and, possibly, returns.

In conclusion, working with IngramSpark is not for the faint of heart and requires more savvy than working with Amazon. Whether or not it is worth it depends on your long-term plans. We'll talk more about getting into bookstores and libraries later.

Are there other options than KDP and IngramSpark?

Yes, at the very least there's Lulu and BookBaby, but those are a bit more into the services side—setting you up with editors and cover designers, etc. They have many options (different trim sizes, hardback and paperback, color, etc.) for printing, but they do cost more per book.

They might be the best option for specialty books, though, such as cookbooks or picture books, or for authors who only want a few copies of their book and don't want to sell it online. You can print but not sell books through Ingram as well.

There's also Draft2Digital print beta and Barnes & Noble Press (this is not a surefire way of getting into Barnes & Noble stores, just so you know, and I've never known anyone to use it). You can also use local printers.

KDP and IngramSpark are the main players, though, and they are the ones I will focus on from here on out.

References and Resources

Alliance of Independent Authors. "Which is better: KDP Print or IngramSpark?" August 21, 2021. https://selfpublishingadvice.org/use-both-kdp-print-and-ingram-spark-together/.

Amazon KDP. "Format your paperback." https://kdp.amazon.com/en_US/help/topic/G201834190.

Amazon KDP. "Hardcover." https://kdp.amazon.com/en_US/help/topic/GAVW3FZZAKA2KY3B.

Barnes and Noble Press. "Print Personal Books." https://press.barnesandnoble.com/print-on-demand.

Barnes and Noble Press. "How to Self-Publish with Us." Accessed March 21, 2022. https://press.barnesandnoble.com/how-it-works.

BookBaby. https://www.bookbaby.com.

Draft2Digital. "D2D Print Price Calculator." https://draft2digital.com/podcalc.

IngramSpark. "How It Works." https://www.ingramspark.com/how-it-works.

IngramSpark. "Print and Ship Calculator." https://myaccount.ingramspark.com/Portal/Tools/ShippingCalculator.

Kuiken, Sarah. "Everything You Need to Know About D2D Print." *Draft2Digital*. September 9, 2021. https://www.draft2digital.com/blog/everything-you-need-to-know-about-d2d-print/.

Lulu. https://www.lulu.com.

Tumlinson, Kevin. "D2D Print now in beta! Here's what you need to know..." *Draft2Digital*. October 30, 2018. https://www.draft2digital.com/blog/d2d-print-now-in-beta-heres-what-you-need-to-know/.

Young, Debbie. "Are Bookstores Worth it for Indie Authors?" *Alliance of Independent Authors*. January 25, 2021. https://selfpublishingadvice.org/are-bookstores-worth-it-for-indie-authors/.

Chapter 12

Concluding getting yourself ready

Indie publishing is a lot like preparing a fancy meal—you have multiple things in the oven at once while a few things are in the fridge and on the table and a few on the counter that you're still working on. You've asked yourself a lot of questions. While those are simmering, let's talk about scheduling, budgeting, and organization. Having an understanding of these ahead of time will be tremendously helpful as you go through the process. With that, we'll wrap up the "Getting Yourself Ready" part of the guide.

These are the questions you should have answered or be considering after reading this section:

- What are your goals as an author? Audience reach and income?
- What is your author name?
- What is your publishing company name (imprint)?
- What are your business plans? Sole proprietorship or LLC?
- What tax information and licenses do you need to be aware of for your location and business plans?

- Will you file a copyright for each book?
- Do you need to include your intellectual property in your estate planning?
- What plans do you have for your intellectual property?
- Which book formats do you want?
- Which retailers will distribute your ebook? Will it be wide or KU?
- Will you print your book solely through KDP or use IngramSpark as well?

Part Three

Schedule and Budget

Chapter 13

Schedule

Scheduling is a huge part of the indie author's job. Scheduling writing time; scheduling edits, beta-reads, cover design, ARCs, promotions, sales, and the book release, among other things.

One of the first big questions of indie authors is when they can release their book. So let's take a moment to discuss book releases, and then we'll go over all the things that need to be scheduled to make that happen.

SCHEDULING AND BOOK RELEASE

In the traditional publishing world, waiting a year or more for a favorite author's next book is common. We know this wait as readers, how it strains our patience and builds anticipation, but authors feel it as well. They turn in their manuscript and may wait a year or more before it's published. They may only be allowed to publish one book a year, no matter how many they can write a year.

In the indie publishing world, though, releases often happen much more frequently than once a year and in a much shorter time frame between completion and book launch. Depending on the author, this can be freeing or terrifying. Some authors publish a book a month, or every three or four months, or one every year or two. I don't understand the former and honestly worry about the quality of a book every month, not to mention the possibility of burnout. A book every four months I can understand and hope to achieve one day, with discipline and a good team to help with editing and cover design.

But that's me.

Don't ignore those three words. What other authors do and hope for doesn't have to matter to you. Each author must determine what works for him or her—the pace that allows for enjoyment and quality work. Stressing out and burning out to keep up with the high-producing, high-earning authors isn't worth it. If you plan on making a successful career or a profitable hobby of publishing, though, you don't have to publish every month, but you will need to be *consistent*. This may mean one book a year or three a year, or one every two years. Readers just need to know what to expect from you (your publishing history, newsletter, and social media announcements can help them figure this out). They'll wait for great books.

Why do I mention the frequency of book releases, since this is a book on getting set up as an indie author and not strictly a marketing book or make-a-living-as-an-author book? Because I think it's important to help people understand the world they are getting into when they publish, and because an author's mindset influences both the type of release they do and the scheduling of it.

Some writers run on very tight schedules, especially the full-time authors whose livelihood depends on frequent releases. They may be finishing the manuscript three weeks before the release date and completing the edits the day the pre-order manuscript must be uploaded. This works for some people, but I don't recommend it, especially for beginners. The stress usually isn't worth it. Give yourself (and those whose work or feedback you depend on) time and grace. When you've grown enough in the craft that your books don't require much revision, and you have a steady team to help you, then you can speed up your schedule. For your first few releases, I highly recommend taking your time and not setting up a pre-order until everything but the final proofread is completed (if you set up a pre-order at all).

If the book you're releasing is part of a series, there is another decision you need to make, and that is whether or not you want to do rapid release.

Rapid release is a strategy where books in a series are released rapidly until the entire series is available, often with only a month, or less, between releases. This strategy plays into the binge desire, as people don't have to wait long to read more. The pre-order for book 2 is ready when book 1 releases, and the pre-order for book 3 is ready when 2 releases, and so on. Soon, you have a completed series, and some people won't read a series until it's complete, so you catch those readers early on. You're effectively building your backlist very quickly, which leads to more marketing opportunities.

Many authors have used this strategy, in combination with marketing and advertising, to boost their careers and find success. There are drawbacks, however: the entire series will need to be ready ahead of time to not miss the deadlines; the buzz surrounding the books might be high initially, but it won't have any natural stimulants later due to additional book releases in the series; and rapid release creates an expectation of frequent releases the author might not be able to follow up on, leading to burnout. You will also need to pay for all the covers and editing ahead of time, instead of using the earnings of earlier books to pay for later ones. You don't have feedback from early books to determine if the series is worth it. Having all the books ready before release does allow you to ensure continuity within the series, however.

Case study: A popular author recently did a rapid release of an urban fantasy series that is the third series in her story world. She released these new books about three to four weeks apart. During book 1's release, she did a sale on the first series in that story world (free book 1 and $0.99 on books 2 and 3). Around the release of book 3, she did a sale on the second series in that story world. So while she doesn't have later books in that particular series to boost sales of earlier books, she's using related series to boost each other. She's a popular author in a popular genre, and within a month had over 1,500 reviews of book 1 in the new series.

However, before you get too excited, I've heard of several authors who go the rapid release route only to burn out. It's gotten a lot of hype, but that doesn't mean it's for everyone, or everyone all the time.

The alternative to rapid release is to publish the books the old-fashioned way, as you finish them. One a year, for example, or one every nine months. It's very important to set an expectation for your readers and be dependable. You might lose some fans if you publish book 1, then wait two years for book 2, and three years for book 3, for instance. Or publish three books one year and make them wait a year for the next book. People don't like waiting, but if they know there's going to be a wait ahead of time, they won't complain as much.

The benefits of this slower method are (hopefully) less stress overall, a spreading out of your expenses, more reader feedback, a longer-lasting interest in your series as people talk about it and potentially re-read book 1 as book 2 releases, and so on. You do have to plan ahead more thoroughly if you write series to make sure nothing in book 3 will require a change in book 1, for instance.

In conclusion, rapid release is a popular strategy and has kick-started or boosted many careers, but it does have drawbacks and shouldn't be rushed into. Look into which method you think will work best for your writing habits and career (if you intend to continue publishing). It's also possible to use both strategies, such as rapid release with a series of shorter books yet have some series that are published at a slower pace. Publishing is more a series of choices you don't know the outcome of rather than right-and-wrong decisions. One choice may work for one author and not another, and you won't know until you've tried.

———

So now that that bit of publishing philosophy is out of the way, let's look more closely at things you need to schedule: things you might want to do one at a time and things you can have going at the same time. There are a lot of things to do, but don't get overwhelmed. They don't all have to be done at once and are all very doable.

The main categories of "to-dos" are *getting the manuscript ready*, *getting the book ready*, *publishing and legal*, and *marketing* (pre-, launch, and post-).

Things to do throughout the process:

- Keep on writing.
- Study the craft.
- Keep track of your expenses, contacts, registrations, passwords, and so on.
- Keep up with marketing trends at least a little (consider listening to one or two podcasts or reading a blog post or two a week).
- Network with other authors (pop into a Facebook group once a week or so; go to a conference or local writers' group once a year, if possible, and learn from their experiences).

From the book's finish to publication, here's what needs to happen. I can't give you an actual timeline because there are too many "what-if's." For example, what if the cover designer you want is booked for a year in advance? What if that editor had a cancellation and can take the project next week instead of two months from now?

Just as a guess, though, for a new author with a good handle on the craft and a *publishable* manuscript, allow at least nine months to publication. This will give you time for all the scheduling of edits and cover design, getting those back, writing the reader magnet, setting up the website, and so forth. Better to plan ahead and have a professional launch than rush.

If your manuscript hasn't gone through a critique group or a developmental edit—meaning the overall structure and story hasn't been checked and the book isn't publishable yet—then you'll need to add in however long it takes to do that. This is basic craft. It might take years or a few months, depending on how much you've studied the craft of writing and how much time you have to devote to it.

If you're only in this as a onetime deal or light hobby, rejoice! A lot of the market research here can be skipped, as can writing the reader magnet.

The following is a task list that might help you gauge in what order things need to be done, but this is a suggested order only. Every author's schedule will vary depending on many factors, including their craft level, finances, available time, and availability of their chosen editor, cover designer, book formatter, and beta-readers. If you're not familiar with some of the terms mentioned, that's fine. We'll get to them.

TASK LIST

1. Let your finished manuscript sit for a month and "grow cool." While it's doing this, you can start on the market research and the "Getting Yourself Ready" decisions. You will have several other breaks in which to work on this, so don't feel you must do it all at once.

Market research

- Look for comparable books.
- Study good covers and blurbs.
- Start working on your cover brief.
- Write your book's back cover copy and tagline.
- Determine pricing based on comparable books.
- Research keywords and categories.
- Choose your keywords and categories.

Start building your team

- Look for cover designers and editors and ask about availability and pricing.
- Look for beta-readers or a critique group.

Getting Yourself Ready decisions

- Author name.
- Book formats.
- Distribution methods.
- Decide on your budget.
- Strategize your record-keeping and employ those tactics as you go along.

2. Get your manuscript back out and read over it. Check for continuity, character arcs, story structure, and so on yourself. Fix any issues and do an informal edit.

3. Send it through a critique group or beta-readers or hire a developmental editor. A chapter-by-chapter critique group takes time. Beta-readers will likely need four to six weeks. A developmental editor may take a few weeks too and will need to schedule you in advance. So plan ahead for all of these options. It's important that you get the story structure or organization of your fiction or nonfiction right before you worry about the line editing and grammar. Also, continue with the marketing research, team building, and research for other decisions while your manuscript is off with others.

4. Review the feedback on your manuscript and apply. If it seems you're not as ready to publish as you thought you were, that's normal. It's better to keep learning the craft and re-writing until you have a good manuscript than publish too soon, get horrible reviews, and have to take down your book to fix it. People have done that and come out okay in the end, and in the early days of indie publishing, that was more common. But it's a competitive, professional marketplace now, so starting off right, with a quality manuscript, is important.

5. Decide on your top editors and cover designers. Contact them about cost and availability. Choose the ones that fit with your budget and schedule and then ask them to put you on their calendar. Get an estimate of when you'll receive the finished product for each. Allow a couple of months for applying edits and for delays instead of setting your release date immediately after you expect to receive your final edits or cover design. It's better to have extra time than miss your deadline or have to move it. Voice of experience: one month isn't a sufficient buffer.

6. Decide if you are going to format the book yourself, use software, or hire someone, and proceed with that, as appropriate.

7. Write a short story or appropriate nonfiction to be used as a reader magnet.

8. Work on cover, blurb, and editing for your reader magnet.

9. Send your book to a line editor and start the cover process, as appropriate.

10. Set up a website.

11. Set up a newsletter (and PO Box). Set up an automated welcome newsletter and decide on your newsletter strategy. Set up a newsletter signup page on your website.

12. Set up social media accounts for your author self.

13. Get a professional author photo and write a short author biography.

14. Work on a media kit for your website (discussed later).

15. Set up accounts on retailers, such as Amazon KDP. Start the book setup, but only save as a draft. Don't publish yet. Use the keywords, categories, etc. already determined to set up your book page. If doing a pre-order, set that up and make the pre-order live whenever you're ready.

16. Set up your Goodreads author page, BookBub author page, and Amazon Author Central page.

17. Complete your reader magnet (editing, cover, formatting, front and back matter). Make sure it has information on your future book and your newsletter sign-up.

18. Set up your reader magnet on a platform such as BookFunnel or StoryOrigin to deliver it and connect it to your welcome newsletter.

19. Start building your newsletter list and sending newsletters, as appropriate.

20. Set up cover reveals, guest blogging opportunities, and a blog tour (being featured on many blogs), if you're doing this.

21. Work on front and back matter for your books (the pages before and after the body of the book, including title page, etc.).

22. Buy ISBNs, if using them. Record them. Generate or buy a barcode (if not using the printer-provided barcode) and give to your cover designer to use on the print cover.

23. Set up ARC readers and ask for endorsements (optional). Allow at least a month for this before publication, probably one to three months for endorsers and a month for ARC readers. Give readers a deadline, as that helps many complete the tasks they've agreed to.

24. Get bookmarks and business cards printed, if using them.

25. Format your book and do another proofread.

26. Send it off to ARC readers and endorsers.

27. Write and send guest posts as appropriate.

28. Do a final information check and proofread on the book. Send a reminder a week or two before release about the release and send links to ARC readers to the book's retail page(s) and Goodreads page for reviews.

29. Upload to retailer(s). Register your ISBN once you assign it to a book.

30. Launch! Send your release newsletter and post on social media.

31. Send your book off to the copyright office (within three months of launch).

32. Continuing marketing according to your strategy and always keep track of expenses and earnings. Keep track of stock (print books ordered, sold, given away). Continue with your regular newsletter schedule. Keep writing!

––––––

Before you get too far into planning your release schedule, please remember that many first novels are never published or are re-written much later and then published. The craft of writing must be learned and practiced, and that learning process often results in unpublishable books. That's normal. Your first published book most likely will not be the first book you wrote. It's a good idea to make sure that what you're trying to publish is ready for publication before continuing the process.

References and Resources

Gaughran, David. "Rapid Release and Launching Books - Beast Mode for authors?" (YouTube video). December 22, 2020. https://www.youtube.com/watch?v=Z5TRfB1Lg_c.

Six Figure Authors Podcast. "SFA 119 – Myths About Success in Self-Publishing." February 10, 2022. https://6figureauthors.com/podcast/myths-about-success-in-self-publishing/.

Umstattd, Thomas Jr. "Why Rapid Release is a Risky Book Launch Strategy." *Author Media*. October 7, 2020. https://www.authormedia.com/why-rapid-release-is-a-risky-book-launch-strategy/.

Chapter 14

Budget

When it comes to indie publishing, you can pretty much spend as much or as little as you want.

Could you self-edit the manuscript, format it yourself, use a free ISBN (provided by the retailer), and do the cover yourself? Sure. The cheapness of it would probably be apparent, though. Indie publishing has grown tremendously in the last several years, as have the available resources and the expected quality. There's too much competition for poorly produced books to thrive these days.

Conversely, some of us have the tendency to want to overspend to prove our book is the best by hiring the best editors and cover designers, spending thousands on this and on the launch itself. This isn't necessary and could hurt you in the long run, since there is no guarantee the book will earn out the money you've invested. And if the book is a series, are you willing or able to spend thousands on each book?

If you intend to continue publishing, you need to consider your long-term plans. What can you afford to spend now *and* on future books? Should you go cheap now and improve later, when the book can pay for itself? (There's no guarantee on this, but that's the hope.) If you go all-out now, can you keep that up (readers will expect similar quality)?

Books take time to earn out, remember. How will being cheap affect your readers (as in poor editing) or your team (do your editors and cover designers feel shortchanged?)? Don't skimp in your editing. Better an inexpensive (but decent and marketable) cover than no editing. Covers can be easily changed later. You can also simply delay launch and save more toward the cover design you want.

Also, keep in mind that in addition to the expenses associated with the release of books, you will have other expenses. These *might* include ISBN purchase, website hosting, domain name purchase, memberships, marketing, printing, running ads, joining professional organizations, attending conferences, continuing education (be it courses or books), book formatting, printing the manuscript for editing, writing software, design software for marketing materials, copyright registration, news-letter costs, stock (copies of print books), a good computer, and internet connection.

Not all of these are essential, however. We'll discuss the various expenses throughout the book, and I will only include some in the proposed budget, as examples. Some costs associated with being an indie author are onetime (such as some software), some are per book published (such as cover and editing), some are yearly or monthly (such as hosting, memberships, and some promotion services, such as Book-Funnel). Some are occasional and can be quite large. If you buy ISBNs, for instance, and plan to publish more than one book, it's more economical to purchase the 10 or 100 pack, but this requires a sizable outlay of money ($295 and $575, respectively). And I don't recommend starting with the 100 pack, as you might change your mind about publishing! Editing costs vary widely, depending on the editor, type of edit, and how many edits you get (discussed later). I have example budgets below and mention ways to save money.

Study the budgets below, consider your own, and keep track of potential expenses mentioned throughout the book. Think about not just your first book, but others as well. Don't go into debt thinking you'll make the money back. Even if you do have a killer launch, it takes two months to get paid (Amazon KDP payments take 60 days). Write out your budget and stick to it.

EXAMPLE BUDGETS

Moderate Budget for Serious Hobby/Career Author for Launch Year and Year Two with one book released each year and no ads run. Books had a line edit and proofread at moderate price points. (Estimated book length: 100,000 words)

Moderate Budget: Launch Year

Website hosting for a year: $100 (yearly)
Domain name: $15 (yearly)
BookFunnel or StoryOrigin: $100 (yearly)
Editing for one book: $1,200 (varies greatly)
Cover for one book: $350
Books on the writing craft: $30
PO Box for a year: $100 (yearly, varies by location)
Marketing: $150 (promos, contest gifts, bookmarks)
ISBN, 10 pack: $275
Miscellaneous: $150 (professional memberships, printing)
Buying print editions for stock: $100
Atticus: $147 (onetime payment)
Copyright: $45

Total: $2,762

Moderate Budget: Year Two

Website hosting for a year: $100 (yearly)
Domain name: $15 (yearly)
BookFunnel or StoryOrigin: $100 (yearly)
Editing for one book: $1,200 (varies greatly)
Cover for one book: $350
Books on the writing craft: $30
PO Box for a year: $100 (yearly)
Marketing: $150 (promos, contest gifts, bookmarks)
Miscellaneous: $150 (professional memberships, printing)

Buying print editions for stock: $100
Copyright: $45

Total: $2,340

Small Budget or Light Hobby Author Launch Year for one book released each year and no ads run. Book had an inexpensive line edit. (Estimated book length: 100,000 words). Year One and Two would be the same if the book length is about the same.

Small Budget Estimate Launch Year

Website hosting for a year: $100 (or free)
Domain name renewal: $15
Editing for one book: $400 (varies greatly)
Cover for one book: $150
Marketing and miscellaneous: $150
Buying print editions for stock: $30

Total: $845

———

As an exercise, consider how many books you need to sell to earn back what you spend. Say you have one book priced at $4.99 at 70% royalty and are following the moderate launch with a budget of $2,762. You earn roughly $3.49 per book, so you need to sell 792 copies to earn back what you spent Year One. If you have only one book, that means you need 792 fans to buy your book. If you have two books by the end of Year Two, you have roughly $7 of products available for purchase, and you have $5,102 invested so far (Year One plus Year Two). That works out to 729 fans, if each fan buys both books, or 1,462 individual sales.

If you launch with a budget of around $845, then you need to sell 243 books to break even.

Notice that the more books you have, the more revenue you can achieve through a smaller number of fans, or readers who will buy most or all of your books. This is a good incentive, to my mind, to focus more on building your backlist rather than dancing around social media outlets to gain followers. Just because you have 1,000 followers on a social media platform doesn't mean they will each buy your book, and even if they did, if you only have one book, that is only $3,490 you can earn from them (assuming one book at 70% royalty of $4.99). But if you have five books (so $17.45 worth of product), you only need 200 fans to earn $3,490 (assuming each fan bought all five books). So it really pays (pun intended) to focus more on building your backlist than on building your social media following, especially early in your career. This goes for advertising as well.

How to save money on your book launches

Ways to save money include using pre-made covers and going with less expensive designers and editors. This doesn't mean low quality. Some are highly skilled but don't charge very high fees. Some are new and so don't have the experience to charge high prices. If you choose a high-skill, low-cost professional, be warned that they may increase their price as their portfolio and the demand on their time grows. I had a cover artist increase her price from $100 to $400 in two years! Also, schedule ahead of time so you don't have to pay rush fees to get your edits done in time.

If you have a professional skill, such as editing, cover design, or marketing, you might try trading skills with someone else. You do edits in return for a cover, or something of that nature. Another way is to study the craft of writing and editing, and get good at it, so that your stories only require a light copyedit instead of a line edit and a developmental edit. Swapping beta-reads and critiques with other authors can save on a developmental edit. You can also get ARC readers to help with the final proofread.

For marketing, you don't have to run ads or use promotion services, or you can use the less expensive promo sites, like ENT and Book Barbarian (which are about or less than $100), rather than using BookBub and paying hundreds of dollars (the cost of a fantasy Featured Deal for a $0.99 book is over $700). You also do not have to have character art for your release, or do expensive giveaways or a launch party. You don't have to do an audiobook. You can even use the free ISBNs instead of buying them (we'll cover ISBNs later). It's probably best not to run ads or do too many promotions until you have multiple books to funnel people through (at least five books is recommended before you do ads). You'll get more return on your investment that way.

This isn't specifically for book launches, but you will need a word processing program of some kind to write your books or view your editor's or others' feedback (usually involves the use of the comment and track changes features in word processors). And in case you didn't know, Microsoft Word is not your only option! There are many options and price points, but here are a few. You can pay for Microsoft's products (a yearly subscription or a one-time purchase, roughly $70 per year or $160 onetime, respectively, for one user) or utilize an open source (free) word processor such as Google Docs, Apache OpenOffice, and LibreOffice. Pages is free for iOS (Mac) users. You can write in Scrivener (which I do currently; it's only a onetime cost of around $50), but you will need to export your manuscript as a docx or doc file to send to your editor or beta-readers and then utilize a word processor to see their feedback. If you use Atticus (useful for writing and formatting), it has collaboration tools for working with editors and beta-readers.

Earnings

You've put your book out and it's selling, but when and how do you get your money? This depends somewhat on the distributor and your chosen settings. I use direct deposit into my checking account. Some may allow you to request checks. Some may use PayPal. Some may only pay once a certain threshold has been reached (such as $10).

Either way, the money is not paid immediately, as sales occur, but monthly. With Kindle Direct Publishing, my earnings are directly deposited at the end of the month *two months* in arrears. This means that whatever is earned in January won't be received until the end of March. If you're counting on this money, be sure to allow for the delay.

Also know that income taxes will not have been deducted. KDP and other retailers will send you a 1099-MISC each year, and you will be responsible for including that income in your taxes and paying taxes on it. If you intend to write off your writing expenses as business expenses, you will need to keep good records of them. It might be helpful to establish a separate bank account to help you keep track of earnings and expenses and to just keep things separate from your personal money.

So before you rejoice too much over your book earnings, remember this is a business. You will need to take money out to pay yourself back for your book's expenses, save for the next book's expenses, pay for your continuing education or networking (conferences support both these endeavors), and to pay taxes.

Chapter 15

Organization

As an indie author, you are a small business owner (you might as well get used to hearing that). You may or may not choose to claim your author business expenses on your income tax, but you will still have a lot of information to keep track of, from manuscripts to receipts to dozens of usernames and passwords.

As it's much easier to set up an organization plan ahead of time than to sort through tons of stuff to organize later, let's take a moment to mention some things you will need to organize, how to organize, and tools to do so.

ORGANIZE

1. Your manuscript files and name them carefully. Always name your files carefully. You do not want to have to figure out which of your ten different files is the final one, or accidentally upload a typo-riddled one thinking it was the final file and get complaints about the editing (this happened to a writer I know).

You can use whatever naming system you want, just find one that works for you. As an example, I name a file with the name and date, such as PublishingGuide_edited_2-15-2022. I know what the file is, that it's the edited version, and that it was created on 2-15-2022. If I change this file and then save a new version, I would use the new date in its name. In addition to carefully naming your files, you can use folders to help stay organized, moving older files into a separate folder so they don't get mixed up with the new file.

Speaking of multiple copies of your book file. *Make sure you have backups, and backups of your backups.* You never know when accidents will happen. I once accidently saved a lengthy school assignment as a blank document, losing all my work. Others have had computer failures and cloud issues. You can save files on your computer, on an external hard drive that you store in a firebox, in the cloud, or send as email attachments to yourself or a trusted friend. You don't want to lose all your work due to negligence in the extra work to protect it or cheapness.

2. Passwords. You will likely create dozens of website accounts for your author business, on top of all the accounts you have for your personal life. Remembering all those usernames and passwords, if you use unique ones, is nigh impossible for normal mortals. Using the same or similar passwords for different sites is risking hackers getting your information for one site and then causing trouble on many.

Fortunately, there are apps that help you keep track of passwords, even when they are long, convoluted ones. LastPass and OnePass are two that were recommended on the *Novel Marketing Podcast* to help protect your passwords. LastPass is also part of the software recommended by and offered for free to students and employees at the university where I went to school. These apps help by generating unique passwords for each website (or using ones you give them) and autofilling them into the websites as needed. They can be long, convoluted "safe" passwords and all unique because you don't have to remember any of them. You only have to remember one master password to get into the password protection app.

Not only does using such an app help protect you from hackers, having all your usernames, websites, and passwords stored in one protected space—easily accessed by you and whoever you share your master password with—is a help in times of trouble. If something happens to you, thanks to the app and your master password, your family will be able to access all your accounts with one password instead of hunting down dozens of usernames and passwords for websites they might not even know they need to get into. So be sure to have your master password stored in a safe place.

3. Income and expenses. Save all information regarding expenses, income, print copies purchased and what happens to them. Save paper receipts and electronic ones however works best for you, be that Microsoft Excel, Google Docs, Scrivener, or a dedicated expense program. Even if you don't need this for your taxes, you'll probably want to know if you're turning a profit or still trying to pay yourself back for your books two years later.

4. All publication information. Keep track of book links, ISBNs, blurbs, taglines, ad copy, release dates, retailers, cover designers, editors, cover reveal participants, beta-readers, ARC readers, endorsers, and reviewers (bloggers, newspapers, etc. you asked to review your book). You might need this information for promotional opportunities in the future, for social media posts, to know who to contact for the cover of the next book in the series or who to ask or not to ask for feedback on your next manuscript. When you get ready to release later books, you might want to contact your ARC readers or those who hosted you as a guest blogger or who reviewed your book on their website to see if they would like to help with the next book's launch. This is much easier if all the information is in a designated space.

You can do this with a file for each book or series or a file per topic (such as a "links" file). You can also use folder trees. You might have a folder with subfolders for all the marketing files for your books, or you might keep the marketing information in the folder with the rest of the book's files. For example,

Fiction —> Series 1 —> Book 1 —> final files —> print PDF

Fiction —> Series 1 —> Book 1 —> marketing —> blurb and ad copy

5. Your network. You will meet a lot of authors, editors, reviewers, cover designers, influencers, and others in your author career. It's a good idea to try to remember who is who for later. Also, each time you see a cover you like or character art piece you admire, consider finding out who the artist is and collecting their name and website or Instagram profile into a file for the future. You never know when you might need to change designers, and it's also nice to have a list for when others are looking for recommendations.

You can often find this information on the copyright page of published books. For ebooks, you can use Amazon's Look Inside feature to see the copyright page. (No purchase required.)

6. Your time. If you're going to set up a pre-order or do guest posts or have a cover reveal or do any number of other things, you will need a good calendar to make sure you don't miss something. Preferably, this calendar will let you see your month at a glance and see your week and day, so you will know what is coming up so you can schedule your time accordingly. If, for instance, you're to guest blog on August 26, you can't wait until August 26 to write your post and send it to the blogger. They'll never have you back. Bloggers want materials ahead of time so they can set up their post and schedule it to send at the appropriate time. They are not waiting until the day of to make it. They should give you a deadline to let you know when to send your material, meaning you must schedule time before that to write the post and get any images, links, and so on for it ready.

7. Your ideas and answers. Keep a file for future book ideas, blog post and article ideas, and marketing ideas. Keep a file with canned replies to common questions, including "How can I follow your new releases?" For this question, you will most likely want to mention your newsletter sign-up and choose your most active social media platform or your BookBub or Amazon author page. Give two to three options, but not more, in case they don't want another newsletter. Give links to these. Instead of having to hunt down each link individually, if you have a file with the information ready and easy to find, you'll save yourself much time and energy.

———

Organization: Is there an app for that?

There are common programs authors use for organization, including Excel and Scrivener. I use Excel and the Mac-equivalent Numbers to keep track of my expenses, my stock of books, and my network. I find Excel a little slow and clunky for large files, though, which is why I use the next software a lot.

Scrivener is an amazing software designed specifically for authors and screenwriters. It allows you to create folders and subdocuments within a single project, easily move those around, and easily move between them. No scrolling to find a scene or copy-and-paste to move it! Just find the scene name on the left of your project window, grab it, and drag it where you want. Scrivener is also faster than Microsoft Word and doesn't slow down my computer. I got it for writing novels (being able to quickly find scenes and move them around, or find my notes, is wonderful!), but I now use it as a general life-organizer as well. It can hold *so* much.

I have one Scrivener project file for organizing my life stuff, but dozens of folders and text files nicely arranged within it. No more countless Word documents or sticky notes. I have folders for trip notes, folders for marketing with subdocuments about various ideas, a to-do list, a file for book links, and a folder for book blurbs with a file for each book. It's incredibly handy for both writing and organization. It was designed for Mac but now has a Windows version as well, and it only costs about $50.

However you organize, using folder trees is helpful. You can have a folder for your final files and a separate one for the drafts, for covers, and for marketing materials (blurbs, excerpts, tagline, ad copy, and so forth).

———

However you choose to accomplish it, for your future sanity, work out a method to stay organized. You'll thank yourself later. And don't forget to ask other authors how they stay organized. You can learn a lot just from other peoples' practices.

Chapter 16

Patreon and crowdfunding

One of the drawbacks of publishing a quality indie novel is the upfront cost of the editing, cover design, formatting, and marketing. Some authors have chosen to crowdfund their projects to cover these, or perhaps to produce an audiobook of an existing work. If you're not familiar with crowdfunding, you set up a project page on a site such as Kickstarter, then ask people to contribute to your project: you can ask people you know, post on social media, and so forth. It's also available to anyone who happens to be on the site looking for something to fund. Campaigns often have different funding levels. For example, if the project gets x dollars, then an ebook is produced; if y dollars, then a paperback is released too; if n dollars, then an audiobook version is released as well. Depending on which company you go through, there might be a minimum funding level, and if that isn't reached, then backers aren't charged and you get nothing.

Consequently, you have to give a good pitch for your project and have a large reach. You must also tell exactly what the money is going toward and offer rewards for pledges (a *pledge* is the amount a contributor will give if the project is fully funded). There are different pledge levels, with different rewards at each level, based on the size of the pledge. There's typically a small pledge level ($10 or less, depending on the project) that gets no reward. The reward for higher levels might be a free ebook of the finished book, a free print copy and ebook, a chance to name a character, a personalized poem, and so on. People are essentially pre-buying the book to enable you to produce it.

Crowdfunding is a complicated topic, with many pros and cons, but I wanted to mention it since you will hear of it if you haven't already. You've likely heard of fantasy author Brandon Sanderson's record-breaking Kickstarter campaign for his four "secret" books in March 2022. It earned over $15 million in 24 hours and closed with 185,341 backers for a total pledge of $41,754,153. This is not typical. Sanderson was already a hugely popular, traditionally published author with a tremendous reach (he could let a lot of people know about the Kick-starter campaign) and a great hook: books written in secret that wouldn't be available through traditional publishers and which would arrive quarterly for a "year of Sanderson." People weren't funding his books so much as buying them. By contributing to his campaign, they were purchasing anything from a single ebook to a year's worth of subscription book boxes with premium hardbacks (not POD hard-backs), audiobooks, and swag. It was a brilliant piece of marketing by a talented author and his team, but it is not the typical crowdfunding campaign. Sanderson has spent years building trust with his readers, and they knew he would provide something great (even his announcement YouTube video was entertaining) and so were eager to contribute. Creating something fun for your fans, as Sanderson has, is something to consider if you're planning a crowdfunding campaign.

Back to the crowdfunding of "mere mortals." I know an author who successfully funded a book, but he knows a lot of people and is just one of those people who has lots of friends and followers. He also had an appealing project and reasons to crowdfund. So you have to have a reason to do this; otherwise, people will just think you're being lazy and will want to know why you're not skipping the lattes or working extra to fund this yourself. And remember that many crowdfund contributors get a free copy of the book in return for their contribution, so the cost of that (print and shipping, for instance, for print books and the removal of those people from the list of actual buyers) must be considered.

Another thing to be aware of for the future is Patreon. This site has been around for a while now and allows "patrons" to support the creatives they admire. A creative doesn't make much from that one ebook or print book their devoted fan bought, and fans realize this. Thus some are happy to pay a monthly or onetime amount to their favorite author through sites like Patreon, Buy Me a Coffee, and Ko-fi to help them out, and maybe enable them to spend more time writing and less time at their day job. Authors usually reward their monthly supporters with exclusive bonuses (like short stories) and early access to materials. Translation: this is extra work, not just extra cash. And this isn't something to start immediately, as you need a loyal fan base.

Here are some crowdfunding and patron-support companies, as well as a few articles for more information.

Patreon
Kickstarter
Indiegogo
Inkshares
Publishizer
GoFundMe
Unbound
Ko-fi
Buy Me a Coffee

References and Resources

Bournias, Stephen. "13+ Brilliant Patreon Alternatives to Monetize Your Audience." Accessed March 21, 2022. *AppSumo* (blog). https://blog.appsumo.com/patreon-alternatives/.

Herbert, Patrick. "Crowdfunding for Authors: A Simple Guide for 2022." *Self-publishing.com*. May 20, 2021. https://selfpublishing.com/crowdfunding-for-authors/.

MiblArt. "How Indie Authors Can Use Patreon: Everything You Need to Know." Accessed March 21, 2021. https://miblart.com/blog/patreon-for-indie-authors/.

Sanderson, Brandon. "Most Funded Kickstarter Ever (2022)" (YouTube Video). March 4, 2022. https://www.youtube.com/watch?v=fmj2Mzhlflg.

Sanderson, Brandon. "Surprise! Four Secret Novels by Brandon Sanderson." *Kickstarter.* Accessed April 1, 2022. https://www.kickstarter.com/projects/dragonsteel/surprise-four-secret-novels-by-brandon-sanderson.

Sydner, Lucy. "How to Crowdfund Your Writing With Patreon." December 22, 2018. https://www.writersdigest.com/publishing-insights/how-to-crowdfund-writing-crowdfunding-your-writing-patreon.

Chapter 17

Concluding schedule and budget

Indie publishing can be as simple and cheap or as complex and expensive as you choose, and you have to do a lot of choosing. Fortunately, you don't have to make all the decisions all at once, and in indie publishing, you can often go back and change things or simply start afresh. So don't get overwhelmed. Keep moving on.

With regard to this book and the publishing process, moving on means getting your manuscript ready for publishing. By that I do *not* mean giving it to your English teacher friend to edit before you slap it up on Amazon for sale (this is a common misconception). English teachers are great at what they do, but they may or may not be qualified to edit a book. Writing books is different to writing essays. There's much more involved in editing a novel than most high school English teachers are aware of (unless they're authors who've studied publishing in your genre).

Also, conventions change, and English teachers and your grammar-police friend may or may not realize it. Case in point, like many of us, I was taught to use two spaces after a period—it's one space now. I was given a list of dialogue tags to use in place of *said*: tags like *grunted, shouted, retorted, cajoled*, and so on. Now we're taught to avoid dialogue tags, with the exception of the light use of *said*, in favor of action beats.

You may also think you shouldn't end a sentence in a preposition or use contractions. Think again.

Writing is its own field with its own conventions, vocabulary, and expectations, and must be studied as a professional would study brain surgery, banking laws, plumbing, or anything else.

Part Four

Getting the Manuscript Ready

Chapter 18

Getting the manuscript ready (editing and pre-formatting)

What does it take to get your manuscript ready for publishing? The simple answer is a lot of editing. As Jo Lallo of the *Six Figure Authors Podcast* says, content, cover, and back cover copy are the three essentials of a published book. The content may be the last thing noticed by the person picking up the book from a shelf—real or virtual—but it is ultimately the most important of the three. At least, if you hope to sell more than one book!

So one can't simply type "The End," hand off the manuscript to a grammar-police friend to "edit," slap on a cover, and then publish it. There is much, much more to the editing process than fixing errors in grammar. So let's briefly go over the three main types of edits— developmental editing, line editing, and copyediting—after which comes the final proofread. These are what I call the editing types. The names and distinctions are a bit fuzzy at times, so always check with your editor before hiring them to determine what they actually do in their edits. Fun fact: editors don't agree on whether "copyedit" is one word or two words connected with a hyphen. We'll talk about working with professional editors later.

TYPES OF EDITS

Developmental edit (content edit or substantive edit)

The developmental edit, also called a content edit or substantive edit, looks at the overall structure of the novel or work of nonfiction. Does it flow properly? It is organized well? Is the plot sound? Are the character arcs done well? How is the pacing? Do any parts drag? Does the author have a good voice?

This edit makes sure the story itself is sound. No amount of typo-fixing will save a story with a bad structure or poorly done characters. In fact, many readers will forgive typos if the story itself is riveting.

How do you get a developmental edit? You can hire developmental editors (these are editors who specialize in this type of edit and who may or may not do the other types of edits). If you're more budget conscious, you can study books on the craft (which you should do anyway), participate in critique groups, and have beta-readers. Between your studies and reader feedback, you can, hopefully, get the story itself in good shape. But what are critique groups and beta-readers and how do you find them? We'll discuss hiring editors later.

Critique groups are groups of authors who exchange manuscripts (usually a chapter or so at a time), giving feedback in return for feedback. You critique their submissions and they critique yours. This can be tremendously helpful to a beginning author, and even to an established one. The comments on your manuscript from other authors can be helpful (others see things you might miss), and critiquing others' works, noting the good and what needs improvement, often helps you identify those things in your own work.

However, the critique may or may not be as holistic as a developmental edit or a beta-read. It depends on the skill of the critique partners and the goal of the critique group. These are often more focused on scene level comments since they tend to be an exchange of a chapter or two at a time.

Beta-readers are authors or readers who read the entire manuscript in one go and give broad feedback on the work and possibly on individual scenes as well, depending on the reader. These are invaluable members of your team no matter what publishing level you're at. You will always need other eyes on your work. When looking for and choosing beta-readers, it's helpful if they enjoy your genre, are reliable, "get" your work, and aren't afraid to tell you the bad as well as the good.

I wish I could give you a list of perfect places to find critique partners and beta-readers. But these people are treasures you'll have to hunt down yourself. You might start by looking up local author groups and searching for author and fan groups on Facebook that are targeted to your genre and allow requests for beta-readers. Some writers' associations have critique group options. I learned a lot through the American Christian Fiction Writers and Realm Makers critique groups. Some associations have local chapters that meet regularly and might offer feedback. If you have a newsletter and readers already, you can ask there for beta-readers. If you'd like a local group, ask at your local library or bookstore about writers' groups, as they tend to meet in one of those two places. Author and writing teacher K. M. Weiland has a blog post about how to find great beta-readers. She shares a list of potential places to find beta-readers that her followers shared with her. The link to that post is below.

If you can afford to pay, there are online writing communities that offer workshops and beta-reads. Scribophile is one that I've come across. It describes itself as "a respectful online writing workshop and writer's community. Writers of all skill levels join to improve each other's work with thoughtful critiques and by sharing their writing experience." (https://www.scribophile.com) I haven't used it personally but have seen a few positive comments regarding it.

Tips for engaging with beta-readers and critique groups

You will get lots of advice, some better than others. Many in these groups are still learning and may not know as much as they think they do or have fallen prey to prescriptive teachers who play up "rules" without understanding the principles behind them.

As always, be wise in what advice you choose to apply, but still also be grateful for the time others put into reading your work and providing feedback, even if you find the feedback unhelpful. Also, remember to consider expectations—don't expect a reader to relay the kind of feedback a trained critic would give, or a novice writer to give professional-level, developmental edit feedback. Don't expect a romance reader to love your spy thriller (do expect them to want you to add lots of feelings where they may not belong). Be aware of genre differences between you and your critique partners or beta-readers. What works for one genre may ruin another. It might take a while to find the right readers and critique partners so be patient and don't take bad advice from the wrong reader because it's all you've got.

Critique groups are often "as you go along" groups. You're submitting to the group as you work on the novel (often), or you can finish it, then submit week by week (or whatever the work flow of the group is). Because of this, and because you are also giving feedback to the authors, this is a slow, time-consuming process. Each critique group is different, with its own dynamics, strengths, and weaknesses. Some last a long time and others fizzle out quickly. If you use beta-readers instead, the book needs to be finished before giving it to the reader. I try to give readers a month to get feedback to me. I find it wise to give an actual deadline on when I need the feedback returned. Deadlines help people get things done. Many people, whether beta-readers or editors, request a deadline because they know the work won't get done without one.

Also, know that some authors join mastermind groups. These groups are usually geared more toward accountability or discussing craft or marketing and may not be offering line-by-line feedback on your manuscript. Some critique groups don't even do that, so be sure you understand what the expectations of groups are before joining. Finding the right people—getting good feedback—is one of the hardest parts of being an author. If you have a great critique partner or beta-readers, be sure to thank them often!

Once the overall story of your manuscript is ready, or the structure and voice of your nonfiction, then you can work on the words themselves.

Line editing (sometimes called copyediting)

Once the story itself is in good shape, then you can focus on the words. As suggested by the title, line editing is a broader type of editing. It looks at paragraphs and sentences as a whole. This is the difference between a grammatically correct but convoluted, nonsensical sentence and "writing that sings." That is, writing that is understandable and pleasant to read. Many editors combine line editing with copyediting (grammar nuts and bolts, essentially), as they are closely related.

There are editors who specialize in this type of editing. You can also get this type of help from certain critique partners. Some writing programs, such as Grammarly and ProWritingAid, have tools to help in this. But such programs are no match for a real editor. What works for essays and nonfiction may be terrible advice for fiction, so always study on your own and be careful of software.

Copyediting (sometimes called proofreading)

Copyediting is more what most people think of as "editing," where grammar issues, inconsistencies, and typos are addressed, among other things. This is a final polish.

Many authors are able—through self-study, practice, and talented critique partners and beta-readers—to skip the previous two edits, but don't skip this. There are many tips for self-editing, but it is also well-established that it is difficult to edit your own manuscript because you tend to see what you think is there rather than what is there. You'll have to get feedback on your writing and see what you're capable of doing yourself and what you need to hire out.

Final proofreading

In traditional publishing, where books are typeset, the author receives a final proof of the book, called a galley. This is used for a final proofreading. Only typos and egregious errors are fixed at this step, since changing things might require a great deal of trouble and money because the typeset must be fixed. Things are different for indie print-on-demand books, but a final proofread, perhaps by ARC readers (those who read advance reader copies), is still a good thing. You can also hire proofreaders. Be sure to note whether this is a true final proofread or a light copy-edit, as the terminology has gotten rather confusing over the years.

It's also good to remember that no proofread is likely to be perfect. Many eyes catch more typos, but even many eyes and highly trained ones still miss typos. Don't be too upset if you find typos in your published books. As an indie, it's not difficult to go in and correct them!

———

Once your manuscript has gone through all these stages, then it's ready to turn into a book. But how do you find an editor? We'll talk about that next, then how to self-edit, and finally, how to evaluate feedback. Feedback can make or break a novel, or a relationship, so we must be wise in how we handle it.

References and Resources

Editorial Freelancers Associations. "Editorial Rates." https://www.the-efa.org/rates/.

Editorial Freelancers Association. "Hiring an Editor: A Guide for New Authors." (PDF) https://www.the-efa.org/wp-content/uploads/2020/12/Guidebook-for-new-authors-2020.pdf.

Ide, Kathy. *Editing Secrets of Best-Selling Authors*. LPC, 2020.

Ide, Kathy. *Proofreading Secrets of Best-Selling Authors*. LPC, 2016.

Renni Brown and David King. *Self-Editing for Fiction Writers, Second Edition: How to Edit Yourself into Print*. William Morrow Paperbacks, 2014.

Weiland, K.M. "15 Places to Find Your Next Beta Reader." *Helping Writers Become Authors*. March 4, 2016. https://www.helpingwritersbecomeauthors.com/find-your-next-beta-reader/.

Chapter 19

Finding and working with an editor

Probably the most expensive part of your book's launch is the edit. Depending on the book's length, the price of the edit, and the number of edits, you can spend hundreds to thousands of dollars. Naturally, you want to spend this money wisely. So how do you find and work with editors?

What kind of edit do you want?

The first step is knowing what type of edit you're looking for. Developmental? Line? Proofread? Some editors specialize in a certain type (which we discussed in the previous section). Some specialize in a certain genre as well. So look for an editor who does the type of editing you want and who edits (and preferably reads) in your genre. Experienced editors will typically have a list of services on their website stating what types of edits they do and what each entails. They'll also state their preferred genres. You might need more than one type of edit (a developmental, then a line edit and a proofread), and if so, you can use the same editor for each edit (if the editor does all three), as that saves time looking for editors, and since some editors offer a discount on a second service on the same book. If you want more than one service, see if the editor does them all. However, having the same editor do all three edits is not necessarily a good idea, because they may have seen your manuscript so many times by the final proofread they may not be seeing the typos anymore. You might want one editor to do the developmental and line edits but get a fresh pair of eyes for the proofread. Some editors will also help with brainstorming, writing your blurb, or marketing.

Depending on your skill level, you might need only a copyedit and a proofread. Or you might need a developmental edit and several rounds of line edits before you get to the proofread stage. You might be able to recognize this yourself, or you might need a trusted friend or an editor to tell you. There are always scams and just slothful people, so before you do multiple rounds of edits with the same editor (who claims your writing is terrible and must be fixed many times) or before you choose an editor who gives more compliments and smiley faces than actual corrections and suggestions, get a second or third opinion.

If your work needs that much help, go back to studying the basics of grammar, of writing itself, and of writing fiction or nonfiction. Do what you can yourself, get in a critique group, and then go back to an editor. (Unless you have the money for multiple edits but are low on the time to improve by yourself.) If your writing is so polished your line editor makes hardly any changes, consider dropping from a line edit to a light copyedit—after you've confirmed your skill level warrants it.

You can send the same page to two different editors, and one will make the page bleed with all the digital "red ink" and the other will tell you you've a natural talent and make relatively few suggestions. You need to have studied the craft enough, and be clear-sighted enough, to know which is best for you. Sometimes, it might be the first editor, other times the second. Arrogantly discounting changes is just as foolish as "humbly" applying every single one. Choosing a good editor is a skill and may require practice. We'll talk more about this later.

How much will it cost?

Cost varies tremendously, by type of edit and by editor. To add to this, some editors charge by the hour, some by the page (a standard manuscript page, which is around 250 words), or by the word. Some charge more if the manuscript requires more than the normal amount of work.

I know, I know. That's a really frustrating answer. So here's a few rates I've seen: a proofread/light copyedit for $4/1,000 words; a line edit for $0.0085/word; and a line edit for $.02-.025/word. For a 100,000-word manuscript, that's $400, $850, and $2,000, respectively. Granted, options two and three entail more work on the editor's part, but those two are equivalent edits, only one is well below the standard rate. The experience of the editor and how confident they are in their work (some have difficulty charging what they're worth), as well as the country of origin (some international editors may charge less) influence how much an editor charges. So some new editors will do great work but charge less. If money is tight, look around until you find a quality editor who charges a lower rate. You can also study craft and editing for yourself and polish your manuscript as much as you can so you'll need a less expensive edit.

The Editorial Freelancers Association (EFA) has a rate chart showing the median price charged by editors: https://www.the-efa.org/rates/. The EFA also has a member directory, jobs list, and guides to help authors considering hiring editors. You can find those on this page: https://www.the-efa.org/hiring/.

How to find an editor

Once you know what you want, you can start looking around. Ask your published author friends. Look at the copyright page of published indie books (you can do this using the Look Inside feature on Amazon, as many authors list their editor and cover designer on the copyright page). Ask in the author Facebook groups you're in (if the terms of the group allow). Many groups have set posts of a "rolodex" on editors and cover designers, so all you have to do is use the search feature or find their resources section. You can also employ an internet search, but you will likely get a huge list. You can try narrowing it down by adding your genre. You can also, depending on your genre, use the Christian Editor Connection, which connects freelance editors to authors seeking edits (https://christianeditor.com). You can also look for editors through

Reedsy (https://reedsy.com/editing/book-editor), Upwork (https://www.upwork.com), and, as previously mentioned, the EFA.

Are discounts and coupons a thing in the editing world? Yes, they are. Some editors give discounts to members of certain writer groups (ALLi, for instance, or to members of a Facebook writing group they're a part of). Some give coupons to writers who attend a conference they're also attending. Some create coupons for holidays or for when they want to gain new clients. So be on the lookout. If you can't afford an edit, it's much better to wait, skimp on fancy coffees or work extra hours, or do what it takes to pay for an edit. It's much better to delay publication of a great book than to publish a shoddy book quickly.

How do you choose an editor?

Cost, availability, expertise, references, and a sample of their work should all be considered when choosing an editor.

Cost, we've already mentioned, and only you can determine your budget. As for availability, some editors are booked a year or more in advance. Some require only a few weeks' or a couple of months' notice. Some can start right away. If you're considering an editor, go ahead and ask about their availability before you agree to work with them. Be prepared to ask for an editing slot months in advance to be on the safe side. That may mean working to a deadline to get the book ready in time, or, if you're not good with deadlines, waiting until the book is finished to set a date, then waiting until your editor is ready for it.

When you're asking when a potential editor can start on a project, ask how long it will take to get it back. The turnaround time might be two to six weeks, depending on the length, complexity of the edit, and the editor's workflow. Unless the project is very long or requires a lot of editing, a turnaround of a month or less is likely. Editors with a day job may take longer. They might give you an estimated date to return the work or ask you for one. If the latter, don't set it too long, as some people work better with tight (but fair) deadlines. I once had an editor take months on a 30,000-word edit because I didn't give her a firm date on it. It was Part 1 of a long novel, and I felt bad about setting a strict date for it since I wasn't even finished with the novel. It ended up stressing out both of us since I had to ask multiple times for it, and I nearly canceled on her before she finally got it finished. She had no trouble with the rest of the manuscript. She just needed a firm date to begin with.

In addition to cost and availability, look at the editor's website and see if they list their credentials. Some are self-taught, some have studied the style guides, some may have been interns in publishing houses and so were taught "in-house," and others may have earned copyediting certificates (I have one from UC San Diego's online extension program). A good editor will have this information and mention what style guides they follow (for fiction, this is *The Chicago Manual of Style*). If you're a nonfiction author, check to see what the style guide is for your field. Editors will often have testimonials from clients or a list of books they've edited. Newer editors may not have this, but you can ask what they've edited. You can check out the listed books on Amazon or Goodreads and see if the reviews mention the editing.

One of the best ways of gauging whether an editor is right for you, however, is an actual edit. Most editors offer a free sample edit, which is a short edit to see if you're a good fit for one another. They get a feel for your writing, decide what level you're at, how much work the edit is likely to be, and if they want to work with you. You decide if they do a professional job, work with your voice or try to change it, or miss egregious errors.

Sample edits are usually the first bit of your story, perhaps 2,000 words or the first five pages, depending on the editor. You polish this as you would the rest of your story to give the editor an honest feel for the work to be done. I don't recommend adding typos to "test" the editor. If they discover this, they'll be offended, and if they don't, they might assume your manuscript will need more work and give you a higher estimate!

Even if you know an editor personally, or a friend recommends them, or they have an impressive website and booklist, *always* get a sample edit.

I've had sample edits where the editor returned the sample almost immediately. And while speed may seem like a good thing, I noticed that both editors made bunches of comments, most of which were not true to my voice. They'd rushed through, making changes to suit themselves, missing genuine typos, and didn't take the time to see if their recommended changes fit my voice and the tone of my story. They quoted "rules" at me but didn't stop to think about my writing as an art. Writing is too nuanced for rules alone to guide it. I mentioned this to one young editor—that she was changing my voice and missing typos—and she didn't seem to care! Needless to say, I didn't work with her.

A second case in point, I once worked with an editor based on a recommendation by a mutual acquaintance without asking for a sample edit and ended up getting the wrong kind of edit! I assumed I was getting a copyedit. The editor's website didn't really say, and I just assumed since that's the most common type of edit. She gave me a sort-of developmental edit (mostly opinions I didn't agree with on a book my beta-readers loved), leaving me scrambling to get a copyedit for it in time to publish. Dumb mistake on my part!

So always get a sample edit, a few from different editors, until you find an editor who's skilled, who gets your work, and who makes wise corrections and suggestions. Many editors make positive comments to let you know your strengths as well as comments to let you know where you need to improve.

What to expect

We've already discussed cost and scheduling the edit. But how do you pay, what do you send, and what will you get back?

Payment is often through PayPal. This is a business transaction, so you should pay through the business option (if they send a link rather than an invoice), not the personal option, of PayPal. It does cost the editor a fee, but that's a business expense, a just payment to PayPal for all they do, and not something you should feel bad about or that they should try to get around by being unethical and asking you to send it as a personal exchange. Besides, they can write it off on their taxes. Editors usually state on their website how they want to be paid.

Some editors may not ask for payment until the manuscript has been returned to you. Some edit the manuscript and then ask for payment before sending it. Some ask for half upfront and the other half before sending the finished, edited manuscript. Some allow payment plans. Each editor varies. Some may have a contract. Most do not.

Realize that editors are taking a risk on you by doing the work before all the payment is received, so don't balk if an editor wants at least part of the money before the edit is returned. I'd be leery of someone who wants all the money before the edit is even begun, though.

What do you send to an editor? They may specify the file type and other considerations, or not. However, be aware that there is a standard manuscript format that most editors want or expect. Some even state this on their website. The standard manuscript page is 1-inch margins and double-spaced, 12-point Times New Roman font text. No tabs— use your word processor's indent feature. One space after the period. These pages run about 250 words per page. Most editors work with docx and doc files, though some use Google Docs. Some are willing to work on formatted manuscripts.

Once you send your work and the editor gets started, you may or may not hear from them until the work is finished. If they find your sample edit was misleading and your manuscript needs more work than anticipated, they'll let you know and ask about adjusting the cost to meet the expected timeframe needed to complete the job. Most likely, you won't hear anything except a notice that they're almost finished and will have the manuscript back by such-and-such a date. Most editors do two or three passes through your manuscript for a copyedit or proof-read. If an editor only does one pass (some say this on their website), I'd be leery of this. From personal experience, I'd say this isn't giving the document enough attention.

Once you've paid and the work is returned, you'll get a document with track changes and comments. You may also get a separate document with broader feedback. If you're not familiar with track changes and the comment feature of your word processor, you'll need to learn to use them before getting an edit. (Familiarize yourself with Find and Replace as well, as using it can save you a lot of time and effort.)

You can go through the editing document itself, accepting and rejecting the changes using those features directly, or you can apply the changes to a separate document. I do the latter, as I prefer to make the changes myself. I recommend keeping a copy of the pre-edit document, the editor's document, and the edited document, all properly labeled and in separate folders. Editors are usually open to you asking them questions about their suggested changes, but do be respectful of their time.

That's it for working with an editor. The next few sections have tips on self-editing and evaluating feedback.

Chapter 20

Copyediting

Editing a manuscript may be a pleasure or a pain, depending on your personality, and either affordable or not, depending on your purse. Either way, as writers, it's our job to write the best we can and self-edit the best we can before our material goes to the public—whether the public is the audience or the hired editor. The cleaner your manuscript is, the less work the editor has to do, saving you money. Here are a few tips on editing. Please note, these are for a light copyedit, not a line edit (which is really a medium to heavy copyedit). The text is pretty clean already. Copyediting is the final editing before proofing and should catch all grammatical errors, inconsistencies, usage errors, and so on. The story structure, character arcs, and general clarity of sentences should already have been checked and approved. You should also know the style of your genre. If you write fiction, for instance, you should already be familiar with good practice for fiction writing, including proper point of view, consistent narration, show versus tell, and proper use of dialogue tags and action beats. I highly recommend *Self-Editing for Fiction Writers* by Rennie and King for that.

TWELVE TIPS FOR COPYEDITING A MANUSCRIPT

1. Read very, very slowly on the first pass. This makes it easier to catch missing words as well as other mistakes. Running your finger or a pencil under each word also helps. Printing out the manuscript for your last editing pass (two or three passes is common for editors) is a good idea. A professional editor may skim your manuscript first and then do a slow, thorough edit on the second pass, and then a faster third pass to catch any missed mistakes.

2. Read aloud or listen to a text-to-speech program read the manuscript to you. This is great for catching similar words you may have used incorrectly as well as words used twice or left out. You can also catch accidental rhymes you may not want or long, convoluted sentences.

3. Don't try to binge edit. You'll tire and miss errors—or add them in. Realize that a good edit takes time and divide your editing into chunks, say five pages at a time or a chapter at a time, depending on how good you are at staying in the editor mindset.

4. Create a style sheet and story details file. This is to help you keep track of preferred spellings (like *Alexandria* instead of *Alexandra*), style decisions (Oxford comma or not, italics or quotes), and story details (timing, character hair color, name spelling, and so on) that should be consistent throughout. List problem areas here as well, such as words you overuse or commonly misuse (*whom* and *who*, for instance).

5. Keep your reference guides handy and use them. *The Chicago Manual of Style* (CMOS) is the standard guide for fiction, but it's quite dense. *Proofreading Secrets of Best-Selling Authors* by Kathy Ide is my go-to guide. It references the CMOS and mentions differences between it and other style guides, such as the Associated Press style guide. *Merriam-Webster's Collegiate Dictionary* is the dictionary of choice in the US for fiction. Some genres or niches may have their own style guide. There's *The Christian Writer's Manual of Style* for Christian nonfiction and fiction, and I've heard that there's one for anything to do with baseball as well.

6. Here are some things to look for when copyediting:

- Spelling, hyphenation, capitalization, punctuation
- Treatment of numbers and numerals
- Treatment of quotations within dialogue and character thoughts
- Use of abbreviations and acronyms
- Dialogue tags
- Use of italics for thoughts and emphasis
- Word usage
- Grammar
- Missing words or punctuation
- Redundancies

7. Look up any word that might be misused or otherwise incorrect. Get accustomed to looking up at least one or two words or phrases per page. Spell check is great, unless, of course, you spelled the wrong word the write way (or the right way). Ask of two-word phrases, are they open or closed? Do they require a hyphen? Is it *in to* or *into*? Is it *under way* or *underway*? You may have a one-year-old nephew or a nephew who is one year old, but you don't have a one year old nephew. This can get tiring, but I've been surprised at how many words I've either used incorrectly or written incorrectly (they needed a space or a hyphen or didn't need a space, for instance).

If you're not sure about grammar and usage rules, Kathy Ide's *Proofreading Secrets of Best-Selling Authors* and Patricia O'Conner's *Woe Is I: A Grammarphobe's Guide to Better English in Plain English* are excellent, readable guides. Ide's book also has a list of commonly misused words and common grammar and usage errors.

8. Keep an eye open for consistency. Check for character details (eye color, for instance), spelling of unique words (particularly relevant for fantasy authors who make up words), treatment of sound words (italics or Roman for words like *um, hmm,* and so on), italics or quotes for emphasis in dialogue, italics and present tense or not for character thoughts, and single spaces before and after the ellipsis (but no space between ellipses and punctuation marks or quotation marks).

9. Note any errors or convoluted sentences or paragraphs. If any

larger issues come up, make a note. You may want to fix them right then or wait.

10. Avoid repetition when it's not intended for a particular effect. "I tossed my heavy cloak onto my bed." vs. "I tossed the heavy cloak onto my bed." That's an unimportant example, but get used to thinking about repeated words in sentences and paragraphs and across the entire manuscript. Do you overuse certain words or phrases? Like *turned, looked, glared,* or *raised an eyebrow*?

11. Look for redundancies and cut or replace extraneous words. Do you really need *that* in the sentence? And "she stood" and "she stood up" are the same; you can delete *up*. You don't need "down" in "she sat down."

- Being a gentleman, he stood up to give her his chair. She thanked him as she sat down.
- Light change: Being a gentleman, he stood to give her his chair. She thanked him as she sat.
- Heavier change: Ever a gentleman, he offered her his chair. She thanked him as she sat.

The first sentence was technically correct, but now it's fourteen words instead of eighteen and sounds better. In the same vein, don't be too formal. Use contractions. They're easier for readers to "hear" as they read. Your prose will read more smoothly and naturally, in other words.

12. Remember the Golden Rule of Copyediting: editing is for the reader. Can the reader understand the work and enjoy it? Is the author's message coming through clearly? The minutiae of comma placement, hyphenation, and so on are to serve the reader, not terrorize the author. So don't get bogged down in the rules—or get lazy—but focus on clarity and the reader's enjoyment.

(This chapter first appeared on *Lands Uncharted,* a blog dedicated to young adult fantasy and writing. It was modified slightly and is used with permission. https://www.landsuncharted.com/2018/07/10-tips-for-copyediting-manuscript.html)

Chapter 21

Proofreading tips

Getting your work ready to send off is scary—you want it to be perfect. Which means proofreading is kinda scary because you know someone will catch whatever mistakes you missed and will let you know about them. So here are some secrets about proofreading to help you win the battle for an error-free story.

PROOFREADING YOUR MANUSCRIPT

Here is the first thing to know about proofreading: Half the battle is knowing your enemies. The other half is being able to see them. The other half is having the right weapons. (Yes, there are three halves.)

Knowing your enemies (or knowing what to look for)
When proofreading, pay attention to these three things:

- Style
- Language: grammar, usage, and diction
- Egregious errors: confusing sentences, inconsistencies, and factual errors

Style

Though sometimes neglected in proofreading, style is important, as it influences the look and feel of your manuscript. Is it consistent and professional or inconsistent and unprofessional?

For style, consider whether these areas are properly styled and consistent:

- Headings
- Capitalization
- Spelling (note words with variable spellings)
- Quotes and italics
- Emphasis, quotes within quotes, sound words

Some style issues are governed by a particular style guide, others by personal choice rather than by hard-and-fast rules. So you need to match the proper style or decide on and stick to your own. You can also read your favorite authors and note how they do things.

For example:

- C.I.A. or CIA?
- Copy-editing or copyediting?
- Gray or grey

Language

1. Investigate grammar, usage, and diction. For language, consider these areas:

- Spelling
- Hyphenation
- Capitalization
- Punctuation
- Correct word or phrase
- Numbers and numerals (written out or not)
- Use of contractions (it can be easier to read contractions)
- Idioms understandable to intended audience?

For this section, slow down and question every word or phrase:

- Is it *ink stand* or *inkstand; under way* or *underway; into* or *in to*?
- Is it *it's* or *its; were* or *we're*?
- *Iced tea* or *ice tea*? (one of these is correct; the other is a misspelling)
- *Effect* or *affect; if . . . was* or *if . . . were; who* or *whom*?

2. Get comfortable with hyphenation. "I have a one-year-old nephew" but "My nephew is one year old." Get used to using the dictionary and guides like Kathy Ide's *Proofreading Secrets of Best-Selling Authors* frequently for spelling, usage, and hyphenation.

3. Consider spacing and white space. Use only one space between sentences. Paragraphs shouldn't be too long (intimidating to readers) or too short (a lot of one-line paragraphs is considered overly dramatic).

Spotting the enemy: By sight and sound

1. Read v-e-r-y, v-e-r-y slowly.

2. Read aloud or use a text-to-speech program. This will help you catch missing words (e.g., dropped *the* or *a*), words used twice, words often confused or mistyped (e.g., *that* and *than*). It will also help you gauge the "rightness" and rhythm of the writing.

3. Pay special attention to line breaks (that is, the last word on one line and the first word of the next—it's easy for word repeats to happen here).

4. Use a pencil to guide the eye.

5. Use a print out.

6. Read from the end to the beginning or from the bottom up of each page. This helps keep the brain from reading into the story what it thinks is there (e.g., a missing *a*).

7. Make a list of words that are frequently misused or misspelled. Make a list of words you overuse and need to replace or cut.

8. Read a page or so of Kathy Ide's *Proofreading Secrets of Best-*

Selling Authors or some other helpful book before starting your edit to get yourself in an editing mindset.

9. Let the manuscript get "cold" before proofreading it.

10. Expect to stop and look up words, phrases, hyphenation, and usage frequently.

11. Break your time into small chunks so you won't lose alertness and make mistakes.

The right weapons

Knowing where the rules or the guidelines are is essential. Your grammar police friend probably isn't familiar with publishing standards, nor are your critique partners (we writers tend to think we know what we're doing and give both good and bad advice with great confidence). It's always best to go to the source. Here are some great references (use the latest print edition or the online version):

- *Proofreading Secrets of Best-Selling Authors* by Kathy Ide
- *Merriam-Webster's Collegiate Dictionary*
- *The Chicago Manual of Style*
- *The Christian Writer's Manual of Style*

Also, always use spellchecker but don't rely on it. You can also use writing programs such as ProWritingAid or Grammarly. A drawback of those for some writers is that they are not necessarily for fiction. Some rules and expectations differ between fiction and nonfiction, and these programs are just not the same as a real editor.

In short, the secret to proofreading is this: Read slowly. Question every word. Read your work aloud or listen to it.

(This chapter first appeared on *Lands Uncharted*. https://www. landsuncharted.com/2018/08/secrets-of-proofreading-lizzie.html)

Chapter 22

Evaluating feedback

Feedback is tough to take, but how an author handles feedback often determines the quality of his or her writing, because others' comments can make a book sing like a nightingale or burn like a turkey at Thanksgiving. Not all advice is of equal value, so how do you decide which suggestions to keep and which to ignore? There are no hard and fast rules, but here are some guidelines I've come up with after many years of giving and getting feedback from both other writers and professional editors.

I've divided my comments into two parts—evaluating the evaluator and evaluating the feedback's resonance. Both parts were originally posts on the *Lands Uncharted* blog: https://www.landsuncharted.com/2017/08/how-to-evaluate-feedback-part-1.html and https://www.landsuncharted.com/2017/10/how-to-evaluate-feedback-part-2.html.

EVALUATING THE EVALUATOR

This is about getting context, not hunting for fodder to reject or accept everything the person giving feedback says. Writers get feedback from different sources—critique partners (fellow writers at varying stages of experience and skill), editors (copyeditors, writing coaches, and so on, each hired to help polish the manuscript), publishing professionals (agents and acquisition editors), readers, professional reviewers, and contest judges (who can fall into any of the previous categories and are notorious for giving extremely varied feedback). Each group brings its own background, training, and preferences into their feedback, and it's essential to take that into account because unless an evaluator is unusually gifted in being objective, it will color the critique.

When you evaluate your evaluator, ask these questions:

1. What's the evaluator's experience and skill level?

What's his or her training and grasp of the writing craft and publishing industry?

The average reader can tell you whether they liked the book and, hopefully, what they did or did not like about it (though sometimes they may know something is "off" but not know exactly what). That's valuable, but you can't expect most readers to point out show-versus-tell errors or point of view errors.

A critique partner might know some writing rules but not understand the principles and thus insist on exact adherence to "rules" in a way that would ruin your manuscript. For example, some things should be told because they're not important enough to waste space on (it often requires more words to show than to tell) or because the subject matter is too hard on the emotions to show. A child getting hit by a car might be better told quickly, for instance, despite the general rule of show versus tell.

When someone with professional editing experience (and training) marks an error in grammar or the use of action beats, you should probably change it and look up the rule to imprint it on your mind to prevent further error. When anyone else marks an error, you should look up the rule yourself and then decide whether the feedback agrees with it. It's easy to think we know the rules when, in fact, we don't or we don't truly understand how best to apply them. This leads us to give (and accept) bad advice. Or to apply good advice badly.

For example, a friend consistently changed my usage of commas in a manuscript I later had professionally edited. Because she made consistent changes (implying confidence and knowledge), I thought she must be right and I wrong. I made her recommended changes. However, after the professional edit, I had to reverse the comma usage to my original, correct usage based on the editor's feedback. My friend was well-meaning but wrong, and I was too lazy to verify her suggested changes. Always look it up.

2. What's the evaluator's preferred genre?

The rules and expectations are different for different genres. A romance writer is likely to insist on the addition of a lot more physical descriptions of characters and introspection, the historical writer on more historical details, and the young adult author on slang and immature reactions from characters. The last thing my "Jane Austen with wands" light fantasy novels need are characters who storm out of the room every time someone disagrees with them, spew slang, minutely describe the fabric and style of all outfits, act according to modern manners and expectations, and go around describing every male as having either a strong jaw and chocolate eyes that draw them in (a sign of the hero, apparently) or bad breath (halitosis being the obvious sign of villainy). You must know the rules and expectations for your genre, which you can, happily, learn by reading in your genre.

Also note that book publishers use *The Chicago Manual of Style* as their guide on issues of style, whereas other purveyors of the written word, such as newspaper and magazine publishers, use other style guides. That can lead to differences in particulars (like usage of the Oxford comma), so know which guide your evaluator is likely to be familiar with so they aren't giving you misplaced feedback.

3. What's your attitude toward the evaluator?

As a people pleaser, there are times when I want to accept everything a certain evaluator tells me just because I respect and want to please them. Other times I'm irritated with the evaluator and want to reject all comments. Perhaps they've marked too many things in the past, doing so in a way that tries to make the writing theirs instead of mine.

I've had a critique partner like that. I fought the fires of anger and arrogance every time I got feedback (Who does she think she is claiming that word is better than mine! They mean the same thing! She's trying to change my voice to hers!). I was tempted to ignore even the good advice she gave. If I had, I would have missed some important comments. Evaluating your attitude will help you look at the feedback objectively.

Again, evaluating your evaluator isn't about justifying a rejection of all comments or lazily accepting them all, it's about getting context and objectively determining which suggestions are valid and which are well-meaning but not useful. We should always be grateful someone took the time and made the effort to read and make comments on our manuscripts.

EVALUATING THE FEEDBACK'S RESONANCE

We've talked about evaluating feedback by first evaluating the evaluator, how it's necessary to consider the evaluator's experience and preferred genre and your own attitude toward the evaluator. That gives you context for the feedback. Now, let's talk about evaluating the feedback based on your feelings. That's right. We're getting in touch with our feelings. Mostly so we can then ignore them. But sometimes the feeling is an educated instinct, or a righteous indignation. So let's get started evaluating feedback based on its resonance, or how we feel about it.

The theft

Feedback almost always elicits an emotional response. Someone corrects a typo or marks out one of those words you use way too much and you're both embarrassed at having made such an error and grateful it's been caught. You recognize your embarrassment and move on. Then you get a critique or edit where the evaluator marked out your perfectly good words and replaced them with synonyms for no apparent reason and did other things that stole your personal touch from the writing. You're angry, and a bit guilty at being angry.

But it's okay to be angry (for a short time) if someone is changing things to fit their own taste rather than to fix errors. It's a healthy anger because the evaluator has crossed a boundary line. In short, they are rewriting your grammatically correct work to suit their own style and preferences or genre expectations. In essence, they are making your work theirs. That's stealing. Not in a plagiarism or piracy sense, but in the sense that they are removing the "you-ness" from your work. Good feedback leaves your voice unchanged. It might remove unnecessary words and clarify meaning, but it doesn't harm your voice.

I usually only skim a "theft" critique, change the few glaring errors pointed out, and then put the critique away. Later, I will look back at it and decide if any of the changes are valuable. If so, I will likely take the idea, but not the actual wording, and rework the original so that it incorporates some of the changes but retains my voice.

Before you toss a critique as "stealing your voice," however, double-check that this is what it's doing and that it's not trying to smooth out underdeveloped writing. Read your work aloud and then read the changes. How do they sound? The same, or is one better? If you're still not sure, let it sit and come back to it when you're calmer and see how it sounds then.

One issue I've seen that might warrant rewriting someone's sentences is grammatically correct but bland writing. Are all your sentences structured the same way, or is there variation to make paragraphs flow better? If read aloud, does it sound monotone, or does it flow well and sound good to your ear?

For example: "The doorbell rang. Sandra rose. Sandra stepped away from the desk. A window shattered. Sandra ducked. Sandra hit the floor. Sandra rolled to the left." Notice how all the sentences have the same structure and are nearly all the same length? And all but two start with Sandra? Not all sentences need to be compound and have clauses at the beginning or end, but neither should they all be straight subject-verb-predicate like these. Conjunctions and clauses are your friends. The sentence might be rewritten as: "The doorbell rang, and Sandra stepped away from her desk to answer it. The window behind her shattered. With a cry, she hit the floor and rolled to the left." These aren't the deep point of view sentences some insist on, but at least they are not all the same structure and don't read like a monotone lecture. Was your critique partner perhaps trying to add needed variety to your sentence structure?

Listen also to how the words sound. Do you have too many repeated words or sounds (like *Sandra* in the example above)? Or would repeating a particular sound—using alliteration—make it read better? "Double, double, toil and trouble" wouldn't be as memorable without the alliteration. Was your critique partner trying to make it sound better?

The revelation

Some criticisms come out of the blue. I don't expect them, but after consideration, I either agree or disagree with them and move on. But some criticisms address issues I "had a feeling" about. A strange word, phrase, or scene I thought was clever, but deep down knew wasn't quite right, but that I refused to rewrite. After one or two, or (embarrassingly) every critiquer, circles the issue in red, I change it. Unfortunately, sometimes the "feeling" is about the plot as a whole, a character, or the writing itself. It's not as easily marked or articulated.

An important question to ask is, does the advice resonate with you? Sometimes almost everyone may say they love your work but you still have a feeling something's not right. Perhaps the work doesn't feel like your voice anymore (you may have let too many "thieves" or people in other genres influence you), or the story isn't fun anymore.

Let me share with you two embarrassing, but ultimately freeing, critiques to illustrate.

The first is from a contest. Contest judges are notorious for their opinionated, conflicting scoring. You know those judges who mark that you did everything correctly but still give you a low score because they just don't like your story? Well, that's not what happened here. The initial judges loved the entry and sent it to the final round. Here's what the final judge (a respected literary agent) had to say:

"Disjointed and jerky. Also something in the tone gives too much of a feminine flare for the male characters. Writes well and opening elements have promise but it doesn't hold. The story structure may add to deterioration of the story . . . "

He said this and it was a finalist entry! And the earlier judges loved it! Did I start to seethe and accuse him of being another subjective judge? No. I was embarrassed and pained, but I listened to what he said. For one, because he's well respected in the industry and, more importantly, because his comments resonated with what I'd been feeling. Something wasn't right about the story, but I couldn't put my finger on what it was. His tough words were exactly what I needed. The story's nearly completely different now, but it's so much better.

Later, on another story, an agent (the same one) made these comments about a different story I sent a query about:

"There is a tendency to overwrite. This usually means unnecessary description and trying too hard to 'write.' [The agent] found a recent blog that could be helpful in one area: http://thewritepractice.com/mark-twain-dialogue-tags/. The protagonist, in first person, has a feminine tinge to the narrative. In fact, one review said they had to double check to make sure it was a man and not a woman protagonist. The story idea is fine. It is the execution of the chapters that sends it back for further seasoning."

Again, I was disappointed, but I felt an agreement. I wasn't satisfied with my writing. I had thoughtlessly accepted others' comments and influence even though it wasn't my preferred style or my voice. I'd worked hard on plot (and the plot in that story needed a lot of work to get it where the agent could say that the idea was fine), but my writing had suffered. I took his advice, and the story is better for it.

To sum up evaluating feedback, you have to know the principles of good writing for yourself in order to decide which comments to accept and which to reject. You must know the *principles*, not simply the rules. The principles of good storytelling are derived from great stories. Rules are developed from principles to make applying them easier (more rote and less a matter of discernment). So rules don't make great stories, per se, but great stories make rules.

Sometimes the best thing to do is walk away for a time and then come back. Depending on the issue, you might bring your style guides and recent releases from your favorite publishers with you. Critiques from fellow writers are invaluable, but, ultimately, it's your story and you are responsible for making it the best it can be.

Chapter 23

Concluding getting the manuscript ready

Professional editing is essential for a professional book. There are four main types of editing: developmental (content); line editing (sometimes also called and even combined with copyediting); copyediting (sometimes called proofreading), and final proofreading (the final typo hunt). Terms get a bit fuzzy at times, so it's essential to clarify what edit you are seeking and what editors are offering. The better you are at the craft of writing, the fewer edits you'll need. When you're deciding on an editor, be sure to get sample edits and find an editor who improves your writing and respects your author voice.

Now that we've addressed a number of the bigger decisions of your indie career and the manuscript is off being polished, it's time to turn our attention to our plans for actually selling the book. That's right. We're going to talk about marketing, and yes, you really do need to think about this before the book is released.

Part Five

Marketing Pre-Release

Chapter 24

Introduction to marketing

You may be wondering at this point whether we'll ever start talking about the actual process of building the book and putting it online to sell. Rest assured, we will. In fact, many of the things we'll talk about in this section you'll need when you set up your book on the retailer dashboard. It's better to think about these things now, though, and think about them with a marketing mindset, than to throw them in during a technical section. Some require time and research to do properly, and waiting until you're actually in the process of uploading your book to consider them isn't the best approach.

In this section, we'll talk about branding, or getting your author self ready for readers, creating a website and newsletter, titling your book, and figuring out its genre and target audience (and the keywords and categories that come from that). We'll talk about the cover, what you need to do to build an audience for your book before it releases, and how to get reviews for the launch.

We'll start with you, the author.

Chapter 25

Branding the author and finding the target audience

If you've put together a book proposal for a literary agent, then you're probably either about to start groaning, because you thought you'd get away from things like comparables and marketing plans, or about to sit up in your seat with a gleeful smile, because you've already done a lot of your homework. Either way, buckle up and get out your research hat.

Branding and target audience

I know some of you hate marketing and just want to know how to put your book up on Amazon and other retail sites and are wondering why I'm even talking about that dreaded *M*-word.

Well, if you really want to know, it's because understanding what you write and who your target audience is, is essential to a successful book launch and author career. Readers have to find your books to buy and read them, which means you have to tell retailers where to put them so that the right readers will spot them. Understanding where to put your book and who will like your book is marketing at its core. Marketing isn't about roping unwilling people into purchasing your work. It's about connecting readers in search of great reads in their favorite genre with your great books in that favorite genre. It's a service to readers. (And it doesn't hurt you either.) So marketing is a good thing, albeit difficult.

One of the first topics you'll hear when discussing marketing is author branding. You already understand brand. Consider these three terms: OshKosh, Wrangler, and David's Bridal. What did you think of for each? Baby clothes? Sturdy jeans for the working man? Wedding gowns? These companies have a reputation based on the type and quality of products they produce and who they produce those products for. Men looking for jeans to stand up to the abuse of putting up fences and fixing the tractor won't go to David's Bridal. The blushing bride isn't looking for a wedding gown with OshKosh on the tag. People know by the name, the logo on the tag or storefront sign, what to expect from each brand.

Your author brand is the same, only for books. If you pick up an Agatha Christie book, you know what it will be like—a mystery with an unusual character solving crimes (a retiring little old lady or a fastidious Belgian gentleman). Jane Austen's novels are known for their satire, virtuous characters, and a romance where the heroine always rejects at least one proposal before accepting the hero at the end of the novel. The Star Wars franchise has its own defining characteristics and appeal, and *Downton Abbey* another. As does *National Geographic*.

Branding announces what types of books you write. It also helps you stay on track by reminding you who you are as an author. It's easy to get pulled in different directions when you see books unlike yours doing well or simply read a different kind of book and like that style. There will be growth and change as you mature as an author, but you don't want to change too much because you want your readers to trust you and keep coming back to your books. If you do find you want to write something different, something your current readers probably won't like, consider using a pen name. Readers might be okay following you into a different genre if your style and tone are the same, but if you change tone (such as from clean romance to steamy, or light-hearted to dark, for instance), using a pen name would be better. You're targeting a different audience, so starting over with a pen name makes sense.

As an example of a brand, I write clean stories with a blend of romance, adventure, and humor, set in fantasy worlds. Some are more fairy tale-like, some Regency-ish with magic, some more high fantasy, and some steampunk. But they are all adventure-romance stories with humor and well-rounded characters. I don't write dark or steamy, or books with a heavy focus on either romance or adventure. Knowing my brand helps keep me on track. I'm creating products readers can trust. If they like my brand, they'll keep coming back and will tell others they know who like that brand about it.

So a brand answers the questions, "What can fans expect from my new books? What can potential readers just now picking up my books expect from all of them? What should my next book be like?"

Branding also tells stores where to place your books to reach the readers who like your brand (they want the OshKosh in the baby section, not the teen section, for instance). It answers the keywords and categories you'll have to choose for your books, but we'll discuss this more later.

If author branding is answering the question, "What can readers expect from you?," how do you as an author figure out your brand, and how do you help your readers recognize your brand?

To figure out your unique brand, look at your work-in-progress. Look at your drawer of ideas and see what's there. What's the theme or glue holding your works together? Mostly mystery? Fantasy with a heavy romance angle? Spaceships blowing one another up?

As an example, author Brandilyn Collins's brand is summed up by her tagline: *Seatbelt Suspense*®. She's even trademarked it (which you don't have to do). It's clear what she writes from her tagline. She's tied her brand to her genre (suspense) as well as the feeling of that genre (being at the edge of your seat).

You may know right away what your brand is, or you may need to write a few novels to figure it out. Your readers may figure it out first and tell you in their reviews. You don't have to have your branding complete before your first novel releases, but you need to start thinking about the ideas behind your writing. Some authors stick to one genre their entire career, which makes branding easier. Some don't write easy-to-categorize books, which makes branding more of a challenge. Do you have to stick to one genre or subgenre to have a clear brand? No, but it might help.

Where does branding reveal itself for authors? Some authors have taglines on their bookmarks and websites. Some have themed websites that match their brand (a castle in the background for a fairy tale author, or a spaceship for military science fiction, for instance). Or maybe a dragon in their author logo. You can look up the websites and social media of several authors and see what they do in terms of branding in their design. It might also show up in their author newsletter or social media as part of the design or content. A historical romance author might share historical facts, for instance.

More importantly, though, brand is seen in your book covers (which should be approached from a marketing perspective; we'll talk about this later), but most importantly, it's incorporated into your story lines, characters, writing style, and genre choices.

My brand, as I mentioned, is that I write adventure-romance stories with humor, fantasy elements, and well-developed characters. Some of my stories are fairy tale retellings, some are closer to fantasy romance, and one series is high fantasy. But all of them have my mark on them, regardless of genre. They're all broadly fantasy, but different categories within that; and many of them, to be honest, don't fall neatly into the categories I mentioned. That's why I went with a broader brand of "adventure-romance" for myself. My tagline is "Adventure and romance are only a page away." My readers follow me across my different but related genres because they like my brand.

I'd like to note here that most of my readers don't know my tagline and would simply call me a fairy tale author, because they found my fairy tales first. It's the clearest category I write in and the most popular one. It's easier to find a fairy tale retelling than a "fantasy that feels like a historical romance but with magic and adventure."

That last description might be a brand, and accurately describes some of my stories, but it's not a terribly useful brand. It's not catchy. I could say I write "Jane Austen with wands" or "*Downtown Abbey* with magic" and people would get an idea and might be intrigued. But I'd still have a problem when it comes to setting up the book to sell. There's not a defined market for those things like there is for fairy tale retellings or historical romance or fantasy romance. This is the problem with "not writing to market," as they say.

So while some authors have clear-cut brands built around a well-defined genre, others of us may actually need two brands. One describing what we really write and one that describes the category our novels best fit in, the market we're aiming for. My "adventure-romance stories with humor, fantasy elements, and well-developed characters" may be what I post on my wall to remind me what I've promised my readers, but a tagline built around "fairy tale author" or "fantasy romance author" helps me shelve my books for selling.

In short, your brand doesn't have to match a specific genre, or a specific category within a larger genre (like "billionaire romance" within "romance," for instance), but it does help you sell books to do so. People like safe bets. Which means they want books that are like other books they like.

Or like a movie. Twenty years ago, the live action Lord of the Rings movies released and Orlando Bloom's Legolas became a heartthrob for thousands of women. Now, stories involving humans marrying elves with a remarkable resemblance to the LOTR elves is part of a thriving subgenre of romance, the fantasy romance category (this also includes fae-human romances, among other pairings). Put a pointy-eared, long-haired elf on a cover, and there will be a lot of women who'll snatch it up because it reminds them of other things they like. Pardon the rabbit-trail. I just find it interesting how the subgenre developed.

Anyway, we've been discussing branding with the expectation that you'll write multiple books and that those books are related. You don't have to write related books, of course, but if you write a fantasy romance à la Legolas and then write a hard sci-fi with little to no romance, you're shooting yourself in the foot, marketing wise. People will read both novels, but not the same people. This means you have to find twice as many readers to sell as many books as you would other-wise. If your books have little in common, you don't have a brand people can connect with, and you're better off using a pen name for each type of novel. Otherwise, people won't trust that your next book is something they'll like, and they'll move on to an author they *can* trust.

You also need to make sure you understand what you're writing (as in the genre expectations). If you think you're writing a thriller when you're really writing a contemporary romance with a touch of suspense, for instance, you're in trouble. The people you're trying to sell your book to won't want it, and the people who do want it will never see it. Recognizing your genre isn't always as straightforward as you'd think. Many of us read in many genres, and our favorite reads may not be what we write. So our thinking may be in one direction but our actual stories are leaning in another. Having other people read your books is helpful for figuring out exactly what you write.

As you think about your brand, try to come up with a short, snappy tagline to describe it. You don't have to use it, but it helps to articulate your brand. And while you're thinking about that, delve into the related idea of your *target audience*. Who are the people who will enjoy reading your books? In the same way David's Bridal knows who they're selling to, and thus where to place ads and where not to place ads, you need to know your audience.

Are you writing for women over fifty? Homeschool moms? Teen boys? Men who like cars? Women who like fairy tale retellings? Men who like spaceships and war (military sci-fi), rather than spaceships and melodramatic adventure and romance (space opera)? Entrepreneurs? Aspiring authors?

This isn't always easy, and like your brand, may be something you finesse over time as your readership grows and reader responses and reviews give you a better idea of your readers.

We all want to think that everyone will read our books (doesn't everyone like Star Wars and LOTR, after all?), and maybe they will, but you can't write a book for everyone. Widely popular stories are popular because they did a great job reaching their intended audience, who then raved about it to others, who decided to give it a try. In other words, there are people who will watch Star Wars who will never watch another science fiction movie or show. Or who will watch LOTR but who normally only watch Hallmark Channel and Disney Princess movies. If you write an epic fantasy à la LOTR, you want to target the people who read epic fantasy all the time, not the people who only read what other people are raving about out of curiosity. J. K. Rowling wrote for her daughter but charmed the world. It's easier to charm one person than many. So decide who you want to charm and give them your full attention. If you do your job well, they'll go out and charm others on your behalf.

In summary, figure out what's a "given" for your books and how you can frame that to make each book sell to an established audience, and your entire collection will sell as a package deal because readers know every book you write fulfills a promise—your brand.

———

I don't get into the concept of "writing to market," but it's related to the idea of brand and target audience. If your goal is to be a high-earning career author, and you don't mind writing what's in demand rather than what's on your mind to write, you might want to look into the idea more. I've included a few references on the subject, which also cover dealing with hard-to-categorize books (basically books not written to market).

———

Let's move on now to some of the places where your brand shows up, and which also represent you: your author biography, headshot, website, and newsletter. But first, I'm going to devote a short chapter to a skill you'll need to publish well: market research/finding comparable books.

REFERENCES AND RESOURCES

Erik, Nicholas. *The Ultimate Guide to Book Marketing: The 80/20 System for Selling More Books* (Ultimate Author Guides). 2020.

Fox, Chris. *Write to Market: Deliver a Book that Sells* (Write Faster, Write Smarter 3). 2016.

Gaughran, David. *Amazon Decoded: A Marketing Guide to the Kindle Store* (Let's Get Publishing Book 4). David Gaughran, 2020.

Six Figure Authors Podcast. "SFA 069 – Selling Hard-to-Categorize Books That Aren't Written to Market/Trope." December 17, 2020. https://6figureauthors.com/podcast/selling-hard-to-categorize-books-not-written-to-market-trope/.

Chapter 26

Comparable books

Understanding who does and doesn't read your type of books is tremendously important. If you figure this out, you're well on your way to getting those readers who read your type of book to buy your book and preventing yourself from wasting resources trying to get the wrong readers. But what is your type of book? What are your "comparable books," or "comp books" as they are called?

Literary agent Rachelle Gardner says this about them: "People get all hung up on it, especially with fiction. Do I look for books with the same premise or plot? Same time period? Same writing style? How do I know what to include? I'm going to make it easy for you. Ask yourself, 'Who are my readers? What are they reading right now?' Those are your comparable books." (Source: https://rachellegardner.com/finding-comparable-books/)

Your comp books are the ones you want to be shelved with, to fit in with. You want your cover to announce to readers of Comp A and Comp B that they'll like your book, because it's like those books. You'll target those books/authors/readers in your advertisements and newsletter promotions. You might do newsletter swaps or joint releases with the authors. This is your community.

So how do you find your comp books? Read, hang out in reader groups on social media and on Goodreads, and study Amazon's recommendations and sponsored ads. Ask the people who read your type of book what else they read. What else do *you* read? What books are showing up on Amazon's book pages and in its ads? Pay attention to what books they're trying to sell you based on what they know of your reading habits (which might be the same books they are selling to your readers).

As an example, I write clean YA fairy tale retellings and less-easy-to-categorize fantasy books with magic, adventure, clean romance, and a happily-ever-after. When I look at books on Amazon, the recommendations, also boughts, ads, etc. are full of clean fairy tale retellings; lighter epic fantasy, magic academy, and urban fantasy written by fairy tale authors; and fantasy romance books (some of which are written by fairy tale authors). These are all books and authors I hear my readers talking about. Amazon and my own reading choices (for pleasure and market research) found the books for me, and my readers confirmed them. Keeping an eye on the more successful of these authors—their newsletters, book covers, pricing, type of books, etc.—helps me stay on track. I can listen to what their fans say—since some of them have large, active reader communities—to better understand what readers want. They like stories with romance, adventure, and fantasy elements. They particularly like certain tropes or dislike others. I can learn from them things that will help me write more appealing books in the future, and better target my readers in my cover choices and blurbs.

Okay, we're back to talking about you now—that is, your author bio.

References and Resources

Erik, Nicholas. *The Ultimate Guide to Book Marketing: The 80/20 System for Selling More Books* (Ultimate Author Guides). 2020.

Gardner, Rachelle. "Finding Comparable Books." *Rachelle Gardner.* September 15, 2020. https://rachellegardner.com/finding-comparable-books/.

Chapter 27

Author bio and headshot

You'll need at least one author biography (a short paragraph, not a book) for your writing career. The bio will go on your website, on your Amazon Author Central page (it will show up on all your book pages that way), on any social media platform or other "author" places you choose to put it (including Goodreads and BookBub), and, if you choose, on each of your book covers. You may write only one bio, or you may write many, targeting each one to its audience. If you write both fiction and nonfiction, for instance, you might want a separate bio for each—one that fits the tone of your genre for fiction and one that establishes you as an expert for your nonfiction topic. If you plan on seeking out media opportunities, such as public speaking, podcast or radio guest interviews, and such, you'll probably want a short biography and a long one to give more information to those who want it. This long one will go in the media kit you'll have on your website (more on this later).

Your short (and most commonly used bio) should include your name, what you write, important accomplishments, and something personal that might allow people to connect with you or get a glimpse of your writing style. You might, but don't have to, include your location or family. A length of 60-90 words is good, and definitely less than 300 words. Third person is preferred as it allows you to use your name (repetition aids memory, after all) and is helpful to media persons and bloggers when, for instance, they are introducing you on a podcast or posting your bio in their book review blog post. Include your website and, if desired, your *active* social media accounts (don't send them to a platform you aren't active on). You will also want a professional headshot or, if you don't want to use a headshot, an author logo.

Why bother with an author bio? For one, it's expected, so if you skip it, you look unprofessional at best and sketchy at worst. Readers like to know whose books they are reading and enjoy "getting to know" the author through the biography. They might also want to check out your credentials to determine if your book is trustworthy. Or they may think your name sounds familiar or "see a friend" in your writing and be curious about you. I've actually had people connect with me after reading my bio because not only did they like my book, we had personal things in common. One reader realized we went to college together and contacted me to say hello! She was one of the first people I met in college, and we had the same major. I was thrilled to hear from her. Another lady had a similar background in science, lived nearby, and shared my faith and an interest in writing. We have an enjoyable correspondence.

On the topic of shared faith, another thing a bio might accomplish is letting the reader know you share the same values or beliefs (very helpful for religious books or inspirational fiction). I read only clean and wholesome books, so if I see a fantasy romance that interests me, I'll check the blurb to see if it says whether or not the book is clean, and if it doesn't say, I'll check the author bio to see if the writer specifies that they writes clean romance.

Here are a few tips for writing your author biography:

1. Read several author biographies and note what is commonly said and what you do and don't care for or connect with. You'll notice that many authors mention a love of coffee, their family, and their pets (and their pets are often given a personality as tyrants). You do not have to

include any of these things, but find some way of connecting with readers or making yourself interesting.

2. Include things that add credibility for your nonfiction bio, or interest for both fiction and nonfiction bios. (It goes without saying that you should only include things that are true.) You want the biography to develop you as a person in the reader's mind. So including some activity real people engage in (such photography or coffee-drinking) or something they want (like dreaming of traveling the world or a house that cleans itself) lets them connect with you. You don't want to appear boring (especially if you write fantasy or sci-fi), so letting people know you do more than sit at the computer is good, or at least that you want to do more. We can connect with people's dreams. If you know your fans are also likely fans of a certain show or book, you might include that.

For nonfiction, or fiction genres where credentials would help (such as a police background for thrillers), give your credentials in a succinct way. They don't need your GPA, but if you have a PhD or professional degree and it's relevant, include that.

3. Write your bio in your author voice (with personality) and with your audience in mind. If you write humorous works, make your bio humorous. If you're writing a serious nonfiction book, don't mention your penchant for wild vacations in party locations or be too quirky. You want to connect with your readers, so you must have an idea of who they are and what they would or wouldn't want to learn about you. You can also use the language of your genre. Fairy tale writers, for instance, might mention being married to "Prince Charming."

4. Include what you write. State that you write thrillers or clean contemporary romance, or whatever you write. This is valuable because it can let readers know about any other genres you write and, if they haven't read your book yet, what to expect from your writing. If you write in a different genre with a pen name, you can include that.

5. Include your website and any social media links where readers can connect with you.

6. Include accolades if they are significant to the readers. Winning obscure contests doesn't make you an "award-winning author" to readers who don't know about, and so aren't impressed by, the contests.

It needs to be an award they could easily look up, if they were of a mind to do so. It makes you seem self-aggrandizing otherwise. An award granted by a sizable conference would be worth mentioning.

As for best seller status, some Amazon categories are small, and you might be able to easily get a best seller badge for a short while in one of those for a promotion on a $0.99 book. Doing so doesn't really make you a best seller, though. And if you call yourself a "best-selling author" and don't have enough reviews on any of your books to back up that claim, you're not helping yourself.

So only include meaningful accolades. You can always have a long biography on your website where you include all your awards.

7. Get feedback on your bio. These tend to be hard to write, so don't be upset if it takes several drafts to get it right.

8. Finally, remember to keep your biography updated, and don't stress too much about it. You can always revise it later.

Professional headshot

To go along with your bio, you'll want a professional headshot. People like seeing faces, so a headshot is one way you can connect with your readers. And if you hope to do any public speaking or media interviews, it gives you a chance to show people you are a professional. This means it's not a good idea to use the camera on your computer to take a photo of you making a face. Some do this and their books still sell well (especially if they write in a genre with voracious readers who don't care as much about quality as quantity), but it might turn away media professionals. So get a professional headshot done, or at least look at enough professional headshots to know how to select a background and pose and direct a friend to take one. You don't want to look too formal, and trends change, so keep up with the headshots of savvy authors. Stiff, solid-color-background photos of people in suits aren't the thing these days. As a tip, you can often get a headshot done at a writers' conference for fairly cheap. And as with the bio, keep your headshot up to date, changing it every few years.

If you don't want a photo of yourself floating around online, you can have an author logo created and use that. I've seen this several times, and it's much better than the no-image avatar that will show up if you don't provide a photo. Get something professionally designed that matches your author brand. Since it's standing in for you, and so will represent you, it needs to look nice. If you don't know a graphic designer, you can ask around for recommendations or hire designers through sites such as Fiverr, Upwork, and 99designs. Fiverr is no longer centered around $5 work, so know that it will have a range of prices and talent.

References and Resources

Chesson, Dave. "How to Write an Author Bio [With Examples and Templates]." *Kindlepreneur.* February 7, 2022. https://kindlepreneur. com/write-author-bio/.

Reedsy. "How to Write a Killer Author Bio (With Template)." February 24. 2022. https://blog.reedsy.com/author-bio/.

Wise, Maureen. "How to Write an Author Bio Examples & Tips to Sell." *Self-Publishing School.* December 14, 2021. https://self-publishingschool.com/author-bio/.

Chapter 28

Website and author email

A web presence is an essential these days for any business, and an author business is no different. With changes in social media and some people choosing not to have Facebook or other social media accounts, relying on a Facebook author page, as once suggested, is not wise. It's best to have your own reality, so to speak, on the web. You need a website.

So what goes into having your own website? And what does it cost? Must you hire someone to build it for you?

Websites require hosting, a domain name, and a theme (the coding and general look for the website). You'll also use a website builder, such as WordPress, Wix, Weebly, or Squarespace. For example, I have a self-hosted website through Wordpress.org. It's hosted by True Path, has a domain name purchased through Namecheap, and uses a free WordPress theme.

As for cost, you can get a free website, such as through Wordpress.com, or you can do a self-hosted website, such as through Wordpress.org or Wix.com. The latter option requires a bit more money and expertise, but doesn't need to be too difficult. Nor do you have to hire an individual or company to set one up. There are many resources on setting up your own self-hosted website. As a sidenote, some email service providers offer a free landing page for use in their email services instead of requiring a website. I'm not familiar with this, but it is an option as well.

Why choose one type of website over the other—free or self-hosted? There's always a catch in free. The developers will want to get paid back for their time and effort in some way. This might be through ads on the website, or in the case of apps and Facebook, tracking you on the web and selling that information or using it to target ads. When you choose a free website, there will likely be ads on it. You don't earn money for these, and you don't control what's on there. It also doesn't look professional. If you're on a tight budget, don't plan on using the website for more than a home page and blog, and don't expect much traffic, it might be worth it to you to go with this option.

If you want to look a bit more professional and do more on your website (such as sell direct or host courses), you want a self-hosted website. You can buy hosting for a monthly or yearly cost through companies such as BlueHost, DreamHost, True Path, and others. Hosting costs vary, and sometimes you can get deals. If you're not expecting large amounts of traffic to your website, the yearly cost might only be around $100 or less.

You will also need a domain name. This is the designation in the address bar, such as www.amazon.com. You will likely have the option of using other domains than .com addresses, but unless there is a reason for it, I'd recommend going with .com.

Your domain name needs to be centered around you—your author name—or maybe your book series. Most use their author name alone, or "[name]author.com." Do an internet search on your author name and see what comes up. If the results are strong for someone else, say an actor with a similar name, consider making your website "[name]author.com." Or consider using your initials or a pen name. You don't want people confusing you with someone else or not being able to find you because your website is on page three of the search results. You want to be easy to find.

Once you've chosen your domain name, you can purchase it through any number of sites, including your website hosting company. It might be cheaper through dedicated domain registrars than a hosting service, however. Namecheap and BlueHost are two companies through which you purchase a domain name. You will need to renew the domain every year, so this is a yearly cost. Note that security is an issue to consider, and not just price, when choosing your domain name registrar.

Once you have your host and domain name, you can get your website set up on your website builder. What's the best website builder for you? It depends, and every blog you read on the matter will give different evaluations (as for most topics). Some website builders offer great ease-of-use and require little technical knowledge, but also give few options, or might cost more. So it's best to do your own research, consider your skills and needs, and go from there. Website builders include Wordpress.org (not Wordpress.com), Wix, Weebly, and Squarespace.

You'll need a theme, which is basically the code to set up your website and give it its structure, look, and functionality. You can use the free themes available through your website builder, purchase themes, or hire a company to design your website.

When you have your website ready, go ahead and talk to your host and get your website set up with the *https* (instead of *http*) designation for extra security and the comfort of site visitors. You might also want to reduce spam and add security through using the Jetpack plug-in (Word-press), or an equivalent, and protect your information from loss through a backup plug-in, such as UpdraftPlus.

What goes on your website?

What should go on your website? This depends a lot on your author goals. At the very least, I would recommend a home page, author bio, books page, newsletter sign-up, and media kit (we'll talk about these last two later). You might want a progress bar to let fans know how your book is coming along. You'll also need a privacy policy to let people know what information is collected and what is done with this (if any is collected).

Most of those pages are self-explanatory. Fans come to your website to find out more about you, discover what books you've written, and find out when your next book is coming out. They might also want to sign up for your newsletter, especially if you offer a newsletter magnet, so you need to have that sign-up form on your home page and on its own page. They might be looking for extra information about your story world or resources associated with your nonfiction topic. They might also be looking for writing tips and resources.

So think about what readers want and make those things easy to find. Also think about what industry professionals (bloggers doing book reviews, podcasters wanting to interview you, event coordinators looking to hire you as a speaker, etc.) want and make that—bio, head-shot, books list and links, endorsements, etc.—available together in your media kit.

As your list of books grows, you might add in landing pages for each series. You can have an "extras" section with maps, character family trees, study guide questions, quizzes, resources, deleted scenes, or any other freebies your readers might want. Be sure to include purchase links for your books.

As you choose your theme and design your website, consider your author brand. If you write horror, don't have a website that looks like a spring garden, with blooming flowers and butterflies. If you write romantic comedy, don't have a stark, dark website. Try to match your website to your brand. This doesn't mean you have to go all out and hire a graphic designer, but at least give your brand some thought in your choices.

I recommend looking at the websites of several different authors to see what they have. If you're just starting out, you won't have as much to put up, but you'll have an idea of what to work toward, what you like and don't like.

Your website and GDPR

In 2018, the European Union passed the General Data Protection Regulation (GDPR), "the toughest privacy and security law in the world." The gdpr.eu website says this about the law: "Though it was drafted and passed by the European Union (EU), it imposes obligations onto organizations anywhere, so long as they target or collect data related to people in the EU. . . . The GDPR will levy harsh fines against those who violate its privacy and security standards, with penalties reaching into the tens of millions of euros." While the EU might not have any authority over you (if you are a US Citizen living in the US, for instance), you'll still see a lot about GDPR compliance for your website and newsletter. In general, it's recommended to comply, whether you have to or not. In brief, this means you need a privacy policy on your website, a double-opt-in for your newsletter sign-up, and a one-click unsubscribe for your newsletter, which your newsletter service likely already has in place. You can find out more information on this in the resource section below.

Author email

Let's add a quick word about email here, as it's connected to websites. Many, many years ago, when email was young and AOL was the thing, people were encouraged to use inventive email addresses for privacy (tacomama7 or footballfan1, for instance). Now, that would be considered highly unprofessional. Use your author name or your name with the word *author* after it. People want to know who is emailing them. You will also need to make sure your author name is showing up in the From field when you email people. Check your account settings and ask someone who doesn't have you in his or her address book to see what shows up. Use a professional domain too (no @aol.com addresses). Consider the longevity of the email provider. If you're using your internet provider for your email, will you still be using them ten years from now?

Some newsletter services require a custom email address with your own domain (author@authorname.com, for instance) for setting up a newsletter. You can usually get an email address through your website hosting company. Their email services are often not user friendly, but they are free with hosting. If you choose to buy an email address (which you can customize to match your domain), you have several options, including Google Workspace, Microsoft Office 365, and Apple iCloud+. Having a separate email for personal and business use might also be a good idea.

Website and email checklist:

- Choose a free or paid website option.
- Choose a website builder, theme, host, and domain name.
- Research your domain name before choosing one.
- Create your website with your reader in mind.
- Include your author bio, book links, and newsletter sign-up page, at the least.
- Make it GDPR compliant with a privacy policy page.
- Budget for your hosting, domain name renewal, and related expenses.
- Use a professional email address and check that it shows up with your name when it arrives in email inboxes.

References and Resources

There are many resources online concerning websites, but here are a few that have been helpful for me. They tend to talk more about WordPress than other website builders, so be sure to check out Wix, Weebly, Squarespace and others as well.

Convert Kit. "Landing Pages." https://convertkit.com/features/landing-pages.

GDPR. "What is GDPR?" https://gdpr.eu/what-is-gdpr/.

Hyatt, Michael. "How to Launch a Self-Hosted WordPress Blog in 20 Minutes or Less." (YouTube video) June 20, 2016. https://www.youtube.com/watch?v=OFLk3srgg1M.

Ingermanson, Randy. "GDPR for Authors, Part 1." *Advanced Fiction Writing.* May 13, 2018. https://www.advancedfictionwriting.com/blog/2018/05/13/gdpr-authors-part-1/.

Umstattd, Thomas Jr. "How to Get a Professional Email Address."

Author Media. March 16, 2022. https://www.authormedia.com/how-to-get-a-professional-email-address/.

Umstattd, Thomas Jr. "How to Speed Up Your Author Website." *Author Media.* February 2, 2022. https://www.authormedia.com/how-to-speed-up-your-author-website/.

Umstattd, Thomas Jr. "How to Have an Amazing Author Website: A Guide for Tech-Timid Authors." *Author Media.* https://training.authormedia.com/p/amazing-author-websites.

Umstattd, Thomas Jr. "Why American Authors Don't Need to Worry about GDPR." *Author Media.* May 21, 2018. https://www.authormedia.com/why-american-authors-dont-need-to-worry-about-gdpr/.

Wordpress.com Support. "Wordpress.com versus Wordpress.org." Accessed March 21, 2022. https://wordpress.com/support/com-vs-org/.

Chapter 29

Media kit

If you're planning to ask for help with cover reveals, ask book bloggers to review your book, or anticipate doing media interviews, you will want a media kit (or, more accurately, they will want you to have one!). A media kit is a page on your website dedicated to information needed by industry professionals about you and about your book. A media kit typically includes:

- Author photo or photos
- A short biography and a long biography
- Full-size book images (high quality images)
- A book blurb, taglines, and any other marketing copy you want to share
- Links: retailers, Goodreads, your website, and any social media accounts
- Any graphics you want to share

You want professionals to be able to easily grab whatever they need and get about their business. It's much easier to send a link to a web page than to send attachments via email.

Chapter 30

Newsletter

Connecting with your readers so they know your new books are available is one of the goals of indie publishing. There are many ways this can happen: Readers can follow you on Amazon or BookBub and so get a notice from them when you release a book. Readers can follow you on social media and, depending on the algorithm and their viewing habits, may see your post regarding your book. Readers might see your Amazon ad or Facebook ad, or perhaps your featured deal in the newsletter sent out by BookBub, Robin Reads, or any of the other book promotion services.

Another method—one considered a necessity for career-minded authors—is an email newsletter. You "own" this, so changes in social media won't suddenly block your access to your readers. It's also less likely that readers who sign up for your email newsletter will ignore it. If you don't plan on publishing many books, you can skip this, unless you just particularly like the idea and don't mind the work involved.

A newsletter is essentially an email sent out to subscribers at regular intervals. However, you do *not* use your personal email for this. You'll need to go through an email service provider and follow all the privacy guidelines established to prevent spam and protect subscribers.

Email service providers include MailChimp, MailerLite, SendFox,

ConvertKit, and others. These often have free levels for people with less than 1,000 or 2,000 newsletter subscribers, depending on the provider. Above that, you pay a monthly or yearly fee. They also offer free templates to help make your newsletters look better, so you don't have to worry about designing them.

Your newsletter must include, for legal reasons, a physical address. You can use your own, but for privacy reasons, it might be wisest to rent a PO Box or UPS box for this. Your newsletter must also, again for legal reasons, include an easy way to unsubscribe. Many newsletter service providers automatically add an unsubscribe option to your newsletters to handle this for you.

And don't worry about people unsubscribing from your newsletters. It's better for uninterested people to leave than stay on, thereby lowering your open rate and forcing you to pay for "dead weight." The open rate is the percentage of people who actually open your newsletter, which is tracked by the newsletter company (though not all reads are counted as opens for technical reasons). Sometimes the open rate information is asked for in promotional opportunities. Since you will need to pay for newsletter subscribers over a certain number (usually 1,000 or 2,000 subscribers), it's a good thing for your budget to remove uninterested subscribers.

How do you set up your newsletter? That depends on who you choose to go with, so I'll leave that for them to guide you through. As for which provider is the best, that varies depending on who you talk to. The provider some authors vilify is the one others adore. Check out the ones mentioned above, and maybe even set up a free account with each and see which you like best.

You might be wondering *why* people would sign up for a newsletter. They typically do this for two reasons: they really like your work and want to keep up with your new releases or, if you've offered a reader magnet (a freebie book in exchange for signing up for your newsletter), they want the magnet.

Newsletter sign-up
Once you set up your newsletter on an email service provider, such

as MailChimp or MailerLite, you'll want a way for readers to sign up to receive it. There are four main ways to gain newsletter subscribers:

1. Your website. Set up a page on the website inviting them to sign up. This page will include your sign-up form. You'll need a code from your newsletter service for this, but they will have details on how to do everything. You can have the sign-up form on its own page, on your home page, and/or on a pop-up.

2. Your book's back matter. Include a page asking readers if they want to sign up for your newsletter. You can mention your freebie to entice them. Be sure to let them know here or on your website what to expect regarding the frequency and topics of your newsletters.

3. Reader magnets. These are short stories or nonfiction resources people get for free when they sign up for your newsletter. You can mention these on your website and in your back matter. You can also put these on services such as BookFunnel, MyBookCave, and StoryOrigin. They can be part of promotions with other authors and so be seen by many different readers. If a reader wants the story, they agree to sign up for your newsletter.

Hopefully, they will read your book and like it enough to buy your other books. They may, however, never read it or read it and then unsubscribe at your first email, because they only wanted something free. But this is part of being an author, so we deal with it. We're probably guilty of just wanting free things ourselves . . . We'll talk more about reader magnets later.

4. Giveaways. Somewhat similar to the concept of reader magnets is collecting subscriber email addresses through giveaways. These usually involve multiple authors or a single author giving away many books, sometimes along with book-related products (like a Kindle) or a gift card. For a chance to win, the contestant must agree to sign up for your newsletter. They might also gain additional entries for following you on various social media platforms or inviting friends to the contest. Book-Sweeps and KingSumo are two such companies for giveaways to gain subscribers.

As a closing note, never sign up anyone for your newsletter without their consent or buy subscribers. They must sign up for themselves. It's unethical to sign up people who don't want to be on your list or who don't know you're sticking them on it. That's spamming, and no one wants to be spammed. It won't make them more likely to buy your book. The opposite, I should imagine.

What do you say in your newsletter and how often do you send it?

Now that you have a newsletter and subscribers, what do you say and when do you send your newsletter? That depends a lot on you, what you write, and your release schedule and preferences. You at least want to send newsletters when you have a book releasing. This might mean a newsletter only on release day, or it might mean an email with a cover reveal to let them know the book is coming, one at the release, and another later to thank those who purchased the book and reviewed it (this would also be a third reminder of the release). Some authors only send out newsletters when they have something like this to say. Some marketing experts, however, say to send emails at least every month, since you don't want readers to forget you or only hear from you when you want something (them to buy a book). Consequently, there are authors who send a newsletter every week or two weeks. When you ask people to sign up, let them know what to expect from your newsletters in terms of content and frequency.

Personally, I do not want author emails in my inbox every week. Every month is fine with me. If you have really good newsletters, or frequent releases, or I really, really love your books, then I might be okay with every week or every other week. The important thing is to set an expectation with your readers and stick to it. Tell them how often you will send your newsletters and what you will include and stick to it.

I mentioned I'd be okay with a weekly "good" newsletter. What defines a "good" newsletter varies, but for me, I like seeing book recommendations and to hear about the progress of the author's next release. Some authors talk about historical research, their family, their pets, or whatever fits their brand. Personal appearances are also often included. Sneak peeks, excerpts of the work-in-progress, cover reveals, or a serial story are popular options as well.

What to say in your author newsletter is a difficult thing for many of us to figure out. I recommend subscribing to various author newsletters and seeing what these authors do. Ask yourself what you like, then try out what seems good to you and go from there. There's a lot of experimentation in indie publishing. You don't want to spend so much time writing for or worrying about your newsletter that you slack on your writing or family time, however, so balance that with your bigger goals.

When you set up your newsletter and sign-up, you will (according to many marketing experts) want to set up an automated welcome email, or a sequence of emails (called an *onboarding sequence*). This is an email or series of emails that's sent automatically by your email service provider when someone subscribes to your newsletter. These are often the most opened emails.

In the welcome email or the sequence, you'll want to tell the subscriber a little about yourself, remind them how they got on your list, and tell them what you write and what books you have available. If you promised a free reader magnet for signing up, include the link to that.

Some authors have just one welcome email and some a series of welcome emails spread out over a period of days or weeks. (Personally, I am for one welcome newsletter as I don't want a ton of emails, but some people swear by a long onboarding sequence.) Depending on your newsletter company, you may only have the option of one welcome newsletter.

You may have noticed by some of my comments that there are some of us who are at a disadvantage in this author business because, as readers, we don't want a frequent newsletter, if at all, or ads at all, or any kind of advertising or author contact. We want books and that's it. We grumble and dig in our heels at a lot of marketing stuff because we can't imagine anyone wanting it. Tammi Labrecque says in her popular *Newsletter Ninja* book, "Do not make business decisions based on your own consumer behavior." I'd say, however, to not make business decisions based *solely* on your own behavior. There will be other consumers like you, just as there will be those unlike you.

But you don't have to go by your or an imagined reader's preferences. Tammi Labrecque goes on to say, "You make decisions based on how your readers respond to things you try—by getting reader feedback and by looking at measurable results (open rates, click rates, unsubscribe rates, conversion), not by guessing or defaulting to behavior that accommodates your own biases."

Some authors swear by tactics such as frequent newsletters and long onboarding sequences, and some eschew those tactics and do just fine. Try to find a marketing plan that works for you and your readers, and if you're like me and have a hard time imagining people wanting to connect, talk to someone who appreciates author interactions, and then go do the author-connection/marketing things without guilt. If you're a career-minded author, that is. If not, then you can probably skip newsletters altogether.

When do you set up your newsletter? I'd say a few months before the release, when your reader magnet is ready. You can get your newsletter designed just the way you want it and practice sending a few newsletters to yourself and your friends.

There's a lot to talk about concerning newsletters (people have written entire books on the subject), but these are the basics to get you started.

Newsletter summary:

Most authors will want an email newsletter to keep in contact with fans in a space they own. You should:

- Use an email service provider, not your personal email. Be GDPR compliant.
- Put your newsletter sign-up where it can be easily found on your website and in your book.
- Use a reader magnet.
- Decide on a send schedule and stick to it.
- Make your newsletters enjoyable for both your audience and yourself.
- Budget for your email service provider and PO Box.

REFERENCES AND RESOURCES

Erik, Nicholas. *The Ultimate Guide to Book Marketing: The 80/20 System for Selling More Books* (Ultimate Author Guides). 2020.

Labrecque, Tammi L. *Newsletter Ninja: How to Become an Author Mailing List Expert.* Newsletter Ninja, 2018.

Six Figure Authors Podcast. "SFA 056 - Using Your Newsletter to Sell More Books (Part 1)" September 17, 2020. https://6figureauthors.com/tag/email-newsletters/.

Umstattd, Thomas Jr. "How to Pick the Right Email Marketing Service for You." *Author Media.* August 26, 2020. https://www.authormedia.com/how-to-pick-the-right-email-platform/.

Chapter 31

Reader magnet

A reader magnet is one of your most valuable marketing tools. It's the taste test at Sam's Club. The freebie that leads to sales. Typically, a reader magnet is a free short work (a short story, for instance) available when you sign up for an author newsletter. It's mentioned in the back matter of books as an incentive to sign up for the author's newsletter or is found on services such as BookFunnel to be downloaded for free in exchange for signing up for the newsletter.

A reader magnet for fiction, then, is usually a short story or novella —let's say between 10,000 and 40,000 words long—that is given away for free in exchange for the reader's email address. The reader magnet can be a prequel story, an epilogue, a side story, or a story featuring different characters in the same world. Depending on your genre and audience, this could also be a web comic or artwork or something of that nature. If you have a lot of books and many series, you might create a "starter pack" with a freebie related to each series. Samples and excerpts don't work as well. Stories unrelated to the current story or series may not work as well as those connected to the work the reader just read.

You might consider a separate reader magnet for new readers (made available through services such as BookFunnel), to draw them into your story world to then go visit your main works, and a magnet (mentioned at the end of your books) for those who have already read your main work. A side story or epilogue related to the book a reader just finished, if the short is exclusive, might encourage them to sign up for your newsletter just to get it.

For nonfiction, the magnet could be a short nonfiction book, a workbook, a quiz, a free course, or something else related to your book.

Magnets are not sold in stores but hosted by services such as Book-Funnel, StoryOrigin, and MyBookCave and downloaded for free.

Magnets are popular marketing tools because they help you build your readership and your newsletter list before your first book launches and afterward. They also encourage readers of your published books to sign up for your newsletter to keep up with your new releases. If you create different magnets over the years, be sure to give them away to current subscribers as well as offer them to new ones. This is considered nurturing your newsletter list. Those on your newsletter list tend to be your biggest fans, so treat them well.

Because the magnet tends to be a little book, it will need to be edited, formatted, and covered just like the books you intend to sell. It will need a copyright page, other normal front matter and back matter, and a blurb. You can consider it a practice run for your finished book. It also gives you a sense of how successful your book pitch is—are people downloading your free book? If no one or very few people are downloading it, try improving your blurb-writing skills. Depending on the cost of your cover designer and your budget, you might want to get a cover to match your full book or get a simpler, cheaper cover, so long as it looks nice and is marketable. And do remember to get this edited, since people will judge the quality of all your work by this free sample.

Once you have your reader magnet ready, how do you get it before people's eyes?

1. Mention it on your website and on your newsletter sign-up page.

2. Mention it in the back matter of your book, on your newsletter sign-up page or at the end of your final chapter.

3. Use services such as BookFunnel, StoryOrigin, and MyBookCave to host the magnet. The magnet can also be included in their newsletter subscriber campaigns. BookFunnel and StoryOrigin also have

campaigns for full price, KU-enrolled, and on-sale published books, but the magnet is for the campaigns targeted to gain subscribers. Readers will see a page of free books. If they like yours, they'll agree to sign up for your newsletter in order to download the book. Hopefully, they'll read it and be excited for your next newsletter to find out more about your books.

When do you write and release your reader magnet?

Before you release your first book is great, and after you set up your newsletter. I would recommend having the cover and blurb of your first book in the book matter of the magnet, so people know what is coming. So consider plugging it beginning a few months before the main release. I wouldn't recommend putting it out a year in advance, though, as readers are likely to forget you. Including a pre-order link to your main work in your magnet is a great idea.

A reader magnet is extra work and an extra cost, but it's a great tool for building your newsletter and introducing people to your work. You can list a free book on retailers as a way to introduce people to your work, but a magnet is exclusive to your newsletter subscribers. The goal is not just to reach new readers but to get them to sign up for your newsletter, your own private way of connecting with readers.

Reader magnet summary:

A reader magnet:

- Serves to build a newsletter list and to nurture your current list (a freebie at first and occasional freebies along the way, as you write more books).
- Is usually a short work related to your longer works.
- Is mentioned on your website newsletter sign-up page, in the back matter of your books, and on promotional sites such as BookFunnel, StoryOrigin, and MyBookCave.

- Is a trial run of building a book.
- Is hosted by a service such as BookFunnel and a link to it is provided in your welcome newsletter for newsletter subscribers.
- Requires you to budget for cover, formatting, editing, and hosting.
- Requires you to budget time for writing this and getting it ready to release.

References and Resources

BookFunnel. https://BookFunnel.com.

Chesson, Dave. "The Best Types of Reader Magnets: Both Fiction and Nonfiction." (Blog) *BookFunnel.* May 26, 2021. https://blog.BookFunnel.com/2021/the-best-types-of-reader-magnets-fiction-and-nonfiction/.

Erik, Nicholas. *The Ultimate Guide to Book Marketing: The 80/20 System for Selling More Books* (Ultimate Author Guides). 2020.

Labrecque, Tammi L. *Newsletter Ninja 2: If You Give a Reader a Cookie: Supercharge Your Author Mailing List With the Perfect Reader Magnet.* Newsletter Ninja, 2022.

MyBookCave. https://mybookcave.com.

Stephenson, Nick. *Reader Magnets: Build Your Author Platform and Sell more Books on Kindle.* Your First 10,000 Readers, 2014.

StoryOrigin. https://storyoriginapp.com.

Umstattd, Thomas Jr. "145 – How to Create a Reader (Lead) Magnet." *Author Media.* July 18, 2018. https://www.authormedia.com/how-to-create-a-reader-magnet/.

Chapter 32

Author pages other than your website

In addition to your website and newsletter, there are three main places readers can easily find out more about you and your books: Amazon Author Central, BookBub, and Goodreads. I'll briefly outline each. These are simple, easy ways to increase visibility and connect with readers, and I recommend taking a few minutes to set up each one.

Amazon Author Central

If you've not yet explored an Amazon book page, you should. You'll find that by clicking on the author's name you are taken to a page dedicated to that author. It has all their books listed, a biography and photo, and, if set up, a blog feed connected to their blog. This is assuming they set up their page and claimed their books, as you are about to do.

This page is tremendously helpful to readers wanting to know what books you've written. Doing a search for an author on Amazon will likely bring up a mix of that author's books plus sponsored ad books. But the author page, which is set up through Amazon Author Central, is a clean page where your readers can easily see all your published books and their ratings.

When you set up a book on KDP, you'll receive an email with information geared toward helping you sell books. This information will include a link to set up your author page on Amazon Author Central. Be sure to do this and keep it up to date. When you publish a book, go to your Amazon Author Central page and "claim" the book or make sure it and all versions of it (paperback and ebook, for example) are linked.

The link to your Amazon Author Central account is a handy one to keep in your author toolbox, and a clean link to the page readers see— your author page—is also a good one to tuck into your essential links file. Readers can "follow" you through your author page and so receive an email from Amazon when you release a new book. This is a great option for those who don't want to be on a newsletter list.

Goodreads

Goodreads is a reader community where readers can review and keep track of books read. Reviews on Goodreads are not quite the same as those on Amazon, however, and at first seem harsher because the rating system is different. For instance, three stars means that the reader liked the book, not that it was a mediocre one. This means fewer books get five stars. (Not all readers rate books on Goodreads according to the Goodreads official rating system, however.) I tend to get more reviews on Goodreads than on Amazon, actually.

You may already have a Goodreads account as a reader, and that's great if you do. Either way, set up an author one and then add your books. The user experience for this platform is not a good one, in my opinion, so you might watch a video on whatever you're trying to do first, rather than stumbling through it. The "upload your cover" link, when last I used the site, was almost hidden, and so a few of my book pages went live with no cover, and there was no easy way to fix it. So be warned. Readers can set up a book as well, and some may be set up automatically as they show up on Amazon (Amazon owns Goodreads). This means you might have different versions of your book on the platform. Last I heard, if you need to change the cover for your book's page, you will need to contact a Goodreads Librarian.

Once you have your book set up on Goodreads and have claimed it on your author account, keep the link handy to give to reviewers and to add to your media kit. You want leaving a review to be easy, and sparing professional reviewers and readers the hunt for your book's page assists in this process.

Goodreads is also considered a social media site useful for authors, and I've included a few references on its use in the chapter on social media.

BookBub

BookBub describes itself as "a free service that helps you discover books you'll love through unbeatable deals, handpicked recommendations, and updates from your favorite authors. BookBub doesn't actually sell books. We simply introduce you to books you'll love that are available on retailers like Amazon's Kindle store, Barnes & Noble's Nook store, Apple Books, and others." The reader side of BookBub sends emails with curated lists of book deals in the readers' specified genres. It also allows readers to follow authors, recommend books, and receive updates when a followed author releases a new book. The author side, or the "Partner" side, allows for authors to submit Featured Deals for their books and submit ads.

You can't do a featured deal, of course, until you have a book, but when you have a pre-order or live link for your book, it's a good thing to set up a BookBub Partner account for those who want to follow you or recommend your books there.

We'll discuss BookBub again later when we talk about book promotion services.

In summary, an easy, free way to connect with readers is to set up an author account on Amazon Author Central, Goodreads, and BookBub.

Chapter 33

Concluding marketing pre-release

Are you still with me? I hope so. Marketing is the scariest, most detested part of the indie author business to many of us. Those of you with marketing backgrounds are so lucky! Fortunately, marketing can be learned—and the most important part of marketing is a great book. That's a good thing to remind yourself of when the idea of marketing is getting you down. Great books can sell books; great marketing can sell books; and great books plus great marketing can *really* sell books. Let's make the latter our goal.

So far, we've discussed author branding; websites; author biographies and headshots; media kits; newsletters; reader magnets; and Amazon Author Central, Goodreads, and BookBub author accounts. Those are author career-building tools. Let's move on now to the branding, building, and marketing of your individual titles.

Branding the author key points:

- Figure out what makes your books "yours" to readers.
  That's your brand. Knowing this helps you figure out what

to keep giving your readers book after book so they'll come back for more.

- Discover your target audience so you'll know who you write for and who to focus marketing efforts on (and where to tell the stores to "shelve" your books).
- You need a short author biography and a professional headshot.
- You need a website. Cost and technical knowledge varies, but they can be very affordable and easy to manage.
- Include a media kit on your website.
- Set up an author email newsletter.
- Write a reader magnet and make it available to gain newsletter subscribers.
- Create Amazon Author Central, Goodreads, and BookBub author pages.
- Budget for a website, newsletter, and reader magnet.

Part Six

Branding the Book

Chapter 34

Introduction to branding your book

Finally. The nitty-gritty of the book you've been dreaming of publishing for ages is in sight. Welcome to branding the book itself. We'll talk about titles, series names, keywords and categories, pricing, marketing copy for your book, and book links. Keep a record of your decisions in this section because you'll need these things for when you set your book up on retailers.

As a warning, one thing you'll need to do for this section is research (okay, I tell you this a lot). You need to know what books are comparable to yours. What are the people who'll read your book also reading? This is tremendously important (so important that you are asked to include it in book proposals to literary agents). You want your book to fit in with those books (people like a safe bet and more things like the things they already like) but also to stand out a bit (people don't always want the same-old-same-old, or the same-old-same-old in the same way all the time).

This keeping up with your comparable books should be a career-long habit. It helps you market directly by fitting in well with what books are selling, but it might also help you build a community of authors and to commune with your readers. You can try connecting with the other authors for group promos and newsletter swaps, and you can read those books and talk about them with your fans. Your fellow authors are not your competition so much as your *fellow authors*—your co-laborers in bringing entertainment or [insert your goal here] to the masses. Readers read a lot of books, many more than you can publish. They may love your books but not remember the character names or details, only that they loved it. That's okay and something to get used to. If you talk to your readers, you'll likely find that they will want to talk to you about books they've read (I have a reader who sends her favorite authors alerts when books by other favorite authors go on sale), so know now that you're not a lone god they worship. You're one of many professionals they admire and, for some, want to call friends. The other authors in your genre or topic, your readers—you all share at least one similar interest or passion (clean fantasy romance, elves, investments, spiritual growth, etc.), and it's important to remember that. It should also make interacting with them less daunting.

Anyway, it's time for the obligatory Shakespeare reference: "What's in a name?" Let's move on to book titles and series names.

Chapter 35

Title and series name

A book title is second only to the cover in terms of what readers notice, and covers and titles often work together to tell readers about your book before they get to the back cover blurb. *Harry Potter and the Chamber of Secrets* suggests mystery and adventure, and when coupled with a middle-grade fantasy cover, tells readers who the book is written for and what it's like—and if it's something they want to read. Thus, it's important to make sure your title markets your book well. As with most things, there are theories on how to do this well.

According to the *Novel Marketing Podcast*, "If your book title describes the contents of your book, you will get lost in the noise. Your title must attract attention rather than describe contents."

The title is a promise of sorts. The fiction title evokes curiosity and promises entertainment. It also might evoke a sense of what the book will specifically give, such as a particular feeling. A romance might have *heart*, *love*, *second-chance* or something of that sort in the title. A military science fiction would not. It might have military terms instead. For nonfiction, the title might promise to solve a problem, such as providing all that you need to know to cook quick, healthy meals. Or how to get out of debt now (not in ten years, but *now*). Urgency and numbers are often used in nonfiction titles. Words and phrases like "best," "complete," "now," "today," "in thirty minutes a day," or "in thirty days," are used to add appeal.

Uniqueness, memorability, ease of communication, genre expectations, and search engine rank (since many books are found through search engines on online stores rather than through browsing bookstores) are important considerations when titling your book. Look at the titles of famous books and books similar to yours. What titles catch your eye? What do they have in common? Think about your own book —what makes it unique, what gives a sense of genre and tone, who are the characters, what is the setting, are there any catchy phrases or big ideas attached to it? List these things and then brainstorm titles and series names (if you are writing a series). Write down lots and lots of titles, good and bad, and play around with different combinations. Short titles, long titles. Get feedback. Let it rest. And then make your choice.

Here are a few famous fiction titles to get your ideas going:

Gone with the Wind, 1984, Of Mice and Men, The Fellowship of the Ring (The Lord of the Rings), *The Hobbit, Star Wars: A New Hope, Harry Potter and the Sorcerer's Stone, Ender's Game, Rebecca, Pride and Prejudice, Casablanca, The Screwtape Letters, Jonathan Strange and Mr. Norrell, Heart of Darkness, Dune, The Horse and His Boy, Where the Wild Things Are.*

Here are a few nonfiction titles (notice the subtitles too):

Mere Christianity; How to Win Friends and Influence People; Salt: A World History; Longitude: The True Story of a Lone Genius Who Solved the Greatest Scientific Problem of His Time; The Disappearing Spoon: And Other True Tales of Madness, Love, and the History of the World from the Periodic Table of the Elements; The Simple Path to Wealth: Your Road Map to Financial Independence and a Rich, Free Life; Never Split the Difference: Negotiating as if Your Life Depended on It; Seeking Allah, Finding Jesus: A Devout Muslim Encounters Christianity.

Subtitles

Should you use a subtitle? In nonfiction, probably. In fiction, maybe. It's not that common. You can use subtitles to get more specific and add keywords for the search engine (this is great for nonfiction), and to let the reader know your specific genre, as some genres are difficult to convey in covers. If you have a LitRPG, for instance, you might want a subtitle such as "A LitRPG and Gamelit Adventure" to let readers know that's what your book is and if it's for them. For nonfiction, a subtitle can tell you what the problem to be solved is or who the book is for. A subtitle of "Fast and healthy meals for a busy mom," for instance, would communicate the problem being solved (a struggle to cook healthy, fast meals) and who it's for: moms short on time. Subtitles are also used to explain short, catchy titles.

Series names

If you have connected books, fiction or nonfiction, you'll want a series title that connects them. Sometimes, works are known by the series title more than by the actual book titles (Star Wars, The Lord of the Rings, and Harry Potter are examples of this). Although, I admit there are series I refer to by the title of the first book—because the series title is hard to pronounce or remember. Either way, your series title is important for fans to know what books belong together and for connecting the books in stores. Series names can also be useful for keywords.

As a sidenote, I've noticed that fantasy series names tend to be difficult to pronounce. Some readers are put off by names they can't pronounce (and such names are harder to talk about with friends), so do consider that in titles, series titles, and even character and place names.

As for titling series, apply the same techniques used for your individual book titles.

Part of your book's marketing is its title, so you shouldn't choose the first thing that pops into your mind. You want a title your readers will remember and that will draw them into the book. This will take work and research on your part. Getting other perspectives on your title is a good idea as well. It's often hard for authors to know what is catchy and what is not, what matches the genre and what doesn't.

References and Resources

Bolt, Chandler. "Book Title Ideas: Choosing Your Own & Generators to Use." *Self-Publishing School.* February 22, 2022. https://self-publishingschool.com/book-title-ideas-choose-perfect-title-book/.

Umstattd, Thomas Jr. "How to Pick a Strong Book Title." *Author Media.* December 9, 2020. https://www.authormedia.com/how-to-pick-a-strong-book-title/.

Chapter 36

Keywords and categories

From the title to the cover to the blurb, branding is about helping the reader fall in love with your book. But how do you get it in front of them to begin with? "Shelving" in online stores is in many ways similar to shelving in physical bookstores. You have mysteries and biographies and children's books and science fiction and so on. But instead of walking through the aisles and picking up whichever spine among the alphabetized offerings catches your eye, or choosing the face-forward or endcap books (positions that cost the publisher extra money), you browse best seller lists or enter search terms into a search bar and browse the results of your query. There are many, many more books to sort through to find what you want, but you can also be more specific in your quest using specific terms. Instead of having an entire mystery section to peruse for what you want, you can tell your favorite retailer's search engine that you want a cozy mystery with cats, and see just those. Plus, whatever sponsored books and incorrectly labeled books show up, but we won't quibble about that right now.

The point is, retailers want not only your book's category (such as mystery or self-help), but also keyword terms that readers will search for. When you set up your book on the retailer, they will ask for the age range of your book, your categories (two), and keywords (seven). These will be used to place the book into the categories that show up on the product page. And they will work together to determine which searches your book shows up in. Which is mildly important . . .

So let's take a brief look at "shelving" for your book and how to choose the proper keywords and categories.

CATEGORIES

I'm sure you're familiar with the different sections of your local library—biography, fiction mystery, fiction young adult, large print, etc. Those shelving choices aren't determined by bespectacled librarians who read every book that comes in but by information associated with that book upon its receipt: its metadata. When publishers put their books into the catalogue that librarians and bookstore employees order from, they include what's known as the BISAC information. This lets them know who the book is for—adults, teens, children—and what kind of book it is—travel reference, science fiction, contemporary romance, and so on. BISACs are important because they ensure books get placed where the readers who want that kind of book will be looking.

If you go through IngramSpark or some of the other platforms, you will be asked to choose two BISAC categories for your book. If you go through KDP, they have their own "shelving" categories, and you pick two from that list. These are basically BISAC categories, just without the unfamiliar acronym attached. According to Kindlepreneur (https://www.youtube.com/watch?v=8wTThtack9I), there are almost 4,000 BISAC categories, but KDP has additional ones for 16,000+ categories. (Before you get overwhelmed, you won't see those or even all the BISACs when you set up your book. You follow the appropriate drop-down lists and so see only a relative few.) Amazon has so many because it uses search data from its store to adapt its categories to what readers are looking for, such as adding a "Gaslamp" (similar to steampunk) option to its fiction categories when it notices people looking for those books. So KDP's categories tend to be more specific than the BISACs.

The categories you find in the book setup page, however, are not always the same as the ones you see for best seller rank on retail pages.

The rank section gets much more nitty-gritty in its categories than you do on the back end (remember those 16,000+ KDP categories?). As a warning, these categories don't always make sense either. The keywords you enter, and keywords pulled from your book title, subtitle, and blurb, affect the categories your book ranks in.

So how do you choose categories on the back end, the part you have the most control over? Must you look up BISACs somewhere and type them in? No, the retailers provide a handy drop-down list for you. The challenge is—for some—choosing the best category from the list.

You get two categories for your book. You can actually request more, and some suggest you do. But for our purposes, we have two categories we need to fill in. Let's say you write clean contemporary romance. When you get to the Categories section in the setup, you can click Fiction from the dropdown menu, then Romance, then Contemporary. That's as far as this category selection goes. That's one of your two categories. For your other, you'd go to Romance, then Clean and Wholesome. That's pretty easy.

But what if your book is more difficult to categorize? Say it's a fantasy that feels a bit like a historical fantasy but isn't based on a real time and place, and has a good bit of romance but maybe not enough for a fantasy romance? And whose readers like fairy tales but your book isn't a fairy tale, though it is a happily-ever-after story? If you have that kind of issue, I feel your pain.

Your best option is to find the most compatible categories, the ones where your readers will be, and use those. For help with this, look at the sales rank categories of your comparable books and go with those. You can also find the categories of your comparable books using the free website BkLnk (https://www.bklnk.com) by pasting the book's ASIN into their category search feature. You can always change your book's categories later, if need be.

KEYWORDS

Keywords are the words or phrases retailers use to comb their catalogue in response to customer search queries and to populate their results. Keywords are pulled from titles, subtitles, the book blurb, and the seven keywords or keyword phrases you add on the back end when you set up your book.

There are entire courses and software programs (including Kindlepreneur's KDP Rocket) to help you choose the best keywords and categories for your book. It's beyond the scope of this book to go into all of the advanced marketing theories and algorithms associated with choosing just the right keywords. But here are a few tips. I've listed references for those who want to dig deeper. This is one of those places where you can spend as much or as little time as you want. If you're planning on hitting best seller lists and doing ads, you'll want to spend more time in this section.

Nonfiction keywords

For your nonfiction keywords, describe the pain points (reoccurring sources of trouble or distress customers want solved), solutions, or results your work is built around. What solutions do you offer? What problem are you solving? What interest or hobby are you writing about?

Brainstorm words and phrases related to these things. Ask yourself and others what search terms would be used to pull up your book (or terms you want your book to show up for).

Fiction keywords

Describe the story, setting, and characters. The tropes and tone as well. Think about the keywords you'd use to describe your favorite books. Enemies-to-lovers romance? Space marines? Urban fantasy, clean and wholesome? Royalty? Redemption? Historical YA fairy tale retelling?

Make a long list of words and phrases, think about that list in terms of how people search for books, and choose the best seven words or phrases. You can always tweak this later.

Categories and keywords take research and practice to do well, but are well worth the effort to get right, as they help the right readers find your books.

References and Resources

Amazon KDP. "Browse Categories." https://kdp.amazon.com/en_US/help/topic/G200652170.

BISG. "Complete BISAC Subject Headings List, 2021 Edition." https://bisg.org/page/BISACEdition.

Chesson, Dave. "BISACs vs Amazon Categories - I Can't Find the Category I Want!" (YouTube) June 5, 2019. https://www.youtube.com/watch?v=8wTThtack9I.

Chesson, Dave. "How to Add More Amazon Book Categories to Your Book (You can Rank For 10!)." (YouTube) February 23, 2018. https://www.youtube.com/watch?v=2GO-XNA0epE&t=2s.

Chesson, Dave. "How To Choose the Right Kindle Keywords." *Kindlepreneur.* October 20, 2021. https://kindlepreneur.com/how-to-choose-kindle-keywords/.

Chesson, Dave. "Kindle Keyword Strategy For Fiction Authors." *Kindlepreneur.* October 20, 2021. https://kindlepreneur.com/kindle-keywords-fiction-author-strategy/.

Gaughran, David. "These Amazon Category Hacks Can Boost Your Book Sales." May 9, 2021. https://davidgaughran.com/amazon-book-category-kindle-categories/.

Six Figure Authors Podcast. "SFA 069 – Selling Hard-to-Categorize Books That Aren't Written to Market/Trope." December 17, 2020. https://6figureauthors.com/podcast/selling-hard-to-categorize-books-not-written-to-market-trope/.

Chapter 37

Book pricing: ebooks

Why is pricing in the marketing category? Because it's one of those things that successful authors don't just set and leave alone forever. It's something you can play with to see which prices get better sales. There's tons of advice on the internet about book pricing, and part of the reason for this is that the market is always changing, so the advice must change with it.

Indie publishing isn't "new" anymore. More and more people are publishing now. You have new authors coming in, traditionally published authors getting the rights back to their older works and putting them up for sale, authors who've learned how to write faster and so publish multiple books each year, and those who've been published and keep publishing.

New opportunities and challenges are part of the game. There are shiny new book formatting programs to make publishing so much easier. There are more high quality (and low quality) cover designers out there, but their prices are going up. There are many available courses, blogs, and podcasts for authors to learn basic and advanced techniques to improve their craft and their marketing. Marketing venues, such as book promotion services and ads, are more competitive. Ads are more expensive. The cost of getting your ad to show in response to certain search terms on Amazon, as part of their ad campaign, can be over $1 per click (you pay per ad clicked) for certain search terms because of the competition for those terms. If a reader clicks your ad and doesn't buy your book, you risk losing money. Authors with big backlists to sell to a new reader might be able to afford the hit of the click-but-don't-buy shopper, but a new author?

With all the changes and challenges, it's easy to get frustrated, but if you want to be a professional, you have to work hard and be adaptable, and learn to see other authors not as competition but as other members of your guild. Readers don't just read one author, and you couldn't write fast enough to keep their shelf filled anyway. You're just one of many favorite authors to readers, and that's something we have to come to terms with.

Okay, tangent done. So pricing strategies change. You'll need to keep a handle on the market and watch what other authors are doing.

Regarding royalty rates and pricing . . . I'm going to state the obvious here: you don't get 100% of the retail price of your book. Surprise! The retailers, in return for what they do (provide a platform, convert files, handle transactions, deliver the book to customers, customer service, etc.), take a cut. You get the rest. In keeping with the traditional publishing terminology (though KDP, Apple Books, etc. are not publishers), they call what you get your *royalty*. Let's delve into ebook and print book royalties and pricing.

———

But first, this is a good place to briefly discuss the length of works of adult fiction and nonfiction, since price often reflects the length of the book. We're all familiar with *short story* and *novel*, but there are other terms, particularly in the "short story" branch, that need defining. This is helpful for pricing and for letting readers know what they're getting.

The standard word count ranges below are a blend of information from these two articles: https://prowritingaid.com/art/1243/genrebook-length-.aspx and https://blog.reedsy.com/word-count-novella-short-story-length/. These are standards for traditional publishing, but as indie authors, we aren't constrained by the expectations of agents and publishing houses in our word counts (not that we should completely ignore them, however!).

General Fiction

- Flash Fiction: 300–1,500 words
- Short story: 1,500–30,000 words, or less than 7,500 words
- Novelette: 7,700–17,500 words (if a separate category to "short story")
- Novella: 30,000–50,000 words, or 17,500–40,000 words (if no novelette category)
- Novel: 50,000–110,000 words (some start this at 40,000; average length is 90,000)
- Epic: 120,000 words and up

Genre Fiction

- Mainstream Romance: 70,000–100,000 words
- Subgenre Romance: 40,000–100,000 words
- Science Fiction / Fantasy: 90,000–120,000 with epics of greater length (150,000 words is not uncommon)
- Historical Fiction: 80,000–100,000 words
- Thrillers / Horror / Mysteries / Crime: 70,000–90,000 words
- Young Adult: 50,000–80,000 words

Children's Books

- Picture Books: 300–800 words
- Early Readers: 200–3,500 words
- Chapter Books: 4,000–10,000 words
- Middle Grade: 25,000–40,000 words

Nonfiction

- Standard Nonfiction: 70,000–80,000 words

- Memoir: 80,000–100,000 words
- Biography: 80,000–200,000 words
- How-to / Self-Help: 40,000–50,000 words

————

EBOOK ROYALTY RATES

Royalty rates are fairly even across the platforms, except for a couple of stores where the rate changes based on the price of the book. Some charge a small file delivery fee based on the size of the ebook file. You set the retailer price for the stores. Here are the royalty rates (as of February 2022) for four of the larger ebook retailers. If you use an aggregator, such as Draft2Digital or Smashwords, there will be differences in the amount earned due to their cost and contracts with the retailers.

Since your ebook will be available for purchase internationally (unless you choose not to allow that), you will need to set a price for each international store (such as Amazon's UK store). Retailers usually suggest a price for each store based on current exchange rates. You can go with that or visit the stores yourself and check out the price of comparable books. Either way, it's recommended you change the price to end with the standard 99 cents. A price based solely on the current exchange rate might yield a price of $3.42, for instance, instead of a standard $2.99 or $3.99 price (whichever way you want to round in that situation). If exchange rates change dramatically, or you sell particularly well in a certain store or want to target that market, you can revisit your prices. Prices are easily changed in the author dashboard.

Amazon KDP

KDP has two different ebook royalty rates and, depending on the royalty rate, a small fee for file delivery that is based on file size. There is no delivery cost for books at 35% royalty rate. For books at a 70% royalty rate, the delivery cost is equal to the number of megabytes in the digital book file after conversion multiplied by the delivery cost rate. The rate for Amazon.com is $0.15/MB. You can find out more on digital pricing, price matching, and the delivery costs at this KDP help page: https://kdp.amazon.com/en_US/help/topic/G200634500. As an example, the delivery cost of my 160,000-word fantasy *Wrought of Serpent and Snow*, which has a title page image, one small publishing logo, a small series logo, and a medium-size reader magnet book cover, has a file size of 0.95 MB after conversion and a delivery cost of $0.14.

Amazon KDP royalty: 35% or 70% royalty for ebooks

- Ebooks priced less than $2.99 or greater than $9.99: 35% royalty rate, no delivery fee
- Ebooks priced $2.99 to $9.99: 35% or 70% (you choose), delivery fee of $0.15/MB for 70% royalty rate

Example: $0.99 x 0.35= $0.35
$1.99 x 0.35= $0.70
$2.99 x 0.70= $2.09
$3.99 x 0.70= $2.79
$4.99 x 0.70= $3.49
$9.99 x 0.70= $6.99
$10.99 x 0.35= $3.85

These numbers do not include the delivery fee, which varies by the size of the book. If the book is normally $2.99 or more and is on sale through the Kindle Select Countdown Deals, you can still get the 70% royalty rate on the sale price (not the original price).

Kindle Select Page Reads

If you're in Kindle Select, and your book is read through Kindle Unlimited, you get paid per page read. The amount varies by how much money the KU program earned that month. It's divided between authors, based on pages read, with a prize bonus going to the authors with the top number of pages read. It's generally estimated at about $0.004 per page read. The KDP dashboard has a beta-version reports feature that gives you an estimated earnings based on your KU page reads and sales combined, so you don't have to do the math yourself to get a feel for your monthly earnings.

Do note that you can't use the Kindle Countdown Deals and Free Days immediately upon publishing. The book must be in the program thirty days (through pre-order counts toward this) before you can do a sale, and you can't do a sale immediately after changing the book's price.

Apple Books

Apple says this about their program: "If you are the rights holder of your book, you determine the customer price. You'll earn 70% royalties on all of your ebook titles, regardless of price point, with no hidden fees or exclusivity requirements. Payments are made within 45 days following the end of each month." (https://authors.apple.com/sales-and-reporting)

Apple Books: 70% royalties on ebooks

Example: $0.99 x 0.70= $0.69
$1.99 x 0.70= $1.39
$2.99 x 0.70= $2.09
$3.99 x 0.70= $2.79
$4.99 x 0.70= $3.49
$9.99 x 0.70= $6.99
$10.99 x 0.70= $7.69

Kobo

Kobo says this about itself: "Kobo offers a standard Independent Publisher Program contract through Kobo Writing Life. You can receive royalty payments from Kobo via EFT (Electronic Fund Transfer) directly into your bank account. Authors are paid 45 days after the end of each monthly period provided they have met a minimum threshold of $50 USD." (https://kobowritinglife.com/2016/03/28/frequently-asked-questions/)

Kobo royalty: 70% if the list price follows these rules
  The price is:

- greater than or equal to $2.99 USD in the US,
- greater than or equal to £1.99 GBP in the UK,
- greater than or equal to $2.99 CAD in Canada,
- greater than or equal to $2.99 AUD in Australia,
- greater than or equal to €1.99 EUR in the European Union,
- greater than or equal to $2.99 NZD in New Zealand,
- greater than or equal to $15.99 HKD in Hong Kong,
- greater than or equal to ¥299 JPY in Japan,
- For original works priced below this threshold: 45% royalty
- For books that are a part of the public domain: 20% royalty

Example: $0.99 x 0.45= $0.45
$1.99 x 0.45= $0.90
$2.99 x 0.70= $2.09
$3.99 x 0.70= $2.79
$4.99 x 0.70= $3.49
$9.99 x 0.70= $6.99
$10.99 x 0.70= $7.69

For payments through Kobo Plus, their subscription program, see this article. They pay per minute read. https://kobowritinglife.zendesk.com/hc/en-us/articles/360059386091-How-does-Kobo-Plus-pay-

Barnes & Noble Press
  Barnes & Noble Press states that you, the author, "will select a List

Price for each ebook. You will, at all times, ensure that the ebook List Price: Is no greater than the ebook's List Price at any other retailer, website or sales channel. Is no greater than the ebook's print edition (if applicable). Complies with the minimum and maximum pricing policy as stated above.

"According to the B&N Press Royalty and Payment Terms, you will be issued a payment a) when you have accrued a minimum of $10 (combined for both ebooks and Print Books) in book royalties, AND b) 30 days after the end of the calendar month in which the sale occurs (i.e. your February payment will be for your January sales)." (https://press.barnesandnoble.com/legal/royalty-payment-terms)

Please note that getting into Barnes & Noble's online store is not the same thing as getting into their physical store.

Barnes & Noble Press royalty: 70%

Example: $0.99 x 0.70= $0.69
$1.99 x 0.70= $1.39
$2.99 x 0.70= $2.09
$3.99 x 0.70= $2.79
$4.99 x 0.70= $3.49
$9.99 x 0.70= $6.99
$10.99 x 0.70= $7.69

EBOOK PRICING

I will list several common ebook prices here and discuss pros and cons and where each price is normally seen.

Price: $0
Free books were once a hugely successful way to market (at least for those with multiple books readers could buy after enjoying the free

one). However, free books aren't a guarantee to get noticed anymore because there are so many free books. That said, it does still work to a certain extent. A free first-in-series book is common. You can do a limited number of free days for your book if you are in KU (Kindle Select allows 5 free days per 90-day term). You can also do "perma-free," which means your book is permanently free. Amazon won't let you set your book's price to free, but many other sites will, which forces Amazon to price match. So if your book is wide, you can go to Draft2Digital or Kobo, or wherever it is available, and set the price to $0. When that change is live in the stores, send a price match alert to Amazon. They will set your book to $0. Sometimes it doesn't go through or the price goes back up, so check it from time to time.

Price: $0.99

The marketing value of pricing your book permanently at $0.99 has declined somewhat for the same reason as the use of free books. For a short story or a first-in-series, this might be a good price as readers don't want to pay much for a short work, and readers who buy a first-in-series for cheap will, hopefully, go on to purchase the rest of the series. You can also use temporary sales at this price point to attract readers to your work. Kindle Select gives authors seven days a term for sales and lets them keep the 70% royalty rate for those sales.

One catch of pricing permanently at this level is the royalty rate, at least for Amazon KDP and Kobo, which, at this price point, is 35% and 45% respectively.

Price: $1.99

Same as for the $0.99 price. For short works or a first-in-series, this might be a good price. You do only get the 35% or 45% royalty rate, though, for KDP and Kobo.

Price: $2.99

You're up in the 70% royalty rate now. For a while, this was a sweet spot for selling novels. It was essentially the new $0.99, and the higher price gave the books a more respectable feel. That's not so true anymore, as prices for books, as for most things, have gone up. The $2.99 price point is generally used now for novellas, short novels, first-in-series novels and short nonfiction. It's a good price if you're looking to reduce the barrier-to-entry and still earn the 70% royalty.

Price: $3.99

You're in the 70% royalty rate still. This is a fairly common price right now for novels, for standalones, first-in-series, and later books in the series where the first book is equal or lesser in price.

Price: $4.99

Same as for the $3.99 price point—70% royalty rate and a common price for novels. Longer novels are usually at this price. At the moment, $2.99 to $4.99 is the most common price range, with the length of the novel and series placement being a determining factor in price choice.

Price: $5.99 to $9.99

You're still in the 70% royalty range. Some might consider indie novels priced $5.99 and up too high. Some well-established authors, who know their readers will pay to get their books, are pricing at $5.99 or higher now. Lengthier or more technical nonfiction is priced in this range. Longer fiction works, particularly box sets, are priced in this range, so once you have three or more books in a series and want to bundle them into a box set, you can set the price for the bundle within this range.

As the market changes, the price of a single indie book may fall into this range, so keep an eye open.

Price $10.99 and over

You're back in the 35% royalty rate for KDP (but not for wide stores). If you were thinking of doing a box set at this price range, you'd have to price it really high to make what you would at the 70% royalty rate. Or you can sell it wide through the other retailers. Just know that you can't have individual novels in KU and sell the box set elsewhere.

Pricing a series

The first book in a series is typically the cheapest book in the series and the one that gets the most marketing attention. It's usually in the free to $3.99 range. Book 2 is usually higher than book 1, and book 3 in a series may be the same as book 2 or higher.

When sequent books are released, the price of book 1 (if it's not free already) is often dropped so that the book is free or $0.99 permanently or for a short time. Some authors will make book 1 free, book 2 $0.99, and book 3 full price permanently or only during sales.

If you are co-authoring a book and want to know about royalty sharing, references for that are in the anthologies and group release chapter.

References and Resources

Altair, Zara. "What's the Right Length for My Book?" *Pro Writing Aid.* May 25, 2020. https://prowritingaid.com/art/1243/genrebook-length-.aspx.

Amazon KDP. "Digital Pricing Page." August 14, 2020. https://kdp.amazon.com/en_US/help/topic/G200634500.

Apple Books. "Sales and Reporting." Accessed March 22, 2022. https://authors.apple.com/sales-and-reporting.

Barnes and Noble Press. "Barnes & Noble Press Royalty and Payment Terms." Accessed March 22, 2022. https://press.barnesandnoble.com/legal/royalty-payment-terms.

Kobo Writing Life. "Frequently Asked Questions." March 28, 2016. https://kobowritinglife.com/2016/03/28/frequently-asked-questions/.

Kobo Writing Life. "How does Kobo Plus pay?" Accessed March 22, 2022. https://kobowritinglife.zendesk.com/hc/en-us/articles/ 360059386091-How-does-Kobo-Plus-pay-.

Reedsy Blog. "Word Counts: How Long is a Novella, Novelette, and Short Story?" June 13, 2021. https://blog.reedsy.com/word-count-novella-short-story-length/.

Chapter 38

Book pricing: print

A major factor to consider in your print book's retail price is the cost of printing the book itself. This cost is determined by the book's format (such as hardcover or paperback), page count, and interior options, including ink, paper type, and trim size (the book's dimensions). The cost will also vary by printer. Some have tools that will estimate the print cost based on the aforementioned factors. Because of the cost to print the book, retailers and printers will give your book a minimum retail price. Remember that the print cost of POD books is greater per unit than for offset printing, but there's less risk and no storage required. I discuss the price considerations of your book formatting decisions in the section on formatting.

It's important to note that if you order author copies, you will pay only the cost of the printed book plus shipping, handling, and applicable taxes. You will not get a royalty.

Print royalties

The information below is for the POD services already mentioned: Amazon, IngramSpark, Barnes & Noble Press, and Draft2Digital Print.

There is only one print royalty rate, of 60%, on Amazon KDP (we'll cover Expanded Distribution in a moment). There are no charges associated with changing your print file after the title is live.

Barnes & Noble Press pays a 55% author royalty rate on the book's list price, minus the per book printing cost.

Draft2Digital Print offers a 45% royalty rate (like IngramSpark, they work to make your book available to Amazon, Barnes & Noble, Walmart.com, and other bookstores that choose to order it). D2D does charge a small change fee for re-uploaded manuscripts because the printers charge them if changes are made. They do cover one update per 90-day period for each book. So you must wait 90 days after publication to fix a typo or make any changes for free.

Pricing and profit are much more complicated on IngramSpark due to their different business model. You set a retail price and choose a wholesale discount. Remember that IngramSpark serves as a printer and a way of getting your book into a catalogue for libraries and businesses to order from. It doesn't have a general storefront as KDP does. IngramSpark was discussed earlier, so I won't go into detail about it again here.

Print book cost

What's the wholesale cost of a book? It depends on the printer. IngramSpark, D2D, and Amazon all have price calculators to help you determine this. But just to get a better feel for the cost and how it's determined, let's take a closer look at KDP's print book cost.

For KDP, printing costs vary based on page count, ink type (black ink or color ink), and Amazon marketplace (US or UK, for instance). Trim size, bleed settings, and cover finish don't affect printing cost directly, though trim size does influence the number of pages. KDP automatically calculates your printing cost and shows this in the Rights & Pricing section of your title setup, but if you want to get an estimate beforehand, you can use their calculator (referenced below) or calculate it yourself using this formula: fixed cost + (page count x per page cost) = printing cost. The fixed cost per book and the per page cost depends on the variables mentioned above, but for books ordered in the US marketplace, using blank ink and having 110-828 pages, the fixed cost is $0.85 with per page cost of $0.012. Plugged into our formula, for a 300-page book, this is 0.85 + (300 x 0.012) = $4.45 per book.

Shipping, handling, and taxes are an added cost if you order author copies. If you have a very long book, consider whether it might be better to split it into more than one book (as appropriate to the story structure, of course), based on pricing, durability of a book that large in paperback, reader preference, etc.

Print book pricing

I think you know what I'm going to say here: look at your comparable books and see how they're priced. Very good! You're learning!

Because KDP and the others supply print-on-demand books, the cost will be higher per book than for the mass-produced, traditionally published books. To price your book competitively with traditionally published books, you won't make much profit for books sold through retailers. Some authors price their print books such that they make about the same as from an ebook (around $3-4 profit). Others take a much smaller return (around $1) to make the book more competitive. They use a lower price, higher volume approach as traditional publishers do. The cost of printing your book is subject to change, as the printers' costs are influenced by paper shortages and supply chain issues.

In the print pricing section of your KDP dashboard, you will also see a rate of 40% for something called Expanded Distribution. This is KDP's way of getting your book into stores other than their own. You really get very little money for this option (in the range of $0.70 per book, in my experience). Expanded Distribution also requires a higher minimum price. Many authors use IngramSpark or Draft2Digital Print instead of KDP's Expanded Distribution.

As mentioned, you can buy author copies for the cost of printing, plus tax and shipping and handling. You can sell these direct, through your website, or in-person at events. Since you've cut out the middleman, you make a much higher profit this way. You will be responsible for state and local sales tax, though, depending on where you live and where you sell the books. You can also arrange with local businesses and bookstores to sell them through consignment. We'll talk more about selling your author copies later.

Here's an example of print book cost, pricing, and profit for one of my books, a roughly 90,000-word novel, a fairly common size. The total cost varies with the number of copies ordered, more copies making the shipping less per unit. This book, priced $14.99, actually has a higher profit from retailers than most of my books. A comparable size trad pub book I found was priced at $16 on Barnes & Noble but $14.29 at Christianbook.com and $10.99 at Amazon.com. If I price matched for Amazon, I would get $1.77 in royalty, which is more than traditionally published authors get per print copy.

Format: Paperback
Trim size: 5.5 x 8.5 inches
Paper and ink: cream, black-and-white
Page count: 331
Print cost: $4.84
Retail price: $14.99
Profit @ 60% royalty: $4.17
Author copy cost: If 5 copies ordered, total is $6.50 per unit.
Profit if sold in person: $8.49

That's ebook and print pricing. Remember that you can adjust book pricing as the market changes. Choose a sweet spot between lower cost to readers to encourage them to buy and a decent royalty for yourself.

And speaking of encouraging readers to buy, next up is the back cover copy and tagline. These are both marketing copy for your book. *Copy* is writing designed to promote or sell a product. It's important to keep this in mind as you work on your book's back cover copy and tagline.

REFERENCES AND RESOURCES

Amazon KDP. "Printing Cost and Royalty Calculator." Accessed

March 22, 2022. https://kdp.amazon.com/en_US/help/topic/GSQF43YAMUPFTMSP.

Amazon KDP. "Paperback Printing Cost." Accessed March 22, 2022. https://kdp.amazon.com/en_US/help/topic/G201834340.

Apple Books. "Sales and Reporting." Accessed March 22, 2022. https://authors.apple.com/sales-and-reporting.

Barnes & Noble Press. "Barnes & Noble Press Royalty and Payment Terms." Accessed March 22, 2022. https://press.barnesandnoble.com/legal/royalty-payment-terms.

Draft2Digital. "D2D Print Price Calculator." https://draft2digital.com/podcalc.

IngramSpark. "Print and Ship Calculator." https://myaccount.ingramspark.com/Portal/Tools/ShippingCalculator.

Tumlinson, Kevin. "D2D Print now in beta! Here's what you need to know..." Draft2Digital. October 30, 2018. https://www.draft2digital.com/blog/d2d-print-now-in-beta-heres-what-you-need-to-know/.

Chapter 39

Back cover copy and book description

Have you ever picked up a book, read the back cover copy, and said, "Wow! I want to read this book!" Then you read the book, and not only was it a fantastic story that fulfilled all the promises in the copy, but it had *more* great stuff you didn't know was coming?

You did? Many times? That's wonderful! Hold that thought.

Writing marketing copy (which includes the back cover copy and tagline) is a different kind of writing than writing novels and self-help books. You're basically writing an ad, a sales pitch.

This can insult our author sensibilities because we think the back cover copy ought to be about the book. In truth, it is and it isn't. It's about both the book *and* the potential reader.

Before readers spend their time and money on a book, they want to know what the book will do for them. Will it help them solve the problem they've been struggling with? Will it tell them what they need to know? Will it deliver the kind of entertainment they want? It's the back cover copy that answers these questions.

Another issue we authors have with writing back cover copy is that we know so much about the book, and love it so much, it's hard to distill our beloved child into a 200-word blurb. There are so many cool things we think need to be included, so many important things the reader must know! But they don't. Not to sell them the book.

Remember that great back cover copy you thought about at the beginning of the chapter? The one that sold you on a book, delivered what it promised, and left surprises for when you read the work? That's what you want. That's what readers want, so keep that in mind as you work on your back cover copy.

Why do I tell you this? Because many authors hate writing back cover copy and approach it more like a book summary than marketing copy. It's a mental switch you have to make to create effective copy. Your great book won't sell if your blurb doesn't appeal to readers. Rest assured that this does *not* mean saying things like "Best book ever! You must get this book!"

The first step in creating an effective blurb is to read several. Find five or so best-selling indie books in your genre (the ones that sell well at full price, not the on-sale ones) and trad pub books, or just several books whose blurbs have caught your attention. Study the blurbs and figure out what they have in common and what it is that gets you to pay for the books. Also, read and compare the copy on the back of printed books and the book description on the product page.

Done? Now that you have an idea of what a good blurb is, here's a handy list to summarize the core points, then we'll go over a couple of formulas.

Writing back cover copy

- Blurbs are typically less than 250 words, with 150 to 200 words being the ideal length, as this is all that will fit on the back cover without looking too crowded.
- Remember that many readers will be shopping online, on phones or e-readers. Format and write your blurb to catch their eye—having your blurb grab their attention "above the fold" (above where they'd have to click to see more).
- Short sentences and sentence fragments are fine.
- Make it easy to read, with white space for fiction and bullet

points for nonfiction, as appropriate. Use bold or italics too, as appropriate.

- Write in the tone of your book—humorous, snarky, dark, engaging, etc.
- The blurb can address the reader with questions.
- It can be written in third person, second person, or first person. Only use first person if your book is in first person.
- The blurb often starts with a tagline or hook. Questions often serve as a hook in nonfiction.
- There are different formulas for blurbs, telling you what to include and where. Devise a formula or two from the blurbs you looked at that match your genre and story tone.
- Write several blurbs, get feedback, rewrite, and repeat until you have a marketable blurb.
- Write a book description.
- Keep your finished back cover copy and book description in a file you can get to easily, as you will need it often—as you set up your book on retailers' websites and for various marketing promotions.

Back cover copy formulas and principles: Fiction

For fiction, back cover copy is somewhat like a flash fiction piece with a cliffhanger ending. Thus, you can use the principles of story structure to write it. Possibly the greatest lesson on story structure is this famous, unattributed adage: "Get a character up a tree. Throw rocks at him. Get him down."

In other words, introduce your character and setting. Introduce the conflict and escalate it. Resolve the conflict.

This formula works well for back cover copy too. Only, you want a cliffhanger at the end rather than a resolution of conflict. So it looks like this: Introduce your character and setting. Introduce the conflict and escalate it. End with a cliffhanger.

How that looks in your blurb is influenced by your genre and tone. Here are a few more tips for writing blurbs. You can also hire editors or copywriters who specialize in this sort of writing to write your blurb for you or help you strengthen your own.

Writing blurbs: Additional tips

- Use a hook or tagline to catch attention.
- Introduce your main character. If it's a romance, you can introduce both the hero and heroine. Choose only one or two main characters.
- If you're writing romance, you might have a paragraph for the heroine and a paragraph for the hero, each including an introduction and conflict.
- Introduce the setting, especially if it's important to the genre.
- Introduce the villain or conflict that is driving the story. Focus on *one* story line, even if your story has many. Which has the greatest conflict or tension? You can also describe the character's current state and how that needs to change; or what they want and why they can't get it.
- Create a sense of curiosity as to how it will end. Will the couple get together, or, more accurately (in romance, at least), how does it happen? How can the hero defeat such a powerful evil? Will she forgive herself, get over her bitterness, and accept her new friends as family? Who murdered whom? Ending fiction blurbs with an actual question used to be popular but seems to have fallen out of favor with some "experts," so remember that you can create the question in the reader's mind rather than actually asking it.
- Include the stakes—what happens if the hero fails? The stakes need to be high and appropriate to the genre. Destruction of a world works for a fantasy novel but isn't quite the thing for a romance. A broken heart and ending up alone are high stakes for romance.
- Try to avoid words that are difficult to pronounce.

Back cover copy formulas and principles: Nonfiction

For nonfiction back cover copy, the principles are actually similar to that of fiction. Nonfiction blurbs use a hook like a fiction blurb. Instead of introducing a story character, though, nonfiction often introduces the reader: the busy executive, the tired mother, the teen wanting to learn guitar, etc. who can benefit from the book. Nonfiction works often address a pain point or problem: How can I eat healthy on a budget? How can I self-publish my book? How do I play the guitar? Some nonfiction entertains and informs, such as biographies and histories.

Instead of a conflict and villain, a nonfiction blurb addresses the problem being solved, the question being answered, or the information given. Instead of a cliffhanger, it might include what the book can do for the reader. It might also include the author's credentials so readers will know what qualifies him or her to write the book. It might ask questions or have bullet points. It might include an endorsement, if the endorser is well-known and valued by the target audience.

Book description

The book description, found on the book's product page online, includes the tagline/hook, blurb, and often some extra information. For fiction, this is usually geared toward making the book's genre clear ("A YA fairy tale retelling"), noting content and tropes (dark, steamy, clean, action-packed, enemies-to-lovers romance, for example), and providing series information (standalone, part of a series, the reading order of the series). It may place the book in the genre by associating it with a particular trope or author. It may say something like, "Perfect for fans of [famous thriller author]," for instance.

———

As a concluding note, because writing the back cover copy and description helps you hone your marketing skills and find the big picture of your story in a few paragraphs that are easy to test on willing friends (who read in your genre), it's good practice to write a book blurb before or early in the process of writing your book. It helps you focus your story, determine if the stakes are high enough, and if the general idea is marketable.

Back Cover Copy summary:

1. Read the back cover copy of 5-10 successful books in your genre and ask yourself what makes them work.
2. Work out the formulas used in the blurbs and what copy they use to set the genre, announce the tropes, appeal to their target audience, and so on.
3. Write a tagline or hook (the topic of the next chapter).
4. Write a back cover copy with the mindset of making a sales pitch rather than writing a synopsis. Write several and rewrite as necessary. Get feedback.
5. Create a tagline and back cover copy for your print book's back cover. Create a book description for your retail page.
6. Keep the back cover copy at 250 words or less.
7. Keep your finished back cover copy and book description in a file you can get to easily.

References and Resources

Chesson, Dave. "How to Create a Back-Cover Blurb that Sells." *Kindlepreneur.* March 2, 2022. https://kindlepreneur.com/back-book-cover-blurb/.

Erik, Nicholas. "Blurb Cheat Sheet." Accessed March 22, 2022. https://nicholaserik.com/start/. (Link to PDF on this page.)

Hoffman, Jessi Rita. "Writing Your Book's Back-Cover Copy." *Jane Friedman.* August 16, 2015. https://www.janefriedman.com/writing-back-cover-copy/.

Chapter 40

Tagline and hook

If you've looked into getting an agent, or learned about marketing at all, you've probably heard about the "elevator pitch": that catchy, short pitch for whatever you're trying to sell. The idea is that you only have an elevator-ride's length of time to get someone interested in your product.

While being an indie author means you don't have to get an agent, it doesn't mean you don't have to think about short pitches for your books. These are often present on the cover itself, especially at the top of the back cover. You use them as ad copy, and book promotion services use short pitches instead of the full back cover copy as part of your book listing. Many authors use catchy taglines at the top of their blurbs and on their retail pages—in bold or italics—to capture readers' attention.

So what kind of short pitches are you likely to need—tagline, hook, blurb? Actually, I don't really know. It depends on who's asking. (Don't you love that answer?) To be honest, terminology tends to get confusing here, as what some people call a *blurb* others might call back cover copy or back cover blurb, while some will ask for a blurb and mean a short pitch and not your back cover copy. Or they might mean an endorsement. And hook and tagline might be the same thing to them, or what one blogger calls a *hook*, another calls a *tagline*. I wish I could give you a cut-and-dried answer, but you'll have to read carefully (noting the pitch's required word length) and figure out what is wanted. Sometimes, it doesn't matter whether you give a hook or tagline, so long as you give something short. But, whatever it's called, you will need some kind of short pitch, and I am going to talk about two short pitches—the *tagline* and the *hook*—and differentiate them based on the definitions given by Tom Ashford in his post on Mark Dawson's website Self-Publishing Formula (https://selfpublishingformula.com/hooks-and-taglines-what-are-they/).

Introducing short pitches: Tagline and hook

A *tagline* is comparable to a flashing light that catches the reader's attention but doesn't necessarily reveal anything about the product. It's like a slogan. Where Nike has "Just do it," The Lord of the Rings has "One ring to rule them all." It doesn't tell you exactly what the book is about (though you understand after you've read the book), but it catches your attention. It creates intrigue, which draws readers to look at your blurb, which will hopefully seal the deal in a purchase (this is called a *conversion* in marketing terms). Here's a tagline from Terry Pratchett's book *Mort*: "Death comes to us all. When he came to Mort, he offered him a job." Definitely grabs your interest, doesn't it? It also sets the tone of the books. And we've probably all heard "May the odds be ever in your favor" from *The Hunger Games*.

A *hook* is designed to both catch attention and produce an expectation—that this book will tell the reader what they've been wanting to know, that it will help them change, and so on. Marketing expert Seth Godin's *Linchpin: Are you indispensable?* has this hook as the first line of its book description: "This life-changing manifesto shows how you have the potential to make a huge difference wherever you are." The title itself feels a bit like a tagline, being very catchy, and the hook tells you enough about the book to know if it's for you (and since it's "life-changing," it likely will be!). In Michael Hyatt's *Win at Work and Succeed at Life: 5 Principles to Free Yourself from the Cult of Overwork*, the subtitle serves as a hook. So a hook might be a separate thing from your back cover copy altogether, or it might be the first line of the blurb or the book title itself.

Taglines and hooks can not only catch attention but also set a tone. Notice these two: from *A Tailor-Made Bride* by Karen Witemeyer, you have "When a dressmaker who values beauty tangles with a liveryman who condemns vanity, the sparks begin to fly!" and from *The Faceless Mage* by Kenley Davidson, "He'll protect her with his last breath . . . Until she becomes his next target." By the taglines, we can guess both of these are romances: the first a lighthearted, enemies-to-lovers romance; the second a story of danger but also with an enemies-to-lovers romance. Add in what the titles and covers tell us, and we know one is a historical, the other a fantasy romance. Here are a few more fiction hooks to show different styles: "Thomas Fawkes is turning to stone, and the only cure to the Stone Plague is to join his father's plot to assassinate the king of England," from Nadine Brandes's YA historical fantasy *Fawkes*; "An army of witches. A world at war. A girl with no name," from the middle grade fantasy *Pennyroyal Academy* by M. A. Larson; and "What do you do when your knight in shining armor lives, literally, in a different world?" from Lisa T. Bergren's YA The River of Time Series.

Taglines, hooks, covers, and book titles individually can each grab our attention; but when taken together, we get a good sense of what the book is like, and if it's like the stories we already like, or is different from our normal reading, yet intriguing.

Some tips for writing hooks and taglines:
1. Expect it to be hard.
2. Look at lots of taglines and hooks and get a feel for what works, what doesn't, and what your comp authors are using.
3. Write a lot of them and choose the best.
4. Be sure it's not only attention-grabbing but also conveys the proper tone (that is, is true to the book) and fulfills the reader promise.
5. Get feedback to make sure you've done a great job.

Writing hooks and taglines is hard work, and you may write dozens of them before you find the right ones, but the effort is well worth it. A good hook can really drive sales. And as a sidenote, the more I write, the more I realize it's wise to start thinking about these things *before* I start a book. Writing a blurb and coming up with a tagline/hook that stands out—a story with a great concept—can guide me to write a book that also stands out. The more marketable your initial idea, the more marketable your book.

References and Resources

Ashford, Tom. "Hooks and Taglines – What Are They?" *Self-Publishing Formula.* February 7, 2020. https://selfpublishingformula.com/hooks-and-taglines-what-are-they/.

Dittemore, Shannon. "How to Craft a Killer Tagline for Your Book." *Go Teen Writers.* May 8, 2020. https://goteenwriters.com/2020/05/08/how-to-craft-a-killer-tagline-for-your-book/.

Chapter 41

Book links and what you didn't know you didn't know

You'll need to keep a collection of all your book links and your website links to share on social media, to put in the back matter of your books, to provide when setting up promotions or writing guest posts, and . . . Let's just say you will need them a lot. You may not have any links besides your website to share at the moment, but I'm throwing this section in here since, eventually, you'll have the links and will be using them for the things we've talked about in this section. Also, links are part of your organizational strategy. You'll want to create a page in your Scrivener file or find some other way to keep them organized and within easy reach. But first, there's something secret and magical about links you may not know.

They don't have to be long and ugly!

What?! It's true. If you want to know the secret to pretty links, read on.

Shareable links

Getting links to share—you'd think this would be a simple matter of looking up the book on your retailer and doing a copy-and-paste from the address bar. Do that and you'll be considered an amateur. Anytime you search for something (at least on Amazon), that search information gets added into the weblink for data processing. That is why you get long, ugly links like this:

https://www.amazon.com/Wrought-Silver-Ravens-Magic-Made-ebook/dp/B08GQ18SFG/ref=sr_1_1?keywords=wrought+of+silver+and+ravens&qid=1640727086&s=digital-text&sprefix=wrought+of+silver%2Cdigital-text%2C67&sr=1-1.

If you go through the link in your Amazon dashboard, you get this: https://www.amazon.com/dp/B08GQ18SFG.

This link will take you to the same page as the long one, but it's much preferred to share this one. This clean link (which is for the ebook) includes the store and the book's ASIN number (Amazon Standard Identification Number). I'm assuming the necessary *dp* refers to *detail page*. Pardon the pun, but in short, the link to your book's Amazon page should be the Amazon marketplace (*amazon.com* or *amazon.co.uk*, for instance), then, for the ebook, */dp/ASIN number*. The ASIN number is the only unique information needed to send readers to the ebook. For the print edition, use the ISBN-10 in place of the ASIN: */dp/ISBN*.

If you want the book title to be obvious so customers will know exactly where they are going, you can include that, as shown below. You can get this address by copying from the long one. Note that the series name is included, as well as "ebook" for the ebook version.

For the ebook: https://www.amazon.com/Wrought-Silver-Ravens-Magic-Made-ebook/dp/B08GQ18SFG.

For the print: https://www.amazon.com/Wrought-Silver-Ravens-Magic-Made/dp/0999350943.

So when sharing a link, always share a clean link. Crop as appropriate, test, then save the short version in your files.

Universal links

But what if your book is in multiple stores? Do you have to share ten different retailers every time you promote your book? What of people who use amazon.co.uk rather than amazon.com, the American store? If all your links are for the wrong store for your international readers, they may not care enough to search for your book in their store.

Ease of purchase—removing barriers to purchase—is a smart thing. Fortunately, there are *universal book links*, provided by such places as Books2Read that solve both of the issues mentioned above.

Books2Read says of itself: "One link for every reader everywhere. With a Books2Read Universal Link, readers can find your book wherever they prefer to shop." (https://books2read.com/)

When you go through a universal link generator, you are sent to a page with links to whatever stores sell your book. So the link for the correct Amazon store, as well as, if applicable, links for Apple Books, Google Play, Kobo, and other stores. Audiobook and print book links are now included as well. If you've not used a universal link before, you're welcome to check out this one built for my "Beauty and the Beast" retelling *Midnight for a Curse*: https://books2read.com/u/4jgLV5. It includes ebook, print, and audiobook links.

Universal links are very handy if you have lots of links. You only have to share one link, and the reader gets their choice of stores.

———

There are "short" links such as bitly links, but the clean store links and universal links are the most important and likely the only ones you'll need. Many people do not trust short links because they can't tell where they are going, and many professionals are warned not to use them or click them.

———

QR code

Another type of "link" that is useful is the QR code, short for *Quick Response Code*. These pixelated square grids are actually barcodes. They store various types of information, such as website links, account information, phone numbers, or even coupons. For our purposes, they work like links. Many smartphone cameras are able to "scan" the code and read the stored website link. The link may show as a banner at the top of the screen, When tapped, the phone's browser opens to that web page. Some phones might need an app to read the code.

This is very useful for promoting digital products—ebooks and audiobooks—especially at live events. You can generate a QR code, print it out on a sign, bookmark, or just a piece of paper, and people can scan it and buy your book then and there.

There are several free and paid QR generators online. A few mentioned in the articles referenced below are Scanova, Visualead, QR Code Generator, and QR Stuff. You will need to decide if you want a static or dynamic code. A static QR code doesn't change. The same QR code goes to the same website permanently. A dynamic code is changeable, allowing the same printed code to go to different sites over time, as it is altered.

You can test your QR code on the screen using your phone, then download it. You can download it in JPEG, PNG, GIF, TIFF, or JPG formats for use on a web page, or PDF, EPS, and SVG formats for print.

References and Resources

Books2Read. https://books2read.com.

Jacob, Ennica. "What is a QR code? A guide to the barcode's basics, why you're seeing it everywhere, and how to scan one." *Business Insider.* May 3, 2021. https://www.businessinsider.com/what-is-a-qr-code.

Sears, Devin. "QR Codes Uses: How To Grow Your Business With QR Code Marketing." *Bluehost.* August 15, 2021. https://www.bluehost.com/resources/qr-code-marketing/.

Chapter 42

Concluding branding the book

I debated including another section here on getting the word out about your book pre-launch, but I thought you might be getting antsy to build your book, so I moved that section to later. For some of those tactics (like the use of Advance Reader Copies), you need an almost-finished book file anyway, and for most of the tactics you need a cover, our next topic.

So far, we've talked about decisions you need to make before publishing, scheduling and budgeting, starting a website and a news-letter, gaining a readership through your reader magnet, deciding on keywords and marketing copy, and other things to get your book ready and appealing to readers. Now we'll move toward getting the actual book file ready, then we'll jump back to more marketing to help you get the word out about your book before its launch. Finally, we'll talk about how to set up your book title on retailers, and hit publish.

There's a lot to do, so do devise a schedule and get organized so you can make the best use of your time and stay on track financially. For instance, while your book is off being edited, you could tackle looking at comps and choosing a cover designer.

Branding summary:

In this section on branding your book, you have:

- Done marketing research to find books comparable to yours.
- Chosen a marketable, appropriate book title, and if applicable, a series title and subtitle.
- Chosen the best two categories and seven keywords for your book.
- Chosen a price for your ebook and your print book.
- Written your marketing copy: a blurb/back cover copy and tagline or hook.
- Learned how to get a clean link, a universal link, and a QR code.

Part Seven

Book Covers

Chapter 43

Covers

Covers are both the most fun and most stressful part of the publishing experience, at least to those of us who love art. I *love* looking at covers and have spent way too much time doing so (and have bought pre-made covers I have yet to use and may never use). But because I love art, and because the cover represents my book baby, a wrong cover can be a heartache. It can be frustrating to look so hard for the right designer, to hope so much for a fantastic cover, and try so hard to communicate what you want, then get something "less than." Communicating the issues with a first draft cover, or even a second or third draft, can be frustrating and time-consuming, and is a skill that will need to be developed. Sometimes, you have to accept something less than or different to what you envisioned, at least for the time being. You can re-cover the book later.

That encouraging intro done, let's talk about the ideas behind the cover design as well as how to find a designer and what to expect from the process. Bottom line, though: covers are about marketing your book, not telling your story. You can commission fan art later to detail all those amazing scenes and show the details of your character's scars and amazing costume, if you want.

Cover as a marketing device: Covers might not be for what you think

Many people really do judge a book by its cover, using it to decide whether or not to read the back cover copy, which might lead to them purchasing the book. This is a huge point to remember—the cover tells a reader whether they are likely to enjoy the book. Not because the cover tells the story, but because it tells the reader what the story is *like*. Whether it is *like* this other story they enjoyed, or *like* this story they did not enjoy. The cover is not a way to tell the story itself, with lots of details you wouldn't understand unless you read the book. As authors, that is what we tend to think, that the cover is about the book. It is, in a way, but if you want people to read your book, then they need to actually pick it up. That means the cover is more about marketing—letting the reader know "this is the book you are looking for."

For instance, military science fiction stories usually have spaceships on the cover. A space opera would likely have people and a space scene on the cover. If a military sci-fi reader saw a cover with spaceships fighting, he or she would think, "Hey! I like books with covers like that. Let me find out more." But if that same reader saw a military sci-fi book with a handsome hero and a lovely woman *and* spaceships, they might assume it was a space opera and never look for more information. If I see a cover with a young woman in a big pretty dress, I assume a fairy tale retelling or YA fantasy of some sort. I like fairy tale retellings and YA fantasy, so I would pick it up. If I see a young woman in a tight black outfit with a leather jacket in a dark city scene, I think urban fantasy, and if I am in the mood for urban fantasy, I would pick it up and look at the blurb.

Note that I am not mentioning anything specific about the cover; not the glowing amulet the heroine is wearing, or the exact type of castle in the background, or the color of the hero's eyes. I might notice those details and be more intrigued, but it's the overall feel that first draws me in. Now, *after* I've read the book, I might take another look at the cover and notice those things, and be pleased by the way it follows the book or disappointed by a lack of adherence. But I will have already enjoyed the book, which is the main point. I say all this to emphasize that covers should represent the book, and be as accurate as reasonably possible, but are mostly about letting the reader know what experience to expect from the book. The romance genre is really good at this; we all know what to expect from books with "man-chest covers" versus covers with smiling, fully clad couples. Just a glance at these books tells us whether we would or would not like them.

This idea is a huge mental hurdle for most authors, which is why I'm stressing it. And as I have said a few times already, you need to do your market research to find out what books/covers are selling well in your genre.

Cover design basics

Covers come in two types based on the origin of the design: pre-made and custom. These designations are self-explanatory. Pre-made covers are already finished when they are posted for sale. The title and author name are changed after purchase, and the designer might allow a few minor changes to the design, but mostly, they are ready to go. Custom covers are designed based on a brief the author gives the designer. Pre-mades tend to be cheaper. Most, but not all, are ebook covers with an option to purchase a print package to go with it.

Covers are also divided into photo-manipulation covers or illustrated. For photo-manipulation covers, graphic designers use stock photos for the elements in the design (photos of people and places, for instance). They can do a lot with the stock images (hence the term *photo-manipulation*), so don't assume these will look just like images from a stock photo website. Also, don't assume it's easy to create a good photo-manipulation cover. Yes, you, with a little practice and Photoshop or an open-source program like GIMP, can move a head to a different body, but making it look natural, making the character fit with the background, requires skill, and it's easy to tell who's a novice cover designer and who's an expert just from these two things. Illustrated covers are hand-drawn and come in many styles. There is a limit to the abilities of photo-manipulation covers (mostly related to getting the right stock photos); you don't have this issue in illustrated covers. Photo-manipulation covers tend to be cheaper than illustrated ones.

Covers can be people-centric or text- or symbol-based. Some genres work best with people on the covers. Other genres trend toward symbols and no people, or a cover that uses the title itself as the main element of the design.

Key elements of a cover are typography, color palette, and imagery. For an excellent article on this and other cover design basics, check out this article by cover design group MiblArt: https://miblart.com/blog/how-to-design-a-book-cover/.

A pet peeve of mine is font usage. In my opinion, a font can make or break a cover. Some covers look great but the font resembles WordArt from Microsoft Word. Or some designs might have great fonts but poor content otherwise. This is because fonts are a separate skill set. If you find a designer you like whose font choices aren't market savvy, you can show them a font you like (on an example cover) or have them do the background design and take the cover to another designer to finish up with the font, and maybe even take care of the cover's technical specifications (spine width and so forth).

As a tangent, there are hundreds of different fonts—whole websites are devoted to fonts. You can download and install them on your computer and use them as you would the fonts already in your word processor. Like stock photos, however, fonts require a license to use. This means that the fonts in your word processor and the fonts you find online may not be free to use for your ebook or print book. You need to check the license (search online for this). Some fonts are for personal use only, and you must buy a license to use them for commercial purposes (in print books, ebooks, or on your web page). Some are free for personal and commercial use. The fonts in formatting programs should be free for personal and commercial use.

The book's front cover will include the title, author name, and series name. It might also include an endorsement or short review ("Best novel of the year!" —Famous Reviewer).

The spine will include the author name, title, and publishing logo.

The back cover generally has the tagline, back cover copy, and barcode (which might be added at the time of printing). It might also include a review, endorsement, or an author biography.

———

Now to the nitty-gritty of the cover process: schedule, budget, choosing a designer, and working with a designer.

Scheduling for a cover

The time needed for a cover can vary greatly. You might spend an hour searching a pre-made cover website, find what you want, get it paid for and the title and author name adjusted, and have it in a few hours or a day. Or you might spend hours or weeks searching for a designer, find that perfect designer and discover she's booked for a year and would then take a month to finish your design, two if you want changes. So know that while pre-mades can be bought and brought home in a short time span, custom designs can require months or years.

But don't panic. Not all designers have a year of work already in their schedule. Many only book a few months out and might need a month to complete the design, depending on how many changes to the initial concept are requested. Consequently, it's a good idea to find a designer well in advance of your release date or cover reveal and get things set up. Get an estimate from the designer for how long the design process takes.

As an example, one designer I work with gives me a date a few months away on which I will receive a cover proposal (the draft of the cover). He also sends a cover design brief, which I must complete and return two weeks prior to the proposal date. So most of the work is done by the date the designer gives me. However, if I request changes, it might be a week or six before the next draft is ready, depending on their schedule and the requested changes. Once the ebook cover is ready, they send the paperback proposal. I accept it. They send the invoice. I pay, then they send the files the next day. It can be a good amount of back-and-forth. I may get my cover a few weeks after the initial proposal date or two months afterward.

So it's a good idea to allow a couple months' buffer between your expected cover date and your release. That means you will need to start looking for a cover designer six months or more before your release, to get on the designer's calendar and get the finished cover. Depending on your marketing plan, if you're doing a cover reveal and lengthy pre-order, then you'll want the cover months before the release and will need to book a designer even earlier in the process.

A warning, however, that you need to be far enough along in your story or series to really understand the title and the genre. If you send a cover design brief too early, your story might change so that it doesn't fit the cover. That said, some authors (myself included at times) find that the right cover (pre-made or custom) can be an inspiration. It can inspire a specific story or bring depth to a current story.

The cover process

The cover process varies by designer, but here is what it often looks like: You contact the designer. They give you a date on which they'll start work on the cover or return a draft to you. You'll fill out a cover design brief or questionnaire, in which you tell them the desired style of the cover, what characters look like, title, trim size, etc. They send a cover proposal (sometimes called a mock-up) on the assigned date. If needed, you suggest changes. Sometimes, you might get more than one concept (design) to choose from. The cover is altered and sent back to you. This revision process continues until the cover is finished. Some designers have unlimited revisions, some not, so be aware of that.

Having a few friends to help you figure out what is good and what needs changing will be helpful, but don't ask more than three market-savvy people, as too many cooks spoil the dish. These early files are all watermarked files. When the cover is satisfactory, you'll receive an invoice. Once you pay that, they will send the final files. It's common to get the cover files before the print version of your book is ready. You may accept the print wrap design of your book, pay, and then when your book is fully edited and formatted, go back and give them the final page count and print information. They'll then send you the final print cover.

Pricing and what you get with a cover

Cover prices vary considerably. You might find a custom or pre-made cover for $100 or less, but many quality designers (as of early

2022) charge $300 and up for ebook and print, with some photo-manipulation designers charging nearly $800. Illustrated covers may cost much more—$1,000 and up—depending on how complex your concept is and how many characters you want on it. Not all are this expensive, so hunt around before you panic and give up your dream of an illustrated cover, if you had a nasty shock there.

As you think about your budget, remember the cost of future covers, especially if you're doing a series. You might want to do a more affordable cover now, then re-cover later after it's earned out, or delay the launch to save up more money and get a better cover. It's okay to re-cover as styles change or earnings justify it; many authors do this.

Before you start searching for a designer, decide which formats and add-ons you want: ebook only, ebook plus print? Title page? Amazon print only or Amazon and IngramSpark? Hardback?

Cover prices are often for the ebook only, not ebook plus print, so check what you are getting. Print is sometimes an extra $50-$70 on top of the ebook cover. The print wrap includes the spine and back cover. Also note that print paperback and hardback require different covers (different in technical details, not necessarily in overall design). This extra work on the designer's part will add to the total cost. This is usually not by much; perhaps $20 for the different format. Amazon KDP and IngramSpark require slightly different cover sizes for even their same format books, so you need to let the designer know which service you are using. IngramSpark requires a template that you will need to download from their cover generator, after providing information to the generator about your print book (trim size, ISBN, etc.).

On a technical note, ebook files and print files are created with a different color profile—RBG for ebook (and internet usage) and CMYK for print files. An inexperienced designer once sent me an RGB file for print, and the file was rejected. This cost me time and caused a bit of frustration, but we got it fixed. This difference in color profile also means there might be a slight variation in color between what you see on your computer and how it prints. This is normal.

Designers also offer a variety of add-ons: title pages, bookmarks, website headers, banners, and so on.

Things to consider

Here are additional things to consider in your cover ponderings: Will you want more covers matching this first one, as for a series? Let the designer know and also make sure they are going to be around for a while and can work on them. One of the drawbacks of going with a friend or college student to design your book (for cheap) is that they might not be available a few years from now when you need another book in that series. They might also not be willing to work for free or cheap then either, since they will have the experience to charge more.

Find out what rights you are getting with the cover. Do you have full rights, such that you could make derivative products? Or does the designer retain those rights? Do you get the source file (the Photoshop file, for instance) or not? Many designers do not give the source file at all or only a flattened version for an extra cost. This prevents you or another designer altering the file.

Find out what the process is for paying (usually through an online means, such as PayPal) and for handling any issues that might come up, such as a failure to finish the product or a cover you cannot approve. Many designers work on the cover until you are satisfied, then send you an invoice. When you pay the invoice, they send the final files. Some might want all or half of the money upfront. I would be wary of paying all the money upfront unless you know the designer is reliable and has a stated way of settling any issues, including an unsatisfactory project.

Do you need a barcode? Most self-publishing services will add that to your cover, but you can buy a barcode, or generate your own, and provide that to the cover designer.

Remember that while some people do not seem to care about cover quality (some books with hideous covers still sell because they hit the popular tropes), many people do, and "the laborer deserves his wages" (Luke 10:7). Don't go too cheap on the cover.

How to find a cover designer and cover design style

How do you find a cover designer? You can do internet searches with specific terms, such as "fantasy cover designer" or "illustrated cover designer" or "pre-made cover designs." You can ask your writer friends.

One way, however, that works very well is to look up the cover designer listed in the copyright page of comparable books or of any book whose cover you like. You can do this using the "Look Inside" feature on Amazon or the old-fashioned method of picking up books at the book store or library. I found one of my favorite cover designers because I looked at the copyright pages of several books whose covers drew me (these were also highly rated books, so checking out the Top 100 list for your genre is a good idea too).

Another method that I have only recently discovered (as of 2021), is to use Instagram and Facebook. Instagram is an ideal spot for artists, especially illustrators. Cover designers are also creating groups on Facebook to gain clients. You can search for designers there. They tend to put their pre-made covers for sale first through those groups. Writing groups often have lists of designers. There are also sites like 99Designs and Fiverr that have many designers to choose from. On 99Designs, you can have a design competition, receive drafts from many designers, and choose from among those, or you can work with a designer whose portfolio you like. As a note about the 99Designs competition, I've noticed that there are a lot of low-quality submissions in the contests, so I wouldn't recommend doing a guaranteed contest (you guarantee that you will choose a design from among those submitted)—not at the lower price contest, anyway. Check out the designer portfolios instead.

When looking for a designer, consider your desired style (such as illustrated, symbol-based, or photo-manipulation), as designers often specialize in certain types of design. Some are great at the image but not so good at fonts, or vice versa. If you really like a designer's work except for the font, you can ask for the background only and hire someone who specializes in fonts to add the title and author name. Some also specialize in nonfiction or fiction, or fantasy or romance, for example. Make sure they understand your genre.

Recognize that not every graphic designer will be a good cover designer. Cover design requires a certain expertise, marketing savvy, and technical knowledge. Any person good at art isn't necessarily a good choice for a cover designer, in other words.

If you're having trouble with your design/designer, go with your gut and don't be afraid to cancel a project if you and the designer aren't meshing well or the project just isn't what you need. Especially if this is a series, it's better to pay for one cover and start over than to struggle with every cover for that series and end up needing to re-cover all the books later.

Don't beat yourself up if things don't work out with a designer. Sometimes, they seem to do great work for some clients but your cover feels lacking, or is wrong for your genre. It happens. Do make sure your expectations are reasonable and that your brief is well done before you decide the designer simply isn't listening to you or able to do what is needed. Remember that a cover is the work of the designer, representing their time and talent, so be kind and professional even in breaking things off.

Writing a cover brief

Your designer will want to know what you want your cover to look like, and, often, they will have a specific questionnaire for you to fill out. You'll need to consider your color scheme (or your favorite colors), the mood or tone of the cover, whether you want people or not, and if you have people, what pose. Plus, how many people and what they look like (in detail).

Pictures are very helpful here, since we may not realize our expectations don't match others'. You may have one color in mind for blond, but there's ash blond, dirty blond, strawberry blond, bleached blonde . . . You get the idea. You need to specify for your designer or be okay if the designer chooses the wrong thing out of ignorance.

Consider the background setting and character costumes. For a fantasy, what time period or culture most closely represents the fantasy culture? What's the book's tone and genre—dark, funny, sweet romance, fantasy romance, action and adventure, cozy mystery, and so on? A pretty cover with the wrong tone is a bad cover. The same applies to a cover portraying the wrong genre. Covers are not an art piece to hang on your wall to admire; they're a marketing tool. That's not to say they won't *also* be works of art.

It might help to ask a few readers how they picture your character.

Sometimes their idea differs from yours—this could be their mistake or a misleading description in your book.

If doing the brief worries you, you might ask the designer for an example of a good brief. If the idea of coming up with a basic design yourself worries you—and many designers will ask you for a basic design that they then build on—look for a designer who will come up with a design themselves based on a summary of your book and the tone/genre. This is a risk, though, so make sure they know the genre.

As you work on the brief, look up images of characters and settings, research your comparable books' covers, and create a Pinterest board of them. Some designers will ask for this. It's also helpful to you in figuring out what kind of cover your readers like.

For your print wrap brief, you'll need to tell the designer who will be printing your book and the book's trim size, format, and page count. Often, they will design the full cover based on the trim size, have you accept the design, and then, when the book's page count is final, complete the cover. You'll also need a back cover blurb for this. If you have a publishing logo (not essential), you can have that added to the cover as well.

Schedule a couple of hours to research for and write the cover brief as well as time later to communicate with your designer about your draft covers.

Conclusions

1. Covers are first of all a marketing tool. They are for three people: those looking for a book, those who've read the book, and the author, but the cover is first and foremost to get people to pick up the book.

2. Don't stress about the details too much. It doesn't need to convey every aspect of the book. It needs to be recognizable to readers (right hair color and general description) but doesn't have to exactly match. It's more important that your cover is accurate marketing so the right people will pick up your book.

3. Covers need to be budgeted for both financially and with regard to time. If you need to cut costs on covers, look for a pre-made cover or a designer who offers simple designs for less than their premium covers.

4. If you're doing a series, consider how the cost of covers over the series will work out. You can't expect earlier books to pay for them. It can take time for books to start earning a profit. Also ask if the designer plans on being around a while, or go ahead and get the rest of the series done. Books in a series need to have similar covers.

5. The copyright of materials (images and fonts) used in the design should be considered. A professional designer will only use images and fonts with a proper license.

6. Be clear about price, revisions, concepts, termination of a project, and timeline.

7. Schedule ahead of time and leave time for extra work or unforeseen delays.

————

In short, covers aren't about your books; they are about the readers' perception of your book. They are a marketing tool.

References and Resources

Amazon KDP. "Cover Image Guidelines." Accessed March 22, 2022. https://kdp.amazon.com/en_US/help/topic/G6GTK3T3NUHKLEFX.

Amazon KPD. "Create a Paperback Cover." Accessed March 22, 2022. https://kdp.amazon.com/en_US/help/topic/G201953020.

Erik, Nicholas. "Author Resources." October 6, 2021. https://nicholaserik.com/resources/.

Erik, Nicholas. *The Ultimate Guide to Book Marketing: The 80/20 System for Selling More Books* (Ultimate Author Guides). 2020.

Hamilton, Jason. "Font Copyright Laws for Books: Your Print Book Could be in Violation." *Kindlepreneur.* February 23, 2022. https://kindlepreneur.com/font-copyright.

Ippolito, Janeen. "3 Tips for Working with a Book Cover Designer." June 5, 2020. https://www.janeenippolito.com/writingmarketinghelp/3-tips-for-working-with-a-book-cover-designer/.

MiblArt. "Fantasy Book Cover Fonts: Professional Tips." Accessed March 22, 2022. https://miblart.com/blog/fantasy-book-cover-fonts/.

MiblArt. "How to Design a Book Cover: The Only Guide You Need." Accessed March 22, 2022. https://miblart.com/blog/how-to-design-a-book-cover/.

Payne, Chris. "Book Cover Design Basics." *IngramSpark*. December 15, 2021. https://www.ingramspark.com/blog/book-cover-design-basics.

Penn, Joanna. "How To Find And Work With A Book Cover Designer." *The Creative Penn*. February 14, 2018. https://www.thecreativepenn.com/2018/02/14/how-to-find-and-work-with-a-book-cover-designer/.

Umstattd, Thomas Jr and DouPounce, Kirk. "Effective Book Cover Design." *Author Media*. March 23, 2022. https://www.authormedia.com/effective-book-cover-design/.

A few design marketplaces:
99Designs. https://99designs.com.

Fiverr Book Cover Design. https://www.fiverr.com/categories/graphics-design/book-design/cover.

Upwork Book Cover Design. https://www.upwork.com/services/book-design/book-cover-design.

Part Eight

Getting the Book Ready

Chapter 44

Formatting your book, part 1

Now that you've done your market research, made a bunch of decisions for your book, and gotten it dressed up with a cover and editing, it's time to start *building* the book. Here, we'll look at the book's content (the types of pages within it, for example, the title page), its identification, how to format it (get it properly styled and with all the right pages), and how to convert it into the needed file types. Then we'll skip back to some last-minute marketing to get the word out about it (you'll want a finished product for some of these), before uploading it to retailers and hitting publish!

The first thing to do here is pick up a few books (preferably ones in the same genre as yours) and flip through them. Take note of the types of pages, the numbering, the font, the chapter headings, and so on.

Back already? If you skimmed enough books, you probably noticed differences in the types of pages present, especially at the front of the book, and that there were Roman numerals for the page numbers at the front and Arabic elsewhere. And you may be wondering how you even build a book and do you need to do it yourself? And what file types do you upload to the retailers to get said books?

Great questions. We'll start with the last: file types accepted by retailers.

File types needed for ebook and print publication

Generally, these are *doc, docx,* or *epub* files for ebook and *PDF* files for print. The PDF/X-1a is preferred for your print file. The retailers usually convert your uploaded file into their desired format to send out to their customers.

That said, files for retailer platforms aren't the only ones you'll need. You'll also want mobi files and generic epub files for advance reader copies (ARCs) of your book, and for direct sales and gifts. KDP formerly recommended uploading mobi files, but now they prefer epub. However, *readers* still want mobi files for ARC copies and freebies as these are the files they will download onto their Kindle or onto their Kindle app. That is, many readers want mobi. Some will want generic epub files for other reading apps and devices. (I like reading in Apple Books and so download epubs.)

In summary, if you plan on selling through KDP, giving away copies of your book to advance readers or giveaway winners, or selling direct, you will want the Kindle epub file (or formatted doc or docx file), the mobi file, and, if you plan to print the book, the PDF file. For other ebook retailers, you'll likely want a generic epub file. Check to see what your specific retailer requires.

You can get the epub and mobi files using a formatting program, such as Vellum or Atticus, or Calibre (an open-source software). Scrivener will also convert your files to epub and mobi.

What you're converting *into* the epub or mobi file is usually a doc, docx, Pages, or InDesign file that has been formatted according to book design specifications.

How do you format the file that you convert to an epub or mobi?

There are four main ways to do this: do it yourself, hire someone, use store-associated software, or purchase book formatting software.

Formatting a book from scratch, also known as creating the interior design, requires a decent bit of knowledge and expertise, especially if you want a pretty, professional book. If you're okay with a simple, clean product, and don't mind the work, then you can certainly format your own book using a word processor or Calibre in a few hours (if you know what you're doing and have a simple book; otherwise, it will take much longer). If you're a fan of Adobe products, you can do a professional format in InDesign (you really need to know what you're doing here, as this is a professional-level skill set). There's also Scrivener and Affinity Publisher.

Smashwords founder Mark Coker has a popular guide (*Smashwords Style Guide: How to Format Your Ebook*) for formatting an ebook within a Word document (what many of us did back in the early days of self-publishing). This is a useful book if you do a lot in Word because it helps you understand more of Word's functionality. Once the book is formatted you can then use Calibre to convert the formatted file to epub and mobi. Apple has a guide on how to format a book using Pages and export it as an epub (https://support.apple.com/en-us/HT202066).

Formatting in a word processor or InDesign is too technical a topic to go through here, but there are excellent references below (and I'll mention a few tips on formatting in the next chapter). But do know that this does require you to understand the workings of your word processor and all the ebook and print specifications. This includes knowing how to create sections within your document (using page breaks and section breaks), how to set different page numbering for different sections, how to set the proper margins for your print book's trim size, how to have different margins for your verso and recto pages, how to use styles, how to create a linked table of contents for your ebook, and much more.

If you want to do it yourself but need a little help, or want some-thing a bit fancier, you can also buy templates for use in Microsoft Word, Apple Pages, Affinity Designer, or InDesign. I've used the Word templates available for sale from Book Design Templates (https://www.bookdesigntemplates.com) and liked them. They offer a decent amount of flexibility on fonts and image placement, and come with all the margins set (a huge help), but I still highly recommend reading the Smashwords guide first. Book Design Templates offers a helpful guide, "The Book Construction Blueprint," on the parts of a book, which I also recommend reading if you plan on formatting your book yourself.

Templates are a great option if you want unique chapter headers, have lots of illustrations, or desire a particular font, and don't mind tedious work. Note, though, that the fonts you choose will not always show up in the ebook version, as not all fonts are "understood" by ebook readers or computers. You actually have a font book on your computer with stored fonts. Any fonts beyond these will be converted to a stored font. If you want a specific font not in your font book, you can purchase it from a stock font site and install it in your font book. You can embed the font in the PDF file for print, but you may still not be able to get the font to show in the ebook version. Also, remember that fonts, like photos, are copyrighted. This means you should check the license of any font you use.

If this sounds intimidating or too tedious and time-consuming, you can also hire people to format your book. The cost and the complexity of the final book will vary by designer. You can find designers on Reedsy, Upwork, Fiverr, and Damonza. Some cover designers also do formatting. Adobe InDesign is the program many professionals use to format books, though some will do a simple formatting job using Vellum and Atticus ("layperson" formatting programs are discussed below). Find out which program the formatter is using beforehand (don't pay hundreds of dollars for someone to format your book in Word or Vellum). Ask what file formats you are getting and what the turnaround time is. Also find out what happens if you realize you have a typo or want to change the back matter of your book later. Will you have the files to do that yourself, or will you need to contact the designer and pay more to get that done? Dave Chesson at Kindlepreneur has an excellent article (though somewhat biased toward his Atticus program) on hiring formatters; it's listed below.

As for utilizing store-associated software, KDP and Draft2Digital (D2D) also have options to format your book for you. For D2D, you simply upload the proper file type (such as a docx file) and they will format it into the template you choose. You select the style of chapter headings (from their list of styles), whether you want drop caps or not, and so on. You don't have great variety, and it doesn't work well with complicated formatting (such as including chapter sayings), but it's simple, free, and easy to use. KDP has Kindle Create, but they warn of requirements and supported features they want you to know about before you download and use the program. You are also limited to using the product only through KDP. D2D is free to use elsewhere, though I imagine they want you to use their aggregator services! Reedsy also has a free Reedsy Book Editor for typesetting PDF and epub versions.

Another popular option (probably the most popular for authors of multiple books) is to buy a formatting program, such as Vellum or Atticus. Vellum has long been loved by indie authors. It saves time and creates simple but professional-looking books. With Vellum, you purchase and download the software, upload a clean docx file of your manuscript, and Vellum creates a lovely book (epub, mobi, and PDF) for you in a jiffy. You then choose and add elements (such as a title page, copyright page, epigraph, etc.) and decide on the book's style from their selection of styles. They have a limited number of styles (it's easy to spot a Vellum book), trim sizes, and fonts to choose from, but they did release new styles in 2021, so future updates with even more styles aren't out of the question. It's very easy to use, and if you need to upload a revised copy of the manuscript, easy peasy! No laborious copy-and-paste and fixing of resulting formatting issues. It only takes a few clicks. It's a huge time saver. That said, there are limited styles and not as much flexibility in image placements, fonts, and chapter heading styles, and it is a significant onetime investment: $199.99 for the ebook formatting program and $249.99 for the print and ebook version, as of 2022. And you do need a Mac for this program, though you can "rent a Mac in the cloud" and use it that way if you have a PC.

A new program fast gaining in popularity is Atticus. It released in 2021 from the Kindlepreneur team. I haven't used it, but it looks like a great tool for formatting your book as well as for writing it. It's essentially a combination of Scrivener, Vellum, and Google Docs; runs on Windows, Mac, Linux, and Chromebook; and only costs $147. Since you can write your book in Atticus, you don't have to export it as a docx file and then import it into your formatting program (which you must do if you write in Scrivener and format in Vellum). If you're comparing Vellum and Atticus, do note that the comparison chart on the Atticus page (as at January 2022) has the comparison for the older Vellum. Vellum released a major update in late 2021, so be sure to check out Vellum more closely, since some things (like the number of chapter themes) have changed.

There are many benefits to using Vellum and Atticus. You have charge of your files and can easily make changes as you find typos or decide to update your back matter with information on new books or reader magnets. It's so much faster than doing the formatting yourself or hiring someone. They will create a linked table of contents for you (a huge time saver!). You can easily move chapters around if you decide you need to after formatting (I do my final editing passes in Vellum, actually). Atticus and Vellum have also done the work of checking font licenses for you and can create a large print edition. They also have templates for the different page types.

What's in a book?

Now that we've talked about file types and how to format, think back to those books you flipped through. Did you notice different pages? What types of pages do you need? Do fiction books have a table of contents? Why are there so many blank pages at the front of the book?!

Book formatting is an old discipline with its own terms and a rich history. If some things about it sound strange, there's a reason for it, but that's a history lesson for another day.

Here are the basic things you need to know as you consider your book's layout. A book's interior is divided into three sections: the front matter, the body, and the back matter. The right-hand and left-hand pages have their own names: *recto* and *verso*, respectively. The verso is the left-hand page and is considered the back page. The recto is the right page and is considered the front page. The title page, first chapter, and certain other pages in traditionally published books are always on the right or recto page. All those blank pages you noticed are added to keep the right-hand pages on the recto page. If you want to look professional, leave those blank pages and have at least the title page, half-title (if used), and first chapter start on the right-hand page.

Let's take a closer look at the front matter now. This is everything before the actual start of the book, so to speak (everything before Chapter 1). It will include many (but not all) of these pages.

FRONT MATTER

Endorsements/blurb: Sometimes the book's first page(s). Includes short blurbs by other authors or professionals in praise of the author or work.

Also by: List of other works by the author. May be near the front or at the back.

Half title: Contains only the title (no author name or publisher) and is often the first page (if no endorsement page is used). It's often eliminated to cut page length.

Title page: Includes the title, subtitle, author, and publisher of the book. May include the publisher's location and the year of publication. Illustrations are also common. A required page.

Copyright page: Found on the verso of the title page. Includes the copyright notice, edition information, publication information, legal notices, and the ISBN. The cover designer, editor, and illustrator, as appropriate, are also listed. Required.

Dedication: Follows the copyright page. Tells to whom the book is dedicated.

Epigraph: This contains a quotation and is found near the front of the book.

Table of Contents: Lists all the major divisions of the book. Needed for all ebooks. Useful for nonfiction and for fiction books with parts or volumes (such as an anthology). Not typically found in print fiction books. If the book has numerous figures (such as illustrations) or tables, a **List of Figures** or a **List of Tables** might be appropriate in addition to a Table of Contents.

Foreword: Provides context for the main work and is written by someone other than the author. It's signed with its author's name, city of residence, and date.

Preface: This is written by the author and may convey the origin of the book idea. It is often signed with the name, place, and date.

Acknowledgements: The author thanks those who helped with the creation of the book. May also be in the back matter.

Introduction: The author introduces the work, its purpose, and its goals, scope and organization.

Prologue: This is for fiction only and is a part of the novel that comes before the first act of the story.

Second Half Title: A second half title (a match to the first) may be added if the front matter is particularly long, as a break before the body begins.

Specialty pages: These might include a map or list of characters, pronunciations, a glossary, or a family tree.

Of these, the only ones you must have are the title page and the copyright page. The others depend on what you write, what you want, and the page length you are trying for. The front matter, because of potential changes to it after the rest of the book has been typeset (such as getting a late preface added), uses a different page numbering system. The front matter uses Roman numerals, while the rest of the book uses Arabic numerals.

BODY

The body of the book includes your actual manuscript, beginning with Chapter One until The End (and no, you don't have to actually write "The End"). It has a header and footer, usually with your name and the book title in the header, and page numbers (Arabic numerals) in either the header or footer. It has chapter headings, sometimes with illustrations, flourishes, or epigraphs. These may be styled or simple, and usually match across the book. The first chapter starts on the right-hand page, but later chapters don't have to. The first line of each chapter may be regular, small caps, or have a drop cap (the large letter that "drops" several lines down at the beginning of some first paragraphs). There are also the scene breaks. You may use # or *** in your manuscript, but in a published book, something more attractive is generally preferred. You can use the ones provided in your template or program, you can have a designer design one for you, or you can find illustrations or flourishes on stock photo websites and use those. Just make sure you know the technical specifications for this and how it affects the file size of your manuscript, as you would with any added image.

BACK MATTER

The back matter is everything after the body. This is a really handy section for the indie author because it's where your personal marketing material goes. You can have a newsletter sign-up page (with your reader magnet mentioned previously to attract readers to sign up), an author bio with a request that people leave a review of your book, an "also by" page that lists your other works, a next-in-series page, or pages advertising your other books. These latter pages might include book covers, back cover copy, taglines, and retailer links or pre-order links.

At the least, for your back matter, you'll want an author bio and an acknowledgments page (if you didn't put it in at first). If you write nonfiction, you might want an index or glossary.

Back matter checklist:

- Author biography
- Newsletter sign-up
- Next-in-series/pre-order page
- Also By
- Index
- Glossary or special information pages
- Request for reviews (this might be in the biography)

––––––

Most of your formatting decisions are best made after looking at several traditionally published books and quality indie books in your genre, and then choosing what your book should have to look professional, be easily readable, and be useful for marketing your future books. The technical aspects of page margins and image placement and so on will be covered by your formatter or formatting software (so most of you won't need to know the details). Thus, I won't walk you through those or the contents of every page. I will, however, address a few general formatting concerns in the next chapter, then spend a couple of chapters on the print edition (regular and large print). After that, we'll look at the copyright page and back matter in more detail before we move on.

Formatting your book summary:

- For uploading your ebook to retailers, you will want either a properly formatted doc, docx, or epub file.
- For uploading your print book to retailers, you will need a PDF file, particularly a PDF/X-1a file.
- For ebooks ARCs and gifts, you will want both an epub file and a mobi (Kindle) file.
- You can format your books yourself using a word processor, Calibre, InDesign, and other programs. You can hire it out. You can use a program designed specifically for easily formatting ebooks, such as Vellum or Atticus. These programs are very popular with indie authors.
- A book is divided into the front matter, body, and back matter. Each has its own unique contents and formatting specifications.

References and Resources

Amazon. "Kindle Create." Accessed March 22, 2022. https://www.amazon.com/Kindle-Create/b?ie=UTF8&node=18292298011.

Amazon KDP. "Format Your Paperback —> Save Your Manuscript File." Accessed March 22, 2022. https://kdp.amazon.com/en_US/help/topic/G202145060.

Amazon KDP. "What file formats are supported for eBook manuscripts?" Accessed March 22, 2022. https://kdp.amazon.com/en_US/help/topic/G200634390.

Apple. "Use advanced book creation options in Pages." Accessed April 11, 2022. https://support.apple.com/en-us/HT202066.

Atticus. https://www.atticus.io.

Chesson, Dave. "How to Hire a Book Formatter." *Kindlepreneur.* March 24, 2022. https://kindlepreneur.com/how-to-hire-a-book-formatter/.

Chesson, Dave. "Parts of a Book [From Cover To Cover]." *Kindlepreneur.* February 7, 2022. https://kindlepreneur.com/parts-of-a-book/.

Coker, Mark. *Smashwords Style Guide: How to Format Your Ebook.* Smashwords, 2012.

Friedlander, Joel. *The Book Blueprint: Expert Advice for Creating Industry-Standard Print Books.*

Hamilton, Jason. "Font Copyright Laws for Books: Your Print Book Could be in Violation." *Kindlepreneur.* February 23rd, 2022. https://kindlepreneur.com/font-copyright.

Reedsy Book Editor. https://reedsy.com/write-a-book.

The Book Designer. "Front Matter: Organizing the Beginning of Your Book." September 20, 2021. https://www.thebookdesigner.com/2021/09/self-publishing-basics-how-to-organize-your-books-front-matter/.

Tumlinson, Kevin. "Draft2Digital Introduces Professional-Quality eBook Templates." August 31, 2017. https://www.draft2digital.com/blog/draft2digital-introduces-professional-quality-ebook-templates/.

Vellum. www.vellum.pub.

Chapter 45

Formatting your book, part 2

Formatting can be an intimidating part of the publishing process. It can also be a time-consuming one. This is why many indie authors are using Vellum and Atticus. You simply upload your clean manuscript into the software, and it creates a book, complete with chapter divisions and headings. You input your title and author name, and the program puts it into the title page and chapter headers. You can easily add the copyright page, dedication, and so on, as you wish, from the available templates. It builds the table of contents for you. You choose the style of the chapter headings, the font and font size, the placement of your page numbers, and so on. You can choose to add images and footnotes and can do simple formatting such as making a bulleted list. You can choose to have some pages only included in the print version, or only in the ebook version, or in both. When you're done, you generate epub, mobi, and PDF files from it, as desired, with the click of a button. You can save your program files and final files on your computer, backup disk, and in the cloud. Vellum is used as a program on your computer. Atticus has a lot of cloud-based features and so can be used on multiple computers. These programs have excellent tutorials on how to use them, so I won't try to describe what you can more easily see in their tutorial videos and image-rich posts. I will, however, address a few common questions related to formatting.

FORMATTING QUESTIONS AND ANSWERS

What size should my book be? This is called your book's *trim size* and is discussed in the next chapter. Trim sizes in the 5 x 8 to 6 x 9 range are the most common.

What font should I use? There are many different recommended fonts. Some fonts are more readable than others and so are better for children or those with vision impairments. Some are better suited to web use while some are for print. Some convey a certain tone and are chosen for that reason (a typewriter-like text for a mystery or a softer style for a romance, for instance). Fonts are generally divided into two major categories you need to be aware of, however: serif fonts and sans serif fonts. Serif fonts have the serifs, or extra strokes on the tips of the letters. These extra little lines are said to help guide the eyes along the page; thus serif fonts are typically (but not always) used for the body text. Times New Roman, Baskerville, and Garamond are common serif fonts. (This book uses EB Garamond.) Sans serif fonts lack the serifs. They are commonly used in headings and for large print editions. Arial and Helvetica are popular sans serif fonts.

What font size should I use?
Books typically use a font size of 10-12. Large print is at least 16. Vellum doesn't use font sizes. Instead, it offers a slider, with the default setting being at the center of the slider. I have used that setting and the +1 setting, and both are readable. When choosing your font typeface and size, note how readable the font is in italics and how the font affects the number of pages (some fonts are effectively bigger than others even at the same font size). You might consider generating a print PDF for your book in different font styles and then printing off a sample page of each and comparing.

What about large print? We'll talk about that in another chapter.

Do I add my cover to my print PDF? No. Your cover is uploaded separately to retailers.

Do I add my cover to my ebook file? Your formatting program will ask for the ebook cover but generates separate body and cover files. You will upload them separately to the retailer.

Must I do anything special to my manuscript before uploading it to a formatting program or sending it to a designer? Yes! You should have a clean manuscript. We've mentioned standard manuscript format before: Times New Roman, 12 pt. font; double-spaced (though the final, formatted version will be single-spaced); 1-inch margins. Use the indent feature rather than spaces or tabs to indent paragraphs. Use page breaks to create new chapters (very important!) rather than hitting enter until you get to a new page. This is a good start. Also do these things: Indicate new chapters using a page break and by placing Chapter # at the top center of the new page. Vellum recommends using your word processor's heading styles to make the chapter headings all the same and thus easy for the program to recognize. You can split, merge, and add chapters as needed once the manuscript is in Vellum or Atticus. Use # or *** to indicate scene breaks rather than blank lines. Vellum and Atticus will replace those with your ornamental scene break of choice. Avoid using two or more blank lines as the programs treat them as scene breaks and will add ornamental breaks there.

How does the formatting program recognize chapters? Usually by the presence of page breaks and chapter headings.

My formatting is doing wacky things! Help! I can't really answer any specific questions here, but I've noticed that a lot of formatting issues can be resolved by respecting the word processor's formatting. This involves *seeing* the formatting. This is done by clicking the pilcrow button (looks like a paragraph symbol and is called "invisible characters" in Vellum). It will cause the formatting to show (typically dots for spaces, the paragraph symbol for where you hit enter, a line for chapter breaks, and so on). If you're always getting blank lines showing up when you copy and paste, for instance, it could be that you are always copying the paragraph symbol when you copy and, consequently, are pasting an extra blank line into the new location. You might be deleting or adding a page break as well, which messes with the formatting.

Can I use links in my book? Yes! However, do know that any retailer links within your Amazon ebook can only be Amazon links or universal book links. Likewise, wide stores prefer your book to not have Amazon links. If you sell wide, this means you would want to create a different file to upload to Amazon and non-Amazon retailers, or use universal links.

Do I need a table of contents? Yes, for all ebooks. For print: generally, yes for nonfiction and no for fiction.

Any final tips?
Once you have all the parts of your book and have formatted it, I highly recommend reading it over again. Errors can be introduced during this time, old ones spotted in the new look, and there might be stray formatting errors or inconsistencies that need to be taken care of. Pro-tip: editing in a different format (Word doc to Vellum file or reading on a computer versus a tablet or on paper) helps you see typos better.
Once your book is formatted and you've uploaded it, it's a great idea to order a proof copy from the printer, such as KDP (you can do this during title setup, as discussed later). Your book is not live at this point, but you can still get a copy to ensure quality and lack of errors.

Chapter 46

Print book decisions

Formatting for print books involves many more decisions than formatting for ebooks. Let's talk about things to consider and the decisions you need to make regarding your print edition.

PRINT FORMATTING

There are a lot of technical things to consider here, from the different margins of your verso and recto pages to how to get the different page numbering systems for the front matter and body etc.; so, again, I will not run through all that. You may not even need it, depending on which route you go to get your formatted book. There are some things, however, that you will need to know no matter which route you take. Keep track of all your print choices and book details (trim size, final word count, etc.), as your cover designer will need them to finish the print PDF. If you are using IngramSpark, you will put this information (along with the ISBN) into their cover template generator and then send the generated cover template to your designer.

Your first decision for print is whether you want paperback or hardback or both, then you will choose options for paper, ink, and trim size (the final size of the book, such as 5.5 x 8.5, representing inches of width and of height). We discussed the pros and cons of paperback and hard-back earlier. In brief, paperback is cheaper and easier to produce, allows for a greater profit at a reasonable retail price, but hardbacks are beloved by many, favored by libraries, and last well.

IngramSpark (IS) has more options for trim sizes and hardback bindings, but the basic decisions are the same for both IS and KDP, so I will go through the KDP list here and add the options for IS where applicable.

Print options: Paperback

One of your first decisions is the color of the paper your book will be printed on and whether it is printed in black-and-white or color ink. Color ink is, of course, much more expensive than black-and-white. The color of the paper, cream or white, doesn't affect price. Here are the paper and ink options for KDP and IS.

KDP Paper and Ink Options

Black & white interior with cream paper
Paper weight: 55 lb., 90 grams per square meter (gsm)

Black & white interior with white paper
Paper weight: 55 lb., 90 gsm

Standard color interior with white paper
Paper weight: 55 lb., 90 gsm. Page count range: 72-600 pages. Max trim height: 11" (279.4 mm)
Suitable for most books with color but not recommended for books with full-page color elements.

Premium color interior with white paper
Paper weight: 60 lb., 100 gsm
Crisp, vibrant colors for illustrations, graphics, and images.
Recommended for books with full-page color elements.

IngramSpark Paper and Ink Options

Ink Qualities

Black-and-white printing
50 lb. / 74 gsm paper in crème or white

Standard color printing
50 lb. / 74 gsm or 70 lb. / 104 gsm white paper

Premium color printing
70 lb. / 104 gsm white paper

Paper Color and Weights

Groundwood 38 lb. / 56 gsm
Available in black-and-white printing and select, small-format trim sizes in the US and UK.

Crème 50 lb. / 74 gsm
Available in black-and-white printing.

White 50 lb. / 74 gsm
Available in black-and-white printing and standard color printing.

White 70 lb. / 104 gsm
Available in standard and premium color printing options.

Most authors and readers I've talked to prefer cream paper over white paper when printing from KDP. I haven't seen the cream and white paper from IS or deduced a general consensus on preferences there. The recommendation is usually cream for fiction or memoir and white for nonfiction. You can order proof copies from KDP in both types to choose between them, if desired.

Trim size

Once you decide on paper and ink, you must choose a book size, called a "trim size." The sheets of paper the text is printed onto are larger than those found in the finished book and are trimmed down to the desired size, hence the term "trim size."

There are many, many different trim sizes. Which one you want depends on the type of book you're writing and your own personal preference (and what's available in your formatting program, if using). Trim size also influences the number of words per page, and thus the number of pages in your book, so trim size factors into the cost of the printed book. Larger trim sizes result in a thinner, cheaper-to-produce book, but production cost isn't everything. Weigh the cost against the look of the final product. Will your reader want a tall, wide, thin book or a shorter, plumper one? It may not matter much for some nonfiction books, but it will affect your fiction readers. They want a book that will look nice on their shelf and match the books there.

What sizes are typical for your genre? Check your bookshelves and measure the books you want yours to be "shelved" with.

KDP recommends the 6 x 9 in. trim option (6 inches wide by 9 inches tall), but you do not have to go with that one. In my experience, 6 x 9 *fiction* books stand out on the shelf, where most are 5.5 x 8.5 in. or smaller. So while it's fine for nonfiction, 6 x 9 doesn't look professional (in my opinion) for general young adult and adult fiction books. Measure your books and figure out which size is best for you.

IngramSpark has more trim size options than KDP, so if you want a certain size that KDP does not have, try IS. Don't forget about Draft2Digital's print option as well. It should be coming out of beta in 2022.

As a note, paperback books are usually *perfect bound*, which means the pages and cover are glued together at the spine. You may also see an option for *saddle stitch*. This is where the pages and cover are folded and connected by stapling at the crease, rather than gluing. This is an option only for smaller works, such as booklets.

Bleed setting

"Bleed" refers to printing beyond the page margin to the edge of the page, even allowing the image to run off the page. This is a term you'll need to understand for printing most types of images, from covers to bookmarks. This is useful if you have an illustration you want to take up the full page, having no white space around it. Even if you don't have this, however, most books use "no bleed."

Paperback cover finish

How do you want your cover to feel and look? You have two options for paperback books: matte or glossy.

KDP says this about its cover finish choices in the title setup:

"Glossy finish is shiny. It makes black covers darker and artwork more striking. It's typical for textbooks, children's books, and nonfiction. Matte finish has minimal sheen and a subtle, polished look. It's typical for novels and other fiction."

I did a survey of my friends on Facebook and the vast majority preferred matte covers to glossy ones. Many like the feel of the matte books and the lack of shine when taking photos of them (such as for Bookstagram). If you're not sure, you can get a proof copy in both cover types before releasing the book. You can always change this setting after publishing the book. Be sure to keep track of your choices so that your future books will match.

Hardbacks

For hardbacks, many of your options are the same, as far as paper and ink go. The trim sizes available may be different from the paperback options.

The main consideration for hardbacks is whether you want the cover to be case laminate, cloth, or dust jacketed. A traditionally published book often, but not always, has a removable "jacket" that wraps around the book and has the cover design on it, whereas the book itself has a plain cloth cover with little besides the title, author name, and publisher. Currently, IngramSpark offers dust jacketed hardcovers, but KDP does not. However, these are actually jacketed case laminate covers, meaning there can be a design on the hardback itself and not only on the dust jacket.

In a case laminate hardback, the design-containing pages are glued to the boards forming the "hard cover." This is the less expensive option and is useful for books where a dust jacket would get in the way.

IngramSpark also offers a Digital Cloth™ Cover, which it describes as a "subtle, cloth-like look (available with or without dust jacket. Textured feel available for hardcover books printed in the U.S. and U.K. only)."

A few tips on formatting for paperback:

Your final file for printing will be a PDF file. The PDF/X-1a is preferred.

An even number page count is preferred, and KDP may add a blank page at the end to achieve this. Your last page is a verso (left-hand page), which is an even number page.

If you are concerned about page count (for cost reasons), you can adjust the font size or style to decrease the page count, but remember to keep the font at a size readers are comfortable with. I do not recommend using very small margins. A standard margin and font gives a professional look and is good for ease of reading. It's better to choose a larger trim size to cut down on printing cost than to make the book difficult to read. A good edit to reduce unnecessary words also helps! In addition, you can check to make sure you don't have unnecessary blank pages in your back matter. I recommend going through the PDF file and looking for blank pages there, as they don't always show in a Word document. Also check for chapters that have only one or two lines on the last page. If possible, adjust the paragraph breaks on the previous page or couple of pages to end the chapter at the bottom of the previous page.

We'll talk about the large print edition in the next section.

Print book options to keep a list of:

- Print vs. hardback
- Trim size
- Paper color (cream/crème or white)
- Black-and-white or color ink
- Bleed setting
- Paperback cover finish (matte or glossy)
- Hardback cover type (case laminate, cloth, or dust jacketed)

References and Resources

Amazon KDP. "Format Your Paperback—>Save Your Manuscript File." Accessed March 22, 2022. https://kdp.amazon.com/en_US/help/topic/G202145060.

Friedlander, Joel. "Casewrap vs Dust Jacket? Shelf-Publishers Make the Hard(cover) Choice." *The Book Designer*. January 14, 2010. https://www.thebookdesigner.com/2010/01/casewrap-vs-dust-jacket/.

IngramSpark. "Inside the Book." Accessed March 22, 2022. https://www.ingramspark.com/plan-your-book/print/trim-sizes.

Chapter 47

Large print

Large print editions are a wonderful way to make your work accessible to those who have difficulty reading standard print books: the visually impaired, the dyslexic, and those who simply find the larger font and smaller word count per page helpful (such as those reading in a moving vehicle or who read while tired). It's also a great way to get into libraries, who often purchase large print editions (especially in hardback).

But, you may be wondering, does anyone *really* buy large print these days when they can just make the font larger on their e-reader? Apparently, they do. Well-known author and book marketer Joanna Penn was surprised to learn that the large print edition of one of her books actually made up 36% of that book's income. Granted, it was a sweet romance featuring more mature characters, so genre may influence large print sales, but there is a market for large print.

If you wish to have a large print edition of your book, however, you will need to do more than simply increase the font size of the text. There are many aspects to consider, including margins and font type.

Here are a few tips on formatting large print books:

1. Use a larger trim size, such as 6 x 9 in. or 6.14 x 9.21 in. Cream paper might be better than white.

2. Ask the cover designer for a separate cover to handle the increased number of pages and consider adding "Large Print Edition" to it, such as in a "sticker."

3. Use a separate ISBN, as this is a different edition.

4. Use a font size of at least 16. A size 18 font or 20 is preferred. And this is for *all* text, including page numbers, copyright information, back matter, etc. Headings are an even larger font size.

5. Use a sans serif font and avoid using italics, underlining, or blocks of capital letters as much as possible.

6. White space increases ease of reading for those with sight issues. Use at least a 1.5 spacing instead of single-spacing.

7. Use block paragraphs instead of indentations. Double space between paragraphs.

8. Margins should be at least 25 mm (1 inch) wide.

9. Left Align the body text and headings rather than Justify.

10. Images should be aligned to the left.

Some formatting programs will automatically adjust your book to a large print format (this setting is usually found in the trim size settings). Vellum and Atticus both do this. However, always check that your chosen style, use of italics within the document, and so forth all match the standards. Some programs may not consider all the facets of a proper large print edition.

You can learn more about creating an accessible large print edition through organizations such as The American Council of the Blind and the UK Association for Accessible Formats (UKAAF).

References and Resources

Hamilton, Jason. "How to Publish Large Print Books and Why You Should." *Kindlepreneur*. February 17, 2022. https://kindlepreneur.com/large-print.

Penn, Joanna. "Why Publish a Large Print Edition of Your Books?" (YouTube) *The Creative Penn.* https://youtu.be/mK1sciYoHlM.

Phillips, Russell. "Book Production: How to Self-publish Large-Print Books." ALLi. November 29, 2018. https://selfpublishingadvice.org/self-publish-large-print-books/.

The American Council of the Blind. "Best Practices and Guidelines for Large Print Documents Used by the Low Vision Community." Accessed March 22, 2022. https://acb.org/best-practices-and-guidelines-large-print-documents-used-low-vision-community-authored-council.

Vellum. "Creating a Large Print Edition." Accessed March 22, 2022. https://help.vellum.pub/guides/large-print/.

Chapter 48

Copyright page

For the front matter, the title page and the copyright page are the only two necessary pages.

The title page contains the title; series information, if applicable; author name; and publisher information. It may or may not have a title design or an image to match that on the cover.

The copyright page is on the left-hand page (verso page), behind the title page. Check out a few traditional and professional-quality indie books to see what's there and get a feel for how it looks and what belongs. Templates and formatting programs often include a disclaimer and copyright statement, which is very helpful.

On your copyright page, you'll have some variation of "Copyright [year] by [your name]" near the "top" of the page. The text on this page is actually justified from the bottom up, so that the "top" will not be the usual top of the page.

As a reminder from the section on pen names, if you use a pen name, your copyright notice should be in your pen name, or both pen name and real name. Register your copyright under both pen name and real name for extra protection. Using your real name in addition to the pen name eliminates the need to prove the pen name was yours in a lawsuit.

The publisher name and, if desired, the address (or city and state), is included on the copyright page. The edition is given as well. There is some flexibility in where things are placed or how they are grouped.

The "all rights reserved" statement or paragraph usually comes next. This communicates how tightly you want to hold on to your exclusive right to make copies or derivatives etc. of your work. If you don't want people reproducing it in part or in whole, say that. If you're fine with people freely quoting you so long as they don't "quote" the entire book, state that. If you want to make sure no one takes your book as legal or medical advice, state that. If you have people, places, or events mentioned, you might state whether these are fictitious or real, or if names or details were changed.

There's no "one statement" for the disclaimers on your copyright page, meaning you can write your own. Author and lawyer Helen Sedwick even includes several humorous ones from famous novels in her *Self-Publisher's Legal Handbook*. Look around at copyright pages, see what's included, and then write your own. That is, if you don't want to use the "vanilla" one included by some formatting templates and software programs.

If you use quoted material, such as scripture from the Bible, put that information on the copyright page too. Check the copyright of anything you include, though, to make sure you can legally include the content without seeking permission. Remember that lyrics are copyrighted, and you'll need to get permission to use them. Bible translations typically have information on how many verses can be quoted before permission should be obtained. I was recently surprised to learn that the King James Version is considered public domain everywhere but in the UK, where the monarch holds a perpetual copyright to it. Always seek permission if in doubt. You don't want to violate someone *else's* copyright.

After your disclaimers, you might choose to give credit to editors, cover designers, or illustrators.

Then, there might be the Library of Congress Control Number (LCCN). I doubt too many of us indie authors bother with this, but since you'll see it in the trad book copyright pages, I wanted to mention it. If you're serious about getting your book into bookstores, then this would set you apart into the category of truly professional indie authors (assuming the rest of your book is tip-top).

The LCCN is given by the Library of Congress to print publications. It requires an ISBN to submit to the Library of Congress for the LCCN, and it's best to apply before the book goes to print (so you have the LCCN to include in it). You'll send a print copy of the book to the Library of Congress upon publication. It's free to request an LCCN, but know that the Library of Congress has two programs responsible for assigning the control numbers: the Catalog in Publication (CIP) Program and the Pre-Assigned Control Number (PCN) program. Small presses and self-publishers use the PCN program. The CIP Program is for larger, pre-approved publishers. If interested, go to https://www.loc.gov/publish/pcn/newaccount.html for more information and to create a new account and obtain an LCCN number.

Finally, provide your book's identification information—the ISBN.

We'll talk about ISBNs and the barcode in the next chapter. That's it for your copyright page. The rest of the front matter is up to you. Oh, the freedom of indie publishing!

"Bare bones" copyright page checklist:

- Title and edition
- Publication year
- Copyright by [author name and year] (use of symbol or words and order of year and author varies)
- Publisher name
- ISBN (necessary if print, optional for ebook)
- Disclaimers

REFERENCES AND RESOURCES

Sedwick, Helen. *Self-Publisher's Legal Handbook*, 2nd edition.

Library of Congress. "Preassigned Control Number Program." Accessed March 22, 2022. https://www.loc.gov/publish/pcn/newaccount.html.

Chapter 49

ISBN, ASIN, and barcode

A title and author name are not your book's most important identifiers, at least not officially. That honor belongs to the ISBN (International Standard Book Number). Each version, edition, translation, format, and so on of your book gets its own unique ISBN. See why the title and author name isn't sufficient?

ISBNs come in a 10-digit and a 13-digit number format. The 13-digit number was introduced in 2007, after the explosive growth of ebooks, and is sometimes the only one given now. We'll talk about how to get them later. For the moment, let's consider when and if to get an ISBN.

Since each format of your book requires a different ISBN, that means the ebook, paperback, and hardback all need unique ISBNs.

That said, most ebook retailers that I'm aware of provide a free store identifier, so you don't have to use an ISBN for the ebook version at all. Some authors say don't bother with ISBNs for ebooks since they usually aren't required and are a waste of an ISBN. Others say include them to be professional, and that some places (such as libraries) may require them.

Whether or not you supply an ISBN, Amazon will give your book a 10-character, alphanumeric, unique store identifier called an ASIN.

You'll want to keep track of this number because universal link builders, promotion services, and others use this number to find your book on Amazon.

Amazon says this in the Learn More display on the ISBN/ASIN section of the ebook title setup page in your dashboard:

> "An ISBN is an International Standard Book Number. You can publish your book without one, but if you do have one, you may enter it here. However, it will only be used as a reference and won't actually appear on the detail page of your ebook (only the ASIN will). Important: Do not use an ISBN from a print edition for your digital edition. If you want to include an ISBN for the digital version of your book, it must be a unique ISBN. You can purchase an ISBN from multiple sources on the Web."

Print formats require ISBNs. KDP offers a free ISBN for this, but if you use it, you can't use that ISBN on IngramSpark or elsewhere. So if you use KDP's free ISBN for Amazon and then another self-publishing service provider's free ISBN to publish in their store, your book—same format—will have multiple identifiers. This might cause it to be listed twice in some catalogs, creating confusion. It's highly recommended to at least buy your own ISBNs for print.

It's important to note at this point that whoever owns a book's ISBN is considered its publisher. That does not give, say, Amazon, any actual rights to your books.

How do you get an ISBN?

Each country has its own company responsible for issuing ISBNs, and in the US, that's R. R. Bowker. Some companies act as middlemen to sell ISBNs from Bowker, but they will charge more. So if you choose to buy ISBNs, and you live in the US, go directly to Bowker at https://myidentifiers.com/. If you live in Canada, visit https://www.bac-lac.gc.ca/eng/services/isbn-canada/pages/isbn-canada.aspx. For the UK, Ireland or a British Overseas Territory, visit https://www.

nielsenisbnstore.com. Elsewhere internationally, visit https://www.isbn-international.org.

Take a minute to calm down after you look at the prices. One ISBN at Bowker, as of early 2022, is $125. But, a package of 10 is $295. Makes sense, right? Not really, but it's a better deal for those of us who publish multiple books and formats. Once you burn through those ten, you might consider the 100 pack for $575.

The other bad news about ISBNs, other than the cost, is that you can't resell or reuse them. (So don't grab that 100 pack right off before you've proven you need it.) If you use an ISBN "given" to you, the book will show up with the publisher name that ISBN is registered under in catalogues. The good news is that you don't have to renew ISBNs; they are permanent, and they are international, so you only need one per version for the entire world forever!

Once you have your ISBNs, keep careful track of them. Don't assign one to more than one book or format. If you publish a book (the same format and edition) on multiple platforms, be sure to use the same ISBN for it. This means that if you publish your paperback on KDP and on IngramSpark, use the same ISBN for both. Once you assign an ISBN to a book, be sure to go back to your Bowker account to register your ISBN. Bookstores use ISBNs to track inventory and sales information, so if you're interested in getting into bookstores, you must have your own ISBN.

———

Certain changes to your book (making it a new product or edition, essentially) will require it to have a new ISBN, but not all changes will. Here's a few common situations and their impact on the ISBN.

Changes that require a new ISBN:

- The book is printed as a large print edition or is published in a foreign language.
- If a significant amount of material is added to the book (for

example, several new chapters are added). The book might be relaunched as a second edition, then.

- If the title or subtitle is changed.
- If the book is published in another size (as in trim size).

Changes that don't require a new ISBN:

- Changing the book price.
- Changing the cover design.
- Switching to another distributor or printer.
- Making minor corrections to the content, such as correcting grammatical errors.

Barcodes

Barcodes are another way in which indie authors are spoiled by Amazon and other companies who want to make publishing easy on authors for philanthropic or business reasons (or both). Technically, authors need to obtain a barcode and have the cover designer add it to the cover, but many places, including Amazon and IS, will add a barcode for you. Unless you provide a barcode to the designer, your cover will have a white box on the back where the barcode will be added at printing.

But what is a barcode exactly and is it worth the trouble to supply it yourself?

A barcode is a machine-reader graphical representation that tells your book's ISBN and price and is found on the back cover of print books. You don't have to have one for ebooks (they won't be scanned at a cash register, after all). If you plan to sell products in physical stores, you need one. It helps the vendor keep track of sales and maintain inventory.

The EAN (European Article Number) barcode format is the required format for barcodes on books to be sold in physical retailers (there are multiple barcode formats, apparently). The ISBN (13-digit) is encoded into the barcode, so you must have your ISBN to get a barcode.

You can also embed a price in the barcode, but if you change your price, you'll need a new barcode. If you have stock copies, they will need a sticker barcode to replace the printed one.

Industry experts can spot an indie book, or a non-professional-standard one, by the lack of an embedded price in the barcode. If no price is embedded, it will read "9000" above the second set of lines. If it has an embedded price, such as $14.99, the code would read "91499." This is for print-on-demand books. Traditional books have a country code in that section of the barcode. Books from the US will have a number starting with "5."

If you're only selling through online retailers, or don't care what bookstores may or may not turn their noses up at, then don't worry about barcodes. If you want to get into the bigger, stricter bookstores, then get a barcode with a price embedded. Barnes & Noble states that for a book to be considered for retail placement in their stores, it needs a barcode with the ISBN and price embedded in it and the price printed on it. Otherwise, you need a pressure-sensitive label for the back cover.

You can purchase barcodes from Bowker (where you got your ISBN) or you can use some of the free barcode generators available online. IngramSpark's cover generator can create a barcode with an embedded price and ISBN.

ISBN, ASIN, and Barcode summary:

- The ISBN is your book's identifier.
- You can purchase ISBNs (through Bowker in the US) or get free ones through self-publishing service providers. It's recommended to at least buy your own ISBNs for your print edition. They are not required for ebooks.
- Each different format and edition of your work requires a different ISBN.
- Changing your cover or making minor edits to your book does not require a change of ISBN.
- Amazon gives each ebook an ASIN as a store identifier.

- Barcodes can be bought or provided for free by KDP and IS (free is more common).
- Proper ISBNs and barcodes are important for getting books stocked in bookstores.
- Budget for ISBNs.
- Keep track of your ISBNs and ASINs.

References and Resources

Allen, Scott. "How to Get an ISBN Number for a Self-Published Book & Other FAQs." *Self-publishing.com.* August 20, 2020. https://selfpublishing.com/isbn-number-self-published-book/.

Amazon KDP. "International Standard Book Number (ISBN)." Accessed April 11, 2022. https://kdp.amazon.com/en_US/help/topic/G201834170.

Barnes & Noble. "BN.com and Retail Store Placement for Books." Accessed March 22, 2022. https://www.barnesandnobleinc.com/publishers-authors/sell-your-book-at-barnes-noble/.

Bowker. "Barcode." Accessed March 22, 2022. https://www.myidentifiers.com/identify-protect-your-book/barcode.

Bowker. "FAQS: Barcodes." Accessed March 22, 2022. https://www.myidentifiers.com/faq/barcodes.

Bowker. "Buy ISBN." Accessed March 22, 2022. https://www.myidentifiers.com/identify-protect-your-book/isbn/buy-isbn.

Chesson, Dave. "ISBN Bar Code Generator." *Kindlepreneur.* January 13, 2022. https://kindlepreneur.com/isbn-bar-code-generator/.

IBPA. "IBPA's Industry Standards Checklist for a Professionally Published Book." Accessed March 22, 2022. https://www.ibpa-online.org/page/standardschecklist.

IngramSpark. "ISBNs: International Standard Book Number Facts for Self-Publishers." December 15, 2020. https://www.ingramspark.com/blog/isbn-facts-for-self-publishers.

Library of Congress. "Preassigned Control Number Program." Accessed March 22, 2022. https://www.loc.gov/publish/pcn/newaccount.html.

For international ISBNs:
For Canada: https://www.bac-lac.gc.ca/eng/services/isbn-canada/pages/isbn-canada.aspx. For the UK, Ireland or a British Overseas Territory, visit https://www.nielsenisbnstore.com. Elsewhere international, visit https://www.isbn-international.org.

Chapter 50

Back matter

This "goodbye" to your book typically includes your biography, acknowledgments, a newsletter sign-up, a list of your other works, and pages dedicated to individual books or series, if you have more to offer the reader. Thus, it serves to finish up the book proper (author bio and the like pages) and acts as marketing space for your other works, with links, ad copy, and, sometimes, images of the reader magnet and other books and series. I recommend you look through the back matter of several ebooks by successful indie authors in your genre. They tend to tinker with the back matter to try to maximize its marketing benefit for series sell-through, reviews, or newsletter sign-ups. Feel free to change things regularly yourself and see what works best for you.

Some authors don't even wait until the back matter to announce their next book or ask for reviews or mention their newsletter sign-up, but ask immediately after "The End." This is due, I suspect, to the fact that on some devices, Amazon throws up a please-review-this-book-and-consider-these-other-books pop-up at the back of your ebook, so people may not actually see much of your back matter unless they are intentional about it. If you read Kindle ebooks, scroll through the back matter and get a feel for where the pop-up appears and make sure anything you really want to be seen is before that. In other words, don't make the newsletter signup page the very last page of your back matter. The question is what your most important call-to-action is: buy your related books, leave reviews, or sign up for your newsletter. It's recommended to limit yourself to two calls-to-action at a time.

As an aside, some readers would like to keep up with your new releases but hate the idea of getting any more emails. Consider helping them out by including a link to your Amazon Author Central page and your BookBub page in your author biography or on the newsletter sign-up page. They don't get extra emails each month and you get a happy fan.

This does mean, however, that those non-subscriber fans can't get your fabulous reader magnet. Not unless they subscribe, download it, then unsubscribe, which some are loath to do as it feels like cheating. You can solve this by offering the magnet for sale. You can do this via the usual retailers, but some readers might be annoyed if they bought it, then found out they could get it for free. And it's not really a reader magnet, then. However, if you sell it directly and only through your website (through a store such as Payhip or Shopify), then that wouldn't be a problem, as they would find out about it only in the back matter of your books or on your website. You don't have to do this, of course, but if someone would rather pay for your story than get it for free and suffer through more emails, why not let them? You both win this way.

Also, when considering your back matter, remember that your digital files will have a delivery cost ($0.15/MB for amazon.com) if you sell through Amazon at the 70% royalty rate. Stuffing the back matter with graphics for your other books will, unfortunately, raise your delivery fee. I recommend only choosing your best series to highlight, if you choose to have any images.

References and Resources

Amazon KDP. "Digital Pricing Page." August 14, 2020. https://kdp.amazon.com/en_US/help/topic/G200634500.

Erik, Nicholas. *The Ultimate Guide to Book Marketing: The 80/20 System for Selling More Books* (Ultimate Author Guides). 2020.

Chapter 51

Concluding getting the book ready

Getting your book ready means getting all the right pages in the front and back matter together and formatting them and the body into a professional style, then converting all that into the appropriate file format for your retailer. You can do the formatting yourself, hire it out, or use a tool such as Calibre, Vellum, or Atticus. The parts of a formatted book may differ, but you must have a title page and a copyright page (with the copyright notice, publisher information, and ISBN) in your front matter. The back matter of your book is helpful for marketing, as it can include a newsletter sign-up, request for reviews, and ads for your other books.

You will want your ebook in both epub and mobi file types, and your print book in PDF.

Once you have your book ready to go, except maybe for that last proofread, you're ready to send it to endorsers and ARC readers. What, who?

Buckle up, we're going back to marketing for a bit, and then we'll be ready to launch your book!

Part Nine

Getting the Word Out: The Launch and Beyond

Chapter 52

Getting the word out: The launch and beyond

We're back to marketing! Aren't you excited? (If not, you should be, because this is how you get your book to the people who are looking for a book like yours.)

This section covers how to launch (release or publish) your book well, get reviews, and keep it selling. Your launch is built on a foundation of the things we've already talked about—chiefly, the reader magnet and newsletter list. It's really important that you've been building an audience and proving to them you can write.

So let's talk about launch strategy, then go into more detail on the parts of it and other ways to grow your audience.

Chapter 53

Launch strategy

Book launches are a fun, exciting, and stressful time. That's what they have in common. Launches vary greatly between authors in the amount of fanfare, money spent, and strategy employed. What you do depends in part on the kind of book you write, your fan base, and the money you have to spend. Aside from a personal celebration, book launches are about letting folks know your book is out there—finding new fans and (for later releases) alerting old ones.

Let's talk about a few general strategies, then move on to tips to make the launch bigger. These strategies are numbered in no particular order and can be blended (some of them!). Note that launching a series is different to launching a standalone book.

Book launch strategies

Strategy 1: Sale-ing to sell. Release your book at a sale price (usually $0.99) and use your newsletter and book promotion services to drive sales during the release. Change the price to full price after a few days or a week. When full price, get into KU (if doing this) and get page reads. Pros: Using promo sites that accept new releases boosts visibility. Early sales boost rankings. Cons: You only get the 35% royalty. You're getting very little per book, unfortunately, and this might be an issue for authors with established fans who would pay full price for the book. If you're starting out with few fans or if you're trying to push a new series, this might be a good tactic to get noticed early. This can be done with or without a pre-order.

Strategy 2: Launch at full price. Launch your book at full price and enjoy greater royalties from those early sales. This approach works well for later books in a series and for authors with established fans. You can launch in KU immediately. This can be done with or without a pre-order.

Strategy 3: Start wide and stay. Launch your book in Amazon, Apple, Kobo, and others. This approach requires more marketing effort but reaches a variety of readers and increases chances of some promotional opportunities (such as BookBub Featured Deals) and best seller lists.

Strategy 4: Start in KU and stay. Stick to Amazon and go exclusive with the Kindle Select program. There's less marketing to worry about, and you can reach the KU readers.

Strategy 5: Start in KU for 90 days, test and prove, then go wide. Get your feet under you by starting in KU, getting reviews, seeing how your book is received, and then go wide.

Strategy 6: Pre-orders on sale. Set up a pre-order at a sale price and announce that readers must buy it within a certain time (the first week or few days, maybe) or the price goes up. Frame the discount as a gift to your newsletter subscribers and ask them to share about the limited-time deal.

Strategy 7: Pre-orders at full price. Set up a pre-order at full price. Pre-orders count as sales on Amazon as they're "ordered," rather than on release day, so you can build the book's rank before it releases using the pre-orders, providing the pre-order period is short (a week or so).

Strategy 8: Rapid release. Release a series in quick succession (with a week to four weeks between books). Have pre-order links ready for the next book. This is a marketing tactic, not simply publishing quickly, so be sure to study Elana Johnson's video or book and other viewpoints to determine if this method might work for you (details in references below).

Strategy 9: Release with pre-orders ready (not-so-rapid release). Similar to rapid release, only the books aren't released quite so close together, say with six months or more between them. The goal is to have a link at the back of each book for fans to go ahead and buy the next book. The reader knows the next book is coming, and anticipation builds during the wait (and the author gets more time to prep the books).

Strategy 10: One and done for a while. Release your one book for now. Let readers know if future books are coming or not. If so, ask them to sign up for your newsletter or have a way for them to know when the next one is released.

Strategy 11: Release at $0.99 or free and stay. Set up your book at a reduced price or free permanently to reduce barrier of entry to your work as a whole or to that series. This also works for people with other products to sell (such as courses), who give the basics on a topic in a free book and then pitch their product or service (where they hope to make their money).

Strategy 12: No pre-order. Release with no pre-order. Pre-orders spread out Amazon's recognition of sales, so you get a stronger boost at release if people wait until then to purchase the book. You have more flexibility in your release date.

Tips for a book launch

Take what works for you and add and change as suits your situation. We'll talk more about some of these topics in later sections.

Book launch summary:

1. Set up a cover reveal ahead of time to generate interest and, if applicable, pre-orders.

2. Set up guest blog posts and interviews for before and around your release date, say for a couple of weeks ahead and a few weeks afterward. This increases interest and pre-orders.

3. Set up ARC readers to post reviews at release and spread the word.

4. Set up reviews from book bloggers.

5. Send out a newsletter a couple of weeks ahead to announce the upcoming release.

6. Consider an in-person launch event, such as at a local bookstore or other venue, where people can celebrate with you and, if interested, buy the book.

7. If your book is releasing at a discounted price, consider using promotion services and ads to advertise the sale (remember how low a return you get on sale books). If you have a related book, consider doing a sale on it to build interest in your work or that particular story world.

8. If you have connections with authors in the same genre, meaning their fans would likely enjoy your book and your fans theirs, consider asking them to mention your new release in their newsletter as part of a newsletter swap.

9. When the book releases, post about it on your social media pages and send a newsletter. Design several good graphics to share. Once reviews come in, you can choose a few succinct quotes and post those on social media or include in your next newsletter. A personal note: when posting about your release, remember to consider your fans and friends on social media, especially if your personal and author accounts are not completely separate. Even if we do read your books, we really don't want to hear about them every single day for the month of the release. So don't be obnoxious, but don't be completely silent either. Not everyone sees every post you make, so making 3-4 posts over a couple of weeks around your release will help people see it (and some don't want to miss the release) but won't be annoying.

10. Consider running ads for it. Study the platforms, keywords, etc. and decide on a budget beforehand to avoid overspending or wasting your money on ineffective ads.

11. Consider doing a giveaway, such as through Goodreads.

12. Continue to promote your reader magnet (with your book's link in it) and grow your newsletter list.

———

Let's look into the parts of a book launch, beginning with the pre-order, and discuss other things to do beyond your launch.

REFERENCES AND RESOURCES

Amazon KDP. "Timelines." Accessed March 30, 2022. https://kdp. amazon.com/en_US/help/topic/G202173620.

Fox, Chris. *Launch to Market: Easy Marketing For Authors* (Write Faster, Write Smarter Book 4). 2016.

Johnson, Elana. "20Books Vegas 2021 Day 1 – Elana Johnson - Rapid Release Marketing." (YouTube) November 10, 2021. https://www. youtube.com/watch?v=yEW3iDtd-HQ.

Johnson, Elana. *Writing and Releasing Rapidly* (Indie Inspiration for Self-Publishers Book 1). AEJ Creative Works, 2019.

Six Figure Authors Podcast. "SFA 084 – Book Launch Check List." April 21, 2021. https://6figureauthors.com/podcast/084-book-launch-check-list/.

Six Figure Authors Podcast (with guest Dave Chesson). "SFA 100 – Improving Organic Book Sales, Book Launch Tips, and How to Use A-Plus Content on Amazon." September 23, 2021. https://6figureauthors.com/podcast/improving-organic-book-sales-book-launch-tips-and-how-to-use-a-plus-content-on-amazon-dave-chesson/.

Six Figure Authors Podcast. "SFA 121 – Tips for Selling Books Outside of Amazon + Draft2Digital/Smashwords Updates." February 23, 2022. https://6figureauthors.com/podcast/tips-for-selling-books-outside-of-amazon-draft2digital-smashwords-updates/. (beginning at about 19 minutes from the end for launch strategy)

Six Figure Authors Podcast. "SFA 125 – How to Launch a Successful

Book Series." March 24, 2022. https://6figureauthors.com/podcast/how-to-launch-a-successful-book-series/.

Umstattd, Thomas Jr. "How to Launch Your Book on a Budget." *Author Media*. February 23, 2022. https://www.authormedia.com/how-to-launch-your-book-on-a-budget/.

Umstattd, Thomas Jr. "Why Rapid Release is a Risky Book Launch Strategy." *Author Media*. October 7, 2020. https://www.authormedia.com/why-rapid-release-is-a-risky-book-launch-strategy/.

Chapter 54

Pre-order

A pre-order is a book sale made before publication, meaning you can sell your book in advance of when readers will receive it from retailers. You can set up the ebook pre-order during your title set up. It's a simple matter of setting the ebook title's publication date in the future. For print books, it's more complicated, as KDP does not allow print book pre-orders. You can, however, set up your book on IngramSpark such that the print pre-order shows up on Amazon and other retailers.

Should you set your books to pre-order, though? It's really a matter of your situation and strategy. Some authors are for setting up pre-orders; some are against. Doing pre-orders allows you to have a retail page link to send out before the release, allowing for early "buys." But having a release date you might need to change or might miss can be a problem (if you think this might happen, request a date change). Pre-orders also affect your sales ranking. On Amazon, pre-orders aren't counted as sales on release day but count as people click the "pre-order" button over a potentially lengthy period of time. You can, however, set a short pre-order time on Amazon (say a week or ten days), building sales up to your release date, then potentially spiking sales with your other launch efforts, boosting the book's ranking at its release. So it's partly a matter of your desire to accumulate sales over time (say as people read the previous book in the series over several months) or your desire to rank high on release. If you plan on doing a cover reveal and guest blogs, having a pre-order link to put in front of readers reached through those means might lead to increased sales.

If releasing on a specific date is important to you, pre-orders do release on the actual date you set, whereas just setting up a book and hitting publish may give you a day's delay, depending on how long it takes for the book to be processed and go live (KDP says it can take up to 72 hours). So if you're not doing a pre-order, it might be wise to publish the book a couple of days before you plan to announce it, just to make sure it's live when you think it will be. You can find out about KDP's timelines for publishing and making changes on their "Time-lines" page (https://kdp.amazon.com/en_US/help/topic/G202173620).

You can do a full priced pre-order or a "limited-time sale" pre-order (you must change the price manually), as per launch strategies for releasing at full price or on sale and using promotions to boost the release.

At this time, pre-orders through KDP are only for ebooks. Ingram-Spark can do pre-orders for print books, and these will show up in the Amazon store if you choose for IngramSpark to fulfill Amazon orders. You will need to work out when or if you intend to have Amazon KDP fulfill Amazon print orders (you make more money having KDP fulfill Amazon-ordered print books).

Some authors do "soft" releases, publishing the print version first so they can order author copies for release day events. Unless you're really, really certain about the lack of typos in your uploaded manuscript, I don't recommend ordering a large volume of author copies immediately after release. Typos are pernicious things.

Some things of note regarding Amazon ebook pre-orders:

- Amazon allows you to set a pre-order date of up to one year.
- Amazon KDP requires that you upload your final manuscript more than 72 hours before the release date.

Nothing can be changed between the pre-order upload deadline and the release.

- You can enroll your pre-order book in KDP Select. You cannot schedule Free Book Promotions and Kindle Countdown Deals until after the book release, but your pre-order period does count toward the required month in KU before you can schedule a Countdown Deal.
- You can move up the release of your pre-order without penalty. You can cancel your release. You can delay your release date up to 30 days once without penalty, but this one time exclusion applies to your entire catalog.

Pre-orders are a popular but not essential part of a book launch. Whether you use one or not depends on your strategy and your confidence in your release date.

References and Resources

Amazon KDP. "Kindle eBook Pre-Order." Accessed March 24, 2022. https://kdp.amazon.com/en_US/help/topic/G201499380.

Amazon KDP. "Timelines." Accessed March 30, 2022. https://kdp.amazon.com/en_US/help/topic/G202173620.

Bylo, Justine. "Setting a Future On-Sale Date as Part of Your Book Marketing Strategy." *IngramSpark*. March 24, 2021. https://www.ingramspark.com/blog/on-sale-date-for-book-marketing.

Chapter 55

Cover reveal

A cover reveal is the grand unveiling of your magnificent cover. Usually, at least for fiction, authors will ask other authors and fans to help with the reveal a few weeks in advance of it, then provide the finished file and information on the book a few days before the event. The reveal itself includes sharing the cover or a graphic showcasing the cover on social media (especially Instagram and Facebook), blogs, and in newsletters. Most people love art, so members of the author and reader communities are generally happy to help with cover reveals. You can ask for help with this in your newsletter and in author groups. You can also approach influencers on social media, such as Bookstagrammers with a large following, to participate. You can hire services to help with this as well, but do your research to make sure they would really help (reach your target audience and reach a lot of them). Reveals are usually a free part of the book launch process.

If this doesn't sound like your thing, or you write nonfiction and the idea of a reveal is strange, skip it.

If you are doing a cover reveal, a couple of days prior, send out the cover file and relevant information. Provide appropriate hashtags for Instagram posts. Include links for the book (if you have a pre-order) and your website for blog and social media posts. A tagline, blurb, and release date are needed as well. You can also include a few pre-made graphics as an option for those who don't want to make graphics themselves. You can include the cover, tagline, release date, and the phrase "cover reveal," as desired, in the graphics. Many cover artists provide 3D renderings of your book on white and blank backgrounds for use in graphics. You can share those for the people who want to make their own graphics. You can send all of this information as email attachments, or you can create a media kit for your book on your website and only send a link to the media kit.

Don't forget to add the cover to the pre-order page on your retailer!

In summary, a cover reveal to show off your fantastic book cover is a great and easy way to generate interest in your book. Traditionally published authors often do this months in advance. Indie authors—at least those who publish often—wait until closer to the release, a couple of months or less, to schedule the reveal. If you've not participated in a cover reveal, consider doing so. You'll learn much in the process, meet fellow authors, and build goodwill for the future.

Chapter 56

ARCs and reviews

As authors, we tend to have stars in our eyes: a blind love for our books; hopes of fame, fortune, and a Hollywood blockbuster; and, the topic of our current chapter, a desire for more and more of those gold rating stars on Amazon, Goodreads, and other platforms.

Why do we talk about reviews before the book has been published? Because you need to set up reviewers to post reviews as soon as it does publish. The sooner you have a good number of reviews (at least ten, more is preferable), the better your book looks to buyers and book promotion services.

Advance Reader Copies (ARCs)

These early reviews are gained through Advance Reader Copies (ARCs). Traditional publishers have long used this method of sending out print copies (and now ebook copies through services such as NetGalley) to book reviewers, media outlets, and even everyday readers (I've gotten a few free books this way). These early copy books aren't always fully edited, but are in a near-publishing state and serve the purpose of letting readers read ahead and write up a review to post as soon as the book releases.

Those who receive ARCs should state in their review that they received a free copy for review purposes but that the opinions expressed are their own.

How many review copies should you send out? Doesn't that cut down on the number of people who will buy your book, since some are getting free copies?

The first question is not a question I can answer. Some authors give out twenty, some much more. It depends on how many people you can reach who read in your genre and how big and how devoted your fan base is. You want the reviews to be coming in quickly at the launch to reader-validate the book, but too many ARC reviews and no organic ones will look bad.

It's probably best to balance the number of ARCs with the size of your launch. If you've already gained a sizable following and have a big launch planned, the more ARCs you can give away, since the ARC reviews and "verified purchase" reviews (those from people Amazon knows bought your book) will balance out quickly. If it's a small launch, try for ten to twenty ARCs.

If you know some of your ARC readers will buy the book when it releases (giving you a "verified purchase" review), then you can try for more. Not everyone given an ARC will read it, or like it enough to leave a review, or read it in time for the launch, so you need to give out more than the number of reviews you want to start out with.

Ten reviews is the figure some promotion sites like to see before they will promote your book (though they may make an exception for new releases), so there is that to consider, if or when you decide to put the book on sale or for free and announce the sale using book promotion services.

As for losing money by giving out free copies, it's true those readers might not buy the book. Some of them will, however, and that plus the early reviews still provides an advantage to giving out ARCs.

Who do you give ARCs to? Look for readers who read in your genre. So don't ask your friend who hates your genre but loves you to read your book. Ask the person who already reads books like yours. Choose these genre-friendly readers because it's more likely they will enjoy your book and leave reviews that will connect to readers with similar tastes. They understand the lingo of that genre and can touch on points in their reviews that others will get. They also know other readers of the genre to talk your book up to. Additionally, choose them because of the way their buying tastes affect the Amazon algorithms. Finally, know that Amazon doesn't like reviews from family and friends.

———

A word about your books and your family and friends. Some of us have very supportive family and friends who will be eager to buy the first book, and maybe even the subsequent books. Others feel horrible about selling things ("using" people) and so for that or other reasons, want to give away copies of their book to family and maybe even friends. Let me say that there is *nothing* wrong with people celebrating your accomplishment by buying your book from you. (You don't have the right to control how they do or don't spend their money, and you shouldn't feel bad about them wanting to buy your book. But you also shouldn't force them into buying your book or make it awkward for them not to.)

If you start the habit of giving away books to family and friends, then you go on to write more and more books, it could get expensive for you. Not to mention it risks you growing bitter that no one is supporting you by *buying* your books.

Conversely, those people who bought your first book because they love you may not want to buy your next ten or twenty books too. Your marketing efforts (if you plan on making a career of writing) should be focused on people who read your genre, not your friends and family. If they are included in that net, you're very fortunate!

———

Back to getting reviews: this tends to be a painful experience. Some reviews won't get published for whatever reason; some are taken down. People may rave about the book to you; it may sell decently well, but it may not get reviews. Most readers don't care enough to leave a review or may feel they don't know how to write a good review and so don't.

This lack of gold stars is one of those things we have to learn to deal with. It took what felt like forever for my second book to get ten reviews. Now it has over fifty, and that number is slowly rising. It's been out over two years, so fifty isn't a great number, but it's nothing to sneer at either.

What helped get those reviews finally coming in? Publishing more books. The more you write, the more likely you are to write something that really appeals to readers. Some of those readers will go back and read your other books, boosting your entire backlist.

Where do you get these early readers, and reviews in general?

Here are a few suggestions:

1. If you're in author groups on Facebook or another platform that allows promotional posts, post in them and ask if anyone wants to be an ARC reader. Give the blurb, content rating, and release date so people can get a feel for if the book is for them and if they have time.
2. There are reader groups on Facebook specifically for ARC/review copies. Ask around your author community to find out which ones are for your genre and if the readers actually leave reviews or just grab free books.
3. Ask in your newsletter if anyone wants an ARC copy.
4. Use a platform such as StoryOrigin that connects reviewers with books.
5. Ask book bloggers to review it. You may need to set this up well ahead of time.
6. Use a service such as BookSirens or Booksprout to find reviewers for you. It's against KDP's terms of service to buy reviews or offer gift cards or incentives in exchange for positive reviews, but for these services, you are paying the service to put your book in front of people looking for free books to read, who then are asked to leave a review, which is acceptable. These services claim a 75% review rate.
7. Follow the retailer guidelines for reviews. Amazon's

guidelines can be found at https://www.amazon.com/gp/help/customer/display.html?nodeId=201602680.

Creating and distributing your ARC

Does your book have to be finished to send out to ARC readers? Your book needs to be at least *almost* ready to upload to retailers—the editing and formatting need to be complete. It can be lacking the final proofread. Be sure to tell reviewers what the books lacks so they won't cut stars for typos. It doesn't have to have a cover. But if you've already had your cover reveal, include the cover in the file so it will look nice in the helpful ARC reader's library.

You will need to generate mobi (for Kindle or Kindle app) and epub (for other e-readers or apps) versions and decide how you will distribute them. Note that PDF files are an option here, but some authors don't use them because of the greater potential for them being uploaded to piracy sites. Never send out a text file for this. You can collect the email addresses of your advance readers and send the desired file format as an attachment, but that's a hassle and, these days, might seem a bit amateurish.

Services like BookFunnel, StoryOrigin, and MyBookCave make this process so much cleaner and professional-looking. You upload the book to their platform, create a landing page, set the options for delivery, then copy the link for the landing page and send that to readers. Readers follow the link to the book page and download the book, easy peasy. I mean that. These sites are very user-friendly.

As for the download requirements, I recommend that you require the downloader's email address before download of the ARC. This allows you to keep track of who actually downloads the book. Don't require a newsletter sign-up, obviously, but set it to require the email for information purposes only.

If you set up directly with Apple Books, you can request promo codes once the book has a status of On Store or Ready for Store. These codes can be given to reviewers, bloggers, etc. to download the book for free and then leave a rating or review. You can even get reviews during the pre-order period this way. Each book has 250 promo codes.

Scheduling

As you are a considerate author, you will ask for reviewers at least a month in advance of the release and will provide the book three to four weeks prior to the release date. You will want to send a thank-you and a reminder a week before release, as many people depend on reminders to get things done. This might be your only reminder about the ARC, or you could send another on release day. Again, thank them for helping to spread the word.

If you have store links to your book, include those in the reminder and release emails, along with a Goodreads link, to make it easier for them to leave reviews.

Future reviews

So you've set up reviews for the release, but how about for the rest of the book's life? Can you encourage people to leave reviews? Yes! A simple way to do this is to ask for reviews in the back matter of your book. Some authors include a quick appeal in the author biography. Some ask on occasion in their newsletter, or mention the reviews they've received and thank people for them, subtly encouraging others to go leave reviews. Even after the release, you can send the book out to book review blogs and try genre-appropriate review groups on Facebook, or try StoryOrigin's review feature.

There are a few caveats regarding reviews—you need to be familiar with your distributor's rules regarding reviews, as well as the Kindle Select rules. You cannot pay for or offer incentives (such as gift cards) in exchange for reviews. This is considered unethical since it may bias the review in your favor. Services such as Kirkus are allowable, but do check the rules of your distributor. You can't hand out hundreds of review copies while in Kindle Select; a few, yes, but not so many KDP would see you as breaking the terms of your contract. You can give copies for free using your Kindle Free Days, but don't overdo any review copy giveaways outside of that.

It's a shared pain among authors that some of our fans will be unable to leave reviews and some reviews will be taken down for no apparent reason. There's no sense in wasting time griping about it. It happens, and we just have to push forward and hope for more to replace those. For Amazon reviewers, the customer has to have spent at least $50 in the store before reviewing, but some who've spent way more than that still get blocked from leaving reviews.

And dealing with the reviews—the ones you get and the ones you don't get—is a challenge, and authors must find their own way of managing it. It's important for us to remember that reviews are, ultimately, for readers, to help *them* determine if the book is for them, to give *them* a space to talk about that world they've just spent hours in. Reviews aren't for our ego boost. We don't have a right to criticize reviewers. Except the occasional really weird or mean one. They can be as entertaining as they are frustrating. But the one with the honest, albeit negative critique of your book? No. You shouldn't go whining on social media about it and telling people they can only leave positive reviews because bad ones hurt your feelings. If only the people who like the book review it, the reviews mean nothing because they're not an honest survey of reader opinions.

That said, savvy authors can use reviews for their benefit. Some readers are better marketers than we are, so we might use what they say to refine our copy, or use quotes from the reviews in promotional materials and ads, or include them in our newsletters. Reviews might tell us if we're marketing to the wrong people. I recently read a post in an author group from a writer who was being docked stars because of how dark his books were. He included a content warning in his blurb and then went to reader groups and specifically promoted it as a dark novel to attract people who wanted that. It helped the book tremendously. So we can also learn what our readers like and want more of by reading what they say. We do have to be discerning, though, not to get dragged the wrong way by a few vocal fans. Dealing with reviews takes discernment.

Some authors choose not to read reviews at all, and if we look to reviews for our personal validation, we're heading for trouble. So if you think reading reviews could be soul-crushing or a potential addiction for validation, it's best to ignore them.

———

In conclusion, include enough time in your launch plan for ARCs and send out as many as you are comfortable with to the *right* kind of readers. Once those reviews come in, figure out the best way to handle them for your sanity and benefit.

ARC summary and tips:

- Get the book out to ARC readers about a month before release. Too early and it will get put off until the deadline, forgotten about, or read early and forgotten. Send a reminder around release day with links to the product page and Goodreads so readers can leave the review as soon as the book is live.
- You don't have to give out an unlimited number of ARCs, only what you're comfortable with. If anyone seems sketchy or like they are only after a free book, explain that you don't have any more ARC copies available, or something to that effect.
- Look for ARC readers in author and reader groups, on StoryOrigin, your newsletter, book bloggers, and through services such as BookSirens.
- Use a platform such as BookFunnel and StoryOrigin to provide ebook copies (both epub and mobi files) for ARCs and require an email address for readers to download the files. This is easier and more secure than emailing the files directly to people.

References and Resources

Amazon. "Community Guidelines." March 23, 2022. https://www. amazon.com/gp/help/customer/display.html?nodeId=201602680.

BookFunnel. https://BookFunnel.com.

BookSirens. https://booksirens.com.

Booksprout. https://booksprout.co/pricing.

MyBookCave. https://mybookcave.com.

Six Figure Authors Podcast. "SFA 055 – Getting Reviews and Starting a Street Team/Review Crew." September 10, 2020. https://6figureauthors.com/podcast/getting-reviews-and-starting-a-street-team-review-crew/.

StoryOrigin. https://storyoriginapp.com.

Chapter 57

Editorial reviews and endorsers

Those gold stars on Amazon and their corresponding reviews do wonders for our author egos (sometimes) and our sales. But those are not the only type of praise for your books you should get if you can. You also want endorsements and editorial reviews. (You don't have to have these, so if you're short on time, skip it. These are nice but not necessary.)

Endorsements

Traditionally published books, and some indie books, have a page or more at the front with short blurbs about how wonderful the book is. These are written by fellow authors, ministry leaders, or business leaders, or whoever readers of the book would care about. These are *endorsements* (and are also called *blurbs*). On your Amazon book page, the endorsements can be listed in the Editorial Review section (reached through your Author Central account, not your KDP dashboard).

So how do you get these endorsements? First, you need to know who your readers value. So it works like this: Person P endorses Author A's book, and you (potential reader) like Person P, therefore you give Author A a chance. So you're looking for that Person P.

The catch is that it's best to ask people you have a connection to. The sort of people who have influence are often busy, so reading books by strangers looking for a favor is low on their priority list (and there are probably a lot of strangers trying to get their limited attention). If you have a connection to an influential person (a non-creepy connection—don't stalk them at conferences or make them feel like you're out to get something from them), he or she might be willing to give your book a try. Of course, be polite and professional when you ask. No one owes you an endorsement. When you ask, offer a free ebook or print copy and give a date to return the endorsement. The date needs to be a few months away. Remember they are busy doing the things that make them valuable influencers (and living their personal lives), so don't be offended or feel rejected if they don't get back to you. It might be helpful to give them an out, so if they need to say no, they have an easy way to do so without hurting your feelings. An "out" might be an acknowledgement of the heavy demand on their time.

Editorial reviews

Editorial reviews might include Kirkus Indie Reviews or book bloggers. Kirkus Indie Reviews start at $425 and take seven to nine weeks, so it's quite a commitment. Personally, I'm not sure how valuable this is for most indie authors, as I don't know how much attention readers actually pay to these reviews.

Endorsements and editorial reviews summary:

- Endorsements and editorial reviews are reviews from professionals and influencers, not the average reader.
- These are added to your book's retail page through your Amazon Author Central account.
- Seeking these is optional.
- If you decide to ask for endorsements, be sure to budget enough time for the endorser to read your book before the launch.

References and Resources

Kirkus. "Indie Reviews." Accessed March 23, 2022. https://www.kirkusreviews.com/indie-reviews/.

Umstattd, Thomas Jr. "How to Get Endorsements for Your Book." *Author Media*. September 15, 2021. https://www.authormedia.com/how-to-get-endorsements-for-your-book/.

Chapter 58

Blogging and social media

There are authors who make their careers through blogging and social media, and there are authors who get nothing but frustration from it. Since this isn't a marketing book, we won't go into detail here on how to use social media. I'll just give a few ideas on the topic to get you started on making your own decisions. In short, social media is often preached as a means to find your audience, and for some, that works. But for many authors (especially fiction authors), it's more of a way to connect with your current readers, encouraging them to continue reading. When you create social media posts and graphics, it also gives them something easy to share with their friends.

Blogging

For a long time, authors were told they had to have a blog, and readers would find them through their blogs. This was their "platform," their stage to get noticed. Nowadays, not so much. Unless you write nonfiction, having a blog probably isn't going to help that much toward gaining readers. Nonfiction lends itself much more naturally to blogging, as it's about information-sharing anyway, so having a blog on which you post regularly might help you gain readers.

Blogging is more of a challenge to fiction writers. Some authors, or groups of authors, review books on their blog, or talk about something related to their books. A historical research blog might work for historical fiction writers. Some authors also do webcomics and serials, if that fits. Fiction authors also like to talk about fiction writing on their blog, but unless their target is other writers who also read their fiction genre, this isn't the best strategy.

So what happened to blogging as a necessary step? This change is probably a combination of the internet becoming very crowded and other social media platforms popping up to get people's attention.

That said, many authors and influencers still have blogs, and they are often hungry for content. They will host authors for guest blogs, author interviews, character interviews, scavenger hunts, or accept books for review. You can be on many of these blogs in a row in a "blog tour" to gain exposure around a book release. There are companies who set up blog tours for you for a fee. You can also ask around and set it up yourself.

But weigh the time spent arranging this, the cost (if you use a paid service to set them up), and the time to create content with the return. Some blogs get few views. Are thirty views a post worth it to you? One hundred? Two thousand? How much traffic does each blog get? Is the blog really targeted to your readers?

I'm not saying the people who are subscribed to a small blog aren't worth your trouble, but you have to consider your time. Is doing a guest post for a blog with thirty viewers worth the time spent away from your children, chores, or next book? If you're time rich, probably yes, providing the blog is a good fit for your readers. If you're constrained for time, it may not be a good decision. You are building relationships with other authors and bloggers, however, and gaining experience for bigger blogs, when you do guest posts. So that is something else to weigh into your decision.

How do you find blogs to guest post on? You can do internet searches, see if authors you know have blogs, and ask in author groups. If an author in your genre posts about their blog tour, check out the list of blogs and see if any would be a fit for you.

In short, blogging is, generally speaking, better suited to nonfiction authors as far as gaining an audience goes. Guest posting on blogs or doing blog tours can be a useful strategy for authors to help build momentum for their book launch.

Social media

How many social media platforms are there now? I've lost count, and there are many I've only heard whispers of, since I have very little to do with the world of teenagers. So let's start with the "old" social media.

Facebook, love it or hate it, is a good way to connect with other authors in author groups (to learn, network, and be encouraged), to find cover artists (and get first crack at their pre-made covers), to join reader groups with readers who enjoy the same books you do, and to create a group page for your own readers to follow you. As for finding new readers, that largely depends on your savvy in marketing and on the willingness of your readers who are on Facebook to share with their friends about your work. The latter depends on whether or not your readers fit into the demographic likely to be on Facebook. You probably won't find teens hanging out on it.

You can also run ads for your books through Facebook. Some people do Facebook launch parties. These can be costly and take a lot of time and effort to run. I don't think they are as common now as they were.

Facebook *is* a good place to nurture your fans. Bigger authors, or groups of authors who write similar books, often start groups that take on a life of their own to become a reader community. The readers talk about the author's books, other books, let people know about sales, share fun or reading-related memes, and so on. Some moderation and the occasional post are required. Some authors hire a virtual assistant to manage their social media accounts. After all, they have books to write.

Facebook is also a place where lots of writers hang out to learn from one another, support one another, share opportunities, encourage one another, and network. Those things have been worth it for me to be on Facebook. I've learned so much and developed author relationships that I both treasure for themselves and have found valuable for marketing. Writers are also readers, and so getting to know other authors might end up gaining you new readers (and finding new authors to read!). So Facebook works for some things. There are plenty of reasons why people leave it or hate it, with politics and unfavorable algorithms and the addictive nature of social media, but it's not dead or useless.

If you choose to use Facebook, I recommend creating an author profile separate from your personal profile. You can create an author page fans can like and that you can post on (essentially an author profile page). This is public. You can also, individually or with author friends, create a private group where fans can interact more. It has more of an "insider" feel, and you can vet those who join.

What about the other platforms? Instagram was the new thing everyone was supposed to be on for a while. At the moment, it's TikTok. Oh, yeah, Twitter is still alive too. Next year, who knows?

There's Bookstagram on Instagram for sharing pretty covers with lovely backgrounds. You can find artists showing off their works there too. There's BookTok on TikTok.

Some authors have YouTube channels, and others have podcasts, or YouTube channels whose content also ends up on podcasts. Discord is gaining in popularity for fans to connect.

Goodreads is considered a useful site. You can put your book in book lists, do paid advertisements and ebook giveaways, and do quizzes and author Q&As, among other things.

Do you need to join them all? Only if you have 48 hours in your day. Seriously, though, different fans hang out on different sites, some on all. Having a presence on each to connect with your array of fans might be worth it if it doesn't put too much of a strain on your energy and time. You can use tools like Hootsuite and others to schedule your social media posts ahead of time and to post to all your social media at once. It's probably wiser, though, to focus on one or two platforms, the ones you enjoy the most, and figure out how to make those work for you. Remember your time is valuable. New social media platforms sprout up constantly. Will you add each to your list?

New social media platforms create a storm of interest, and authors who get on early and have something to say can really change their careers. Then other authors hear about it, and everyone tries it. It gets saturated. A lot of the people on those platforms have nothing to say but "buy my book," and just don't know how to make it work for them. Things eventually level out. Some do really well, a few do okay, many get frustrated and give up or doggedly continue with little to no reward because they were told by marketing experts and authors at conferences that they must have a platform. (I'm pretty sure you have to have a book, preferably more than one, to be an author, so maybe we need to be careful where our focus lies. You can go after more readers for a few books, or go after more books. More books gives true fans more to read, possibly gains new readers on their own, and who knows whether you'll write a blockbuster and get more readers through the strength of your book and readers doing the social sharing for you.)

Now, it's important to note that social media stresses me out and that I'm slightly bitter about the "you must do every social media" approach I fell for earlier in my career. I wondered at the time why anyone would want to listen to me (a new author) anyway, especially since I write fiction and have nothing to say to draw new readers in, so all the advice seemed to go against my reason and my personality. But I struggled to do it anyway. Now, to my relief, that mindset is changing. Social media is more about your fans than about strangers. You have something to talk about with your readers—your books and books that both you and your fans enjoy, and so on. Maybe your crazy cat and adorable dog as well.

The only social media I've really stuck with is Facebook, because I've had the good fortune to find my place there among authors. I also interact with readers in a reader group run by several other authors in my genre. I interact with authors in writer groups and follow cover artists. Social media to market to new readers isn't really my thing. I'm better off using that time to write more books and do book promotions and sales. And that's okay. If social media is your thing, or you don't know if it is and want to give it a try, go for it. As with everything, you need to evaluate as you go along and see if your time and effort are worth it. We all have different skills, so we find what works for us. Social media may give some success, but is it the best use of your time? And if readers love your books, they will do the sharing for you.

References and Resources

Bosken, Nina. "Facebook for Authors: Using Facebook to its Full Potential as an Author." *Self-Publishing School.* December 13, 2020. https://self-publishingschool.com/facebook-for-authors/.

Chesson, Dave. "How to Create a Facebook Author Page (And Tips for Using It Wisely)." *Kindlepreneur.* March 25, 2022. https://kindlepreneur.com/facebook-author-page/.

Chesson, Dave. "Instagram for Writers [2022]: How to Get the Most out of It." *Kindlepreneur.* March 25, 2022. https://kindlepreneur.com/instagram-for-writers-and-authors/.

Chesson, Dave. "The Ultimate Guide to Goodreads for Authors." *Kindlepreneur.* March 25, 2022. https://kindlepreneur.com/how-to-use-goodreads-for-authors/.

Self-Publishing Formula. "How to Sell More Books Using TikTok (The Self Publishing Show, episode 294)." (YouTube) September 3, 2021. https://www.youtube.com/watch?v=7gBcuKQQj_s.

Umstattd, Thomas Jr. "How to Use Goodreads to Promote Your Book." *Author Media.* March 30, 2022. https://www.authormedia.com/how-to-promote-books-goodreads/.

Umstattd, Thomas Jr. "Why Most Authors Don't Need Social Media in 2022." *Author Media.* January 12, 2022. https://www.authormedia.com/2022-social-media-marketing-guide-for-authors/.

Umstattd, Thomas Jr. "What Every Author Needs to Know About Cyber Security." *Author Media.* December 28, 2021. https://www.authormedia.com/what-every-author-needs-to-know-about-cyber-security/.

Chapter 59

Graphics

A picture is worth a thousand words, right? As authors we retort that pens are mightier than swords. Swords can slash pictures, so pens win. Right? Sort of like a game of paper, rock, scissors.

In the realm of book marketing, we'll call a truce on the debate. Images with pictures and few words are useful and expected marketing tools, so pictures and words are mighty together. Graphics are mighty.

For your website, newsletter, and social media, you'll want graphics. A simple graphic with your book cover, tagline, and release date. Or one with an atmospheric background and marketable quote. Or images of your characters and setting. Sale announcements are also good.

Notice the graphics that catch your eye as a reader and decide what kind of graphics you need. Here are a few tips and tools to get you started.

Canva, PicMonkey, GIMP, and Book Brush are popular tools for creating graphics. The first two are found online, while Book Brush and GIMP are programs to download. Canva has a free option and paid subscription plans, which give you access to more stock images and tools. It's fairly simple to use. PicMonkey (by Shutterstock) is paid but has a free seven-day trial. Book Brush is more complicated but has a lot of tutorials. It's designed specifically for authors, allowing them to create covers, box set covers, and even 3D covers. It has free and paid subscription plans. GIMP is an open-source software with Photoshop-like abilities, so it is a more complicated program.

When you make graphics, you'll eventually want to use photographs or images other than your book cover in them. This is where you have to be careful. Not all images are free for the taking, and using them without permission is violating the creator's copyright (if you think this is unfair, think about someone pirating your book and making a profit from it). So don't just grab any image that shows up in Pinterest or an internet search. You'll want to check for copyright information or stick to using images from stock photo websites.

Stock websites have photography, vector illustrations, illustrations, fonts, and even some videos available for use—either for free or paid. Pixabay, Unsplash, and Pexels allow you to download and use images for free, though you have the option to tip the creator. Shutterstock, Depositphotos, iStock, and other stock sites charge for the right to use images. Always check what license you are getting when you purchase a stock photo, as not all licenses are for commercial use and some images have a limit to the number of times they can be used. You typically buy image credits in a pack or pay a monthly subscription in order to purchase stock images. You can purchase one or two images alone, but this is usually more expensive. If you plan to use a lot of images, consider buying an image credit pack or a subscription. These sites often have sales you can watch for. Or you can stick to the free sites.

You can do graphics yourself or you can hire others to do them. Some virtual assistants will make them for a small fee per graphic. You can also hire designers on Fiverr or Upwork.

Another type of graphic I haven't mentioned so far is character art. These are drawings of specific characters from your work, or a scene. Character art is gaining in popularity, at least for YA fantasies. They're fun to have and make useful additions to graphics. They can be used on bookmarks and other promotional material. Some authors even create products—mugs, shirts, or journals, for instance—using the character art. But please know that you do not have to have character art to be a successful author, even in YA fantasy. If it's out of your budget, don't worry about it.

Other popular graphics are author logos and publishing logos. A publishing logo is nice to put on your title page and book spine. An author logo could be a really fun thing to have, to put on your website and marketing materials, and to use as a profile photo, but it's best to wait on this (if you do it at all) until you've written enough books to gain clarity for your brand.

Graphics are useful marketing tools. They don't have to be too complicated or expensive.

Chapter 60

Bookmarks, bookplates, and business cards

Speaking of graphics, one graphic-related tool you'll want is a bookmark, and since we're talking about physical items, I'll throw in bookplates and business cards too.

Bookmarks are fun, inexpensive gifts to give to current or potential fans. You can give them away at book signings and conferences or give them to strangers. When someone I meet learns I'm an author and expresses an interest in reading my books, I hand them a bookmark—showing off a pretty cover and providing a website to check out and a book title/author name to make searching for the book easy. You can also include a QR code they can scan to take them straight to a buy page.

As for the design of your bookmark, cover designers often have an add-on for this, usually for a relatively small charge (mine charges $40). You can also design them yourself or find someone on a site like Fiverr or Upwork to do so. You can use a local printer or one of the many options online to print them. Consider the size, paper weight, and durability you want when you choose a printer: heavier weight paper for durability, or thinner so you can print more for less money?

Bookplates are typically a sticker or card of some kind that an author signs for fans to stick into books they already own but couldn't get signed in person. These vary greatly in design and printed form, from simple pre-made designs ordered as stickers from Zazzle to professionally designed graphics printed on card stock. These are more for later in your author career and are not necessary for launching your first book.

Business cards are for networking with industry professionals, so you'll want your name and contact information (email and website), a professional headshot to make remembering you easier, and a tagline to describe your books. If you offer services, such as editing or book coaching, add that. Again, you can design them yourself, use the free designs on the online printers (these can look very nice), or hire it out.

If you're feeling overwhelmed with all the stuff to do or spend money on, you don't have to have bookmarks, bookplates, or business cards, or have them before your book releases. Bookmarks are standard tools of the trade that you'll likely want eventually, though.

Chapter 61

Newsletter swaps and group promotions

Getting your book in front of readers is a hard task; getting it in front of the right readers is an even harder one. In the next few chapters, we'll talk about specific ways to do this: working with authors in your same genre through newsletter swaps and group releases, using book promotion services, and running ads.

First, we'll talk about working with other authors. If you're published, or you've acquired readers through your reader magnet, you and your fellow authors will each have a fan base. If you write in related genres, it's possible your fans would like the other authors' books and vice versa. So you "share" fan bases. The easiest way to do this is a newsletter swap, which means you are swapping mentions in your newsletter. Author A includes a mention of Author B's book, and Author B includes a mention of Author A's book, usually around a release or sales promotion.

If you have a personal connection to authors in your genre, those whose books you read and whose readers read your type of book, ask them if they would consider a newsletter swap. Many authors have a section in their newsletter where they mention books their fans might enjoy (because those books are like their books). If you're releasing a new book or have a book on sale, consider asking those authors if they would mention your book in an upcoming newsletter. You can ask (if allowed) in online writing groups or via a personal email. In your personal request, include how you are connected to the author (you're in an online group with them or you met at a conference, for instance), as well as information on your book: title, blurb, genre, rating (clean romance or steamy, violence level, etc.), and the preferred date for the mention. Also offer to mention a book of theirs now or in the future. No one has to include a mention of your book because you mention theirs, however.

You can also use a service such as BookFunnel and StoryOrigin and join a group of authors there. These are very useful services for authors because not only do they host and deliver your book files to ARC readers, and host your reader magnet, but they allow you to connect with subscribers of other authors' newsletters through their newsletter promotions. These are paid sites, about $100/year, but they are well worth it. Once you set up your account with them, you can add your books and create sales pages and landing pages. These pages have a cover image and blurb of your book as well as buy links.

For the newsletter promotions, someone sets up a promotion for a certain genre or theme (KU fantasy, freebie sci-fi, or sweet Christmas romances, for instance), sets a date for the promotion to run, sets rules (no erotica or you have to have 500 newsletter subscribers or share ten times during the promotion, for instance), provides a landing page header image, and then opens it up for people matching the criteria to join. BookFunnel/StoryOrigin builds a page with the header image and the book cover of each book in the promo. These promotions typically last a few weeks. Every author sends out at least one newsletter mentioning the promotions in that time (usually including a pre-made graphic and a tracking link). Interested newsletter subscribers of the various authors in the promo click the link, look through the covers, and click on the covers that appeal to them. They are taken to that book's landing page, which has its blurb and download links (for reader magnets) or purchase links for sales promos.

Once your books are set up on your chosen book promotion service, you look through the available promotions and join one or two that work with your newsletter send schedule. When you send your newsletter, you include your personal tracking link. This allows BookFunnel/StoryOrigin to know that you are actually fulfilling your part of the bargain and promoting the promotion to your readers by mentioning it in your newsletter or on social media. The more of your subscribers who click on the promotion links, the better your "reputation" is with the services.

These promotions allow readers to find new authors and authors to get in front of new readers in similar genres, so they are a win-win.

However, don't spam your newsletter subscribers with tons of newsletters so you can participate in tons of promos. That's unfair to your subscribers, who are simply being used. Choose only one or two appropriate promos per newsletter, if you do one every newsletter.

Newsletter promos are a common practice and are likely to continue being useful. If you use BookFunnel and StoryOrigin, you will need to budget about $100 per year. You need only use one. It might be a good idea to swap between them every few years to reach different sets of readers. MyBookCave's book hosting is free. They have some newsletter promotions for growing your subscriber list. They are more focused on their paid book promotion à la BookBub—sending out notices of books on sale and available for free, which we'll talk about soon.

BookFunnel and StoryOrigin are useful for:

- Growing your newsletter list through subscriber-focused promos, which require a reader magnet.
- Promoting books on sale or free as part of a group of similar books.
- Promoting books in KU as part of a group of similar books.
- Promoting books in certain genres or themes.
- Promoting audiobooks.
- Hosting your reader magnet and ARC copies.

Chapter 62

Anthologies, group releases, short fiction, and articles

In addition to the newsletter swaps, you can cross-promote with other authors in group promotions and increase your reach through short works.

For group promotions, you can join with other authors to release a box set of novels, novellas, or short fiction (each author contributing a different story and working to promote the set), or do a group release. A group release is when authors write books around a common theme and do a staggered release of individual titles, each author promoting each book in the release. You can also write for an anthology (a collection of short works in a single volume). You can submit a story to an anthology seeking submissions (and get paid for it) or join with several friends to publish one together.

For short works, you can write fiction or articles for magazines, e-zines, or blogs. These opportunities might be free or paid (you earn money for the article and maybe gain new readers!). If readers like your work, they can check your biography to find out if you've written anything else.

What are these like? I had a short story accepted into the Fellowship of Fantasy anthology *Tales of Ever After* several years ago. Its purpose was to be a group promotion. I think I paid $25 to cover expenses for getting the book cover, editing, and formatting done and for some marketing. The ebook is available for free. I got the rights back to my story in six months and can use it however I like on its own. I can order print copies of the anthology and sell them at events. So the anthology itself is not a direct money maker (except in print), but the author connections I made certainly helped my career, and I imagine some readers discovered me through it.

I participated in another anthology (*Encircled*) with a few critique partners, and while it was fun and gives me another print book I can sell at in-person events, it isn't a money maker either. We each contributed time and some money to create a collection of six fairy tale short stories. We arranged for the editing, cover, and formatting ourselves. It's a quality piece and I'm proud of it, but I don't expect much money from it.

I've also participated in a group release where six authors released retellings (short to full-length) of "The Twelve Dancing Princesses" over a month's time and pooled our marketing efforts to support one another. The coordinator organized blog tours and cover reveals and was paid a small fee for her work. We were each responsible for every-thing for our own books. Only marketing efforts were shared. This was helpful to my career and for motivation to write what turned out to be one of my best books!

A friend has participated in several box sets of contemporary romance stories written around a theme. The books are released in a box set and the rights return to the authors after a certain period of time. At that point, the stories can be published independently.

These types of group projects, however, are like any group project. They can be fantastic if done with the right people, or a terror. There needs to be clear communication about rights, expectations, deadlines, cost, and target audiences. Choose the participants carefully. Do you really want that erotica author who's your friend's friend in a promo for readers of squeaky clean or light-steam fantasy romance?

You also want reliable, easy-to-get-along-with authors, because you will have a lot of decisions to make, including cover design style and designer, who's doing what, marketing strategies, release dates, format-ting, and so forth. If you're the one doing the organizing, do you have the time? Can you count on people to help you (and have they agreed to this—don't volunteer them or make assumptions)? You also need a way to split income, if doing a project that requires it. Currently, Amazon allows you to list other authors on a project but doesn't split royalties for you. There are options for royalty splitting, however, such as using PubShare (formerly BundleRabbit), Publish Drive, and Draft2Digital.

As for writing shorts and articles for magazines, e-zines, or blogs, or for paid anthologies, these can earn you money upfront and possibly gain readers. Writing articles and blog posts is likely most effective for nonfiction writers. As for fiction, the number of paying magazines, anthologies, and e-zines seems to be dwindling, but you can search the *Writer's Market* guide or check your author groups for legitimate ones to submit to. Writing shorter works requires a slightly different skill set than writing longer works, so do consider this. That said, writing short stories is often considered a great tool for learning to write, since you need a full story in a small number of words.

In summary, working with other authors in group releases, anthologies, and box sets can be a good way to combine marketing efforts and reach new readers. Writing articles and short fiction can earn you extra money and possibly find you new readers.

References and Resources

PubShare. https://pubshare.com/about/collaborative-publishing.

PublishDrive. "PublishDrive Abacus and Team Royalties." https://publishdrive.zendesk.com/hc/en-us/categories/4403679961106-PublishDrive-Abacus-and-Team-Royalties.

Tumlinson, Kevin. "Announcing D2D Payment Splitting!" *Draft2Digital*. Nov 18, 2020. https://www.draft2digital.com/blog/announcing-d2d-payment-splitting/.

Chapter 63

Book promotion services, sales, and perma-free

One of the major helps for your author career are book promotion services. These services are geared to alerting readers to book deals. Authors submit their books to be included in the service's newsletter and social media announcements.

Want a way to get your book in front of people actually looking for books? This is it. (Okay, one way.) There are two caveats, though: this method is for ebooks that are on sale or free, and it costs money to use the services. Oh, and, like everything else, things change and services become more or less effective, so you have to keep track of feedback from other authors and give things a try for yourself.

Before we discuss the book promotion services, however, we need to talk about putting books on sale or free, as those are the books the readers using these services are looking for.

BOOK SALES, KINDLE COUNTDOWN DEALS, FREE DAYS, AND PERMA-FREE

As an indie author, you get to set the price of your book. If you use Smashwords, Draft2Digital (when they get it worked out with partner Smashwords), or sell direct through your website, you can create coupons and offer those to readers through your newsletter or other means. You can also put your books on sale. There are two main ways of doing this: by changing the book's price yourself and then, after the desired length of time, returning it to "full price"; or you can use the retailer's method of handling sales, if they have one. Findaway handles promotional sales of its audiobooks. Apple Books has promo codes for free ebooks for reviews, and has other promotional opportunities for authors. KDP Select has Kindle Countdown Deals and Free Days. It also has (in beta) a program that allows you to nominate your ebook for a promotion, either a Kindle Deal (limited-time discount deals offered on ebooks) or for inclusion in Prime Reading. For other retailers, check their websites.

If you put your ebook or print book on sale by changing the price manually, start the price change process a day or two ahead of any announcements of the sale, since you don't control exactly when the price change will be processed and show up. Your book will not show up as on sale, as the "sale" price appears to be the permanent price. You do, however, have greater control over the length of the sale.

Let's talk a moment about Kindle Countdown Deals. These are available for the Amazon US and Amazon UK stores, and you set each individually through your author dashboard. Your book must be in Kindle Select to qualify for this. You have seven days each 90-day term in which you can put your book on sale—the sale price will show up as a limited-time price with a countdown to show when the price will go up. You can set a single price for the entire sale or have one that starts low and goes up each day until the sale ends; so starts at $0.99 and then goes up a dollar each day until it's full price again, for instance. You have seven days, but you can only use your days in one stretch. There are limitations regarding when you can schedule a deal, however, as has already been discussed. These include the necessity of a steady price prior to the sale (you can't run a sale if you recently raised your book's base price to make the sale price seem like a better deal, in other words), a 14-day period between the end of the Countdown Deal and the book's KU term renewal, and no scheduling ahead for the next term. Your book must also have been in the program for thirty days before the Deal (this time can include the pre-order period); this isn't thirty days after each renewal but only for its initial entrance into the program. The benefits of running a Countdown Deal over changing the price yourself are that the sale starts at the specific date and time you choose; it shows up as a limited-time sale price, and you keep the 70% royalty rate.

And for sales, readers tend to want free or $0.99 books, not $1.99 or $2.99. So deeper discounts work best.

As for free books, some retailers allow you to set your book for free, including Apple. If you sell direct, you can do that as well, or give out coupon codes that allow readers to purchase it for free. If your book is in KU, you can give it away for free for five days each term using your Free Days. These days can be spread out or used in a row. Your book must have been in KU for a few days before setting up a free day. KDP does not allow setting the price of a book to free permanently. Many people get around that by putting the book wide and setting the prices on those stores to free, then notifying KDP of the lower price and asking for a price match. KDP will usually then make the book free. Sometimes the price will revert, so if you do this, be sure to check occasionally.

Setting a book's price to be free permanently is called "perma-free," and is popular with those who write series and who want to draw people into their series with a free book 1. How-to guides and other nonfiction books are often set at free as a short lead to interest people in the author's other services, such as courses. However, if your other books are in KU and only the free one is wide, some wide readers will be understandably miffed your other books aren't in their preferred store.

How do you get the word out about your sale or free books? You can send a newsletter to your subscribers and post on social media. It might show up to those who check out the free booklists in stores. However, to many authors, those are just supplements to the use of book promotion services. These services have a large reach and allow you to target specific audiences, such as readers of thrillers or romance.

BOOK PROMOTION SERVICES

The biggest of the book promotion services is BookBub. Their Featured Deal has long been considered the gold standard for book promotion, which means it costs more than the other sites to use, results in a lot more rejected submissions, but tends to get *much* higher download/purchase numbers when an author is accepted. Costs varies by category and the book's sale price, with some deals costing over $700. You can do US or international, with the international deals being much, much cheaper. BookBub tends to favor wide books over KU exclusive but will sometimes include a KU book (my one BookBub Featured Deal was a KU book).

If you try for a BookBub Featured Deal, make sure you have other books to funnel people into after they've read your sale or freebie book. If you're spending $700 to promote just one book at $0.99, it's going to take *a lot* of sales to break even. Where many get their money back is on later books in a series (this is one reason you should consider writing in a series, at least for fiction) and KU page reads.

Don't be discouraged if you submit your book for a deal and get rejected. That happens *a lot*. Be sure to read BookBub's tips for applying and then keep submitting.

Do note that BookBub has other options besides Featured Deals. They have ads, a free new release notice for people who've followed you on BookBub, and a paid New Release for Less option. The New Release for Less is very expensive (over $900 for most categories), and a number of authors on a thread (early 2022) discussing it in the 20BooksTo50K® Facebook group stated they would never use it again. So the current word on the street is to stick with the Featured Deal.

Speaking of 20BooksTo50K®, this is a Facebook author group and a conference dedicated to the idea that it takes twenty books all earning at least $7 a day to earn $50,000 a year, or enough to live on as a full-time author. So while you may hear about single-book authors making it big, most authors publish many books before breaking out or becoming full-time authors.

BookBub is not the only promotion service, however. There are many less expensive ones that work well (though they have smaller lists). Some are general ones with sub-lists for specific genres, while some focus on a particular genre or related genres (such as romance only or science fiction and fantasy). Freebooksy, Robin Reads, BookBarbarian (sci-fi/fantasy specialty), and ENT (EReader News Today) are respected book promotion services.

As with everything, strategy is important when using the promotion services. If you're in KU, many recommend using your Countdown Deal days each 90-day term on your backlist titles to hopefully get the books in front of new readers or boost interest among current fans who missed them. If you're launching a later book in a series, you can put the previous books on sale and promote them using the promotion services to boost the entire series. For instance, if you're releasing book 3 of a trilogy, you might have book 1 free and book 2 at $0.99 and book 3 at full price for $4.99.

Using different promotion services together, over a period of days, is a respected strategy called "promo stacking." The goal is to use promo services strategically to combine attention from the various services' subscribers with retailer algorithms to improve your chances of getting a best seller ranking and being noticed by the stores to get them marketing for you. Retailers like sustained sales, not huge spikes and then nothing. If your sales build over several days without falling, that attracts the notice of the algorithms, which incentivizes the stores to recommend your books, because they like books proven to sell (at least, that's how it works for Amazon).

So you might have a $0.99 sale on a series starter from Monday to Sunday. You could announce it on social media and your newsletter on Monday, use a combination of good-size promotions and smaller ones on Tuesday through Friday, and BookBub on Saturday. Or something like that. You could also include ads in your strategy.

Scheduling your biggest promo site near the end of your sale days, leading to a building of sales before the peak, then a slow lowering in a nice bell curve, is what you want. You will hopefully then get a higher tail of sales thanks to the retailer recommendations, word-of-mouth, and new fans reading through the rest of your backlist. What you ultimately want is not just a spike of sales but a higher base rate after the sale. When you release a book or do a promotion, your sales go up, then after a period of time, they tank. You come down to a base rate, or typical earning.

When you do sales, you want to find new readers who will read through your backlist (all your other published works). Unless you master ads or find some other way to stabilize your earnings, this is the typical pattern: peak at releases or promotions, then a tank and evening out to a base rate. If you want to get a dependable income from writing, you have to get your base rate, not your peak, up to the needed amount. This is why some authors release so rapidly—they are trying to escape that tank in sales by creating a new release peak at the time the tank would normally happen.

———

Just putting your book on sale or for free won't generate that much interest because of how crowded the market is now. Coupling the sale with the use of one or more promotion services, newsletter swaps, and ads helps. When you do sales, your goal is not just to sell books but to find new readers who will read through your backlist (all your other published works). It can be challenging to earn out from a sale of a book you only get about $0.35 for, especially after you paid for book promotion services. Having a backlist to send the readers on to helps. Free books are also used to generate new fans to drive to other books. Promo stacking is a good strategy to make the most of your book promotions and achieve a best seller ranking.

References and Resources

Amazon KDP. "Kindle Countdown Deals." Accessed March 23, 2022. https://kdp.amazon.com/en_US/help/topic/G201293780.

Amazon KDP. "Kindle Free Book Promotions." Accessed March 23, 2022. https://kdp.amazon.com/en_US/help/topic/G201298240.

Amazon KDP. "Nominate Your eBook for a Promotion (Beta)." Accessed March 21, 2022. https://kdp.amazon.com/en_US/help/topic/GHNKT7V426GVDM3G.

Apple Books. "Apple Books Promo Codes." Accessed March 23, 2022. https://itunespartner.apple.com/books/articles/apple-books-promo-codes-2740.

BookBub Partners. "Featured Deals Pricing and Statistics." Accessed March 23, 2022. https://www.BookBub.com/partners/pricing.

BookBub Partners. "Overview." Accessed March 23, 2022. https://www.BookBub.com/partners/overview.

BookBub Partners. "New Releases for Less Pricing." Accessed March 23, 2022. https://www.BookBub.com/partners/new_releases_for_less_pricing.

Erik, Nicholas. "Promo sites." Accessed March 23, 2022. https://nicholaserik.com/promo-sites/.

Erik, Nicholas. *The Ultimate Guide to Book Marketing: The 80/20 System for Selling More Books* (Ultimate Author Guides). 2020.

Gaughran, David. "Best Book Promotion Sites." https://davidgaughran.com/best-promo-sites-books/.

Gaughran, David. *BookBub Ads Expert: A Marketing Guide to Author Discovery* (Let's Get Publishing Book 3). David Gaughran, 2019.

Chapter 64

Pay-per-click ads and author careers

Authors interested in ads tend to be the more career-focused authors, those who want to earn money for their work. So I think this is a good place to step back and mention making a full-time living, or a major side income, as an author. It's not easy. There are no magic bullets. Running ads, getting BookBub Featured Deals, writing in that hot new subgenre or jumping on that new social media, are not guarantees to selling books and making money. There are a lot of factors that play into this, luck being one of them.

One of the best and most realistic "formulas" I've seen for making a living as an author is from Nicholas Erik's *The Ultimate Guide to Book Marketing: The 80/20 System*. This is his formula: "Market research + 3 traffic sources + pro covers + great blurbs + newsletter + 4-6 novels per year consistently for 3-5 years —> full-time author." As you can see, there's no single thing that will make you a full-time author. By traffic sources, he means ways to get "traffic" (potential readers) to your sales pages. This includes ads, book promotions, and social media, among others.

The few authors I follow who write full-time all have large backlists in consistently popular subgenres (like urban fantasy or fairy tales), write consistently (publish multiple books a year), wrote a breakout series, and use ads (what other traffic generators they use, I don't know).

If the idea of doing this scares you or brings the word "burnout" to mind, that's fine. Some of the greatest authors of all time were not full-time authors (C. S. Lewis and J. R. R. Tolkien weren't). If you want to try for a full-time career at this, though, don't forget you can add related skills, such as editing or speaking, to it. And realize that this doesn't just happen because you publish one book, or even ten books. It usually takes years and many books and much trial and error and hard work. I mentioned this in the last section, but you usually get a spike in earnings after a release or a big promotion and then a plummet. Ads and such are used to help drive traffic to your books so that the plummet is less catastrophic.

Ready for ads, now?

Authors who use ads generally use *pay-per-click* ads, such as found on Amazon, Facebook, and BookBub. These ads show up in response to certain keywords or parameters set by the author, and if a reader clicks the ad, which takes him or her to a buy page or the author's website, the author pays the per click amount for that ad (this might be anywhere from $0.15 to over $1 per click).

Amazon ads are targeted via keywords to appear in search result pages and product pages (the sponsored products we've talked about and the lock screen ads on Kindle devices). The targeted keywords might be something like "urban fantasy with vampires" or "how to play the guitar for beginners," or the ads might be targeted to searches for a comparable author. Authors can also target categories for a broader approach.

Facebook has tons of data about its users, not only from their actions and interactions on Facebook but from all over the web. Authors can use this to create ads that target specific readers. A romantic suspense author, for instance, could target those who like both thrillers and the Hallmark channel. Note that a Facebook ad is not the same thing as a boosted page, which is commonly said to be a waste of money. There have been many alterations to Facebook ads (including policy changes) over the years that advertisers have had to work around.

Expect things to be always changing for one reason or another in the book world.

How much does it cost to run ads?

If you hang around certain author spots online, you'll hear about crazy ad spends. You'll see people talking about how they spent $10,000 last month on ads and made $15,000, for a profit of $5,000 (or some other amount). If you think that's a lot, that's actually much less than what some spend (some talk about six figure ad spends). But please, don't start out trying to do that. Learning to use ads well (to write copy, find the best keywords and target audience, etc.) takes time, money, and trial and error. Start small. When you get things to work, then you can go bigger. It's commonly recommended to start at $5 a day on a single platform until you master it. The pay-per-click cost for ads varies considerably, from something like $0.15 per click to over $1 per click, meaning you could burn through your budget very quickly, with or without a return for your investment. How many people click on your ad but don't buy is a factor of how on point your targeting, cover, copy, and blurb are.

Remember that you're paying to acquire readers here. The more books you have out, the more effective your ads will be. Paying $1 to get a reader to buy your $3.99 book doesn't make good sense if ten other people clicked on the ad but didn't buy. If you have many other books to send that one reader on to, then you're more likely to make up for the loss.

———

There are entire books and courses devoted to ads (some notable teachers include Bryan Cohen and Mark Dawson), and this is a beginner's guide to publishing, so I won't go into ads in detail. However, I wanted to cover one platform in more depth, so I chose the one I am most familiar with: Amazon Ads. There are references at the end of the chapter for marketing, specific platforms, and making a living as a writer.

Here's a brief overview of Amazon Ads. You'll need to set up an Author Central Account and link your books. You'll also need an account at https://advertising.amazon.com. Or you can reach this through your author dashboard. Find your title, then choose "Promote and Advertise" under the Kindle Ebook Title Options. There will be a "Run an Ad Campaign" box with information and links to get you started.

You will choose a book from your booklist to run a campaign for. You select the date range the ad runs for and how much Amazon Ads can spend per day for that ad (Amazon has a limit to spend; other platforms may not, so be aware of this). These are pay-per-click ads, so you get *impressions* when the ads show up in response to a reader search, but you only pay when a reader clicks on your ad and goes to your book page. If you get a sale from this *click*, that's a *conversion*. You set the pay-per-click rate. This is actually a bid. It's a bidding process between you and other advertisers to see what product with that keyword shows up, which means the more people using those keywords, the higher the bids will be. Some marketers teaching about Amazon Ads talk about $0.35 bids. The suggested bid mentioned in Amazon Ads is $0.75, but they recommend starting with lower bids. For higher bids, if you don't get good conversion (you have the wrong target audience or your blurb isn't converting well), you can max out your daily budget quickly, and thus lose money quickly. If your book is in KU, you will get some page reads from clicks instead of sales, so that's something to consider as well.

You can select automatic ads for your books (Amazon determines the target of the ads) or target the ads manually, choosing the keywords you want the ad to show up for. These keywords are the words or phrases used in customer searches and which relate your book to other similar books. You can write a short ad copy for the ads or choose not to include ad copy. Take a look at several Amazon book pages and do a search using a phrase readers might use to find your books and look at the sponsored books that show up.

———

Pay-per-click ads with Amazon, Facebook, and BookBub are popular ways to increase traffic to your book pages. Other ways to advertise include paying for an ad in the program of a writing conference you attend, sponsoring a podcast episode (one whose target audience matches yours), and paying social media influencers to promote your books. Don't want to learn TikTok and work to gain your own following? Put your time and energy toward more books or enjoying life and pay someone who already understands the platform and has a market to advertise to for you. You can contact Bookstagrammers and Book-Tokkers yourself and ask them if you can sponsor them in return for them promoting your book. Always make certain the audience is your target audience.

A summary of pay-per-click ads and author careers:

- Ads can be very effective, especially for career-focused authors with many books out.
- Running effective ads is a skill that must be learned through trial and error.
- Don't run ads willy-nilly. Target the right audience, set a budget, be mindful of your spending; pay attention to the data to see what is and isn't effective.
- Budget for ads and only run them if you can afford to lose the money, as it takes time and money to get them to work effectively.
- The more books you can funnel readers through, the more effective your ad spend will be.
- You can pay other people to advertise on social media for you.
- An author career is built on many things. Writing great books consistently, having great packaging, and finding effective ways to drive traffic to your books are essentials for an author career.

References and Resources

Amazon Ads. https://advertising.amazon.com.

Erik, Nicholas. *The Ultimate Guide to Book Marketing: The 80/20 System for Selling More Books* (Ultimate Author Guides). 2020.

Fox, Chris. *Ads for Authors Who Hate Math: Write Faster, Write Smarter.* 2019.

Gaughran, David. *Amazon Decoded: A Marketing Guide to the Kindle Store* (Let's Get Publishing Book 4). David Gaughran, 2020.

Gaughran, David. *BookBub Ads Expert: A Marketing Guide to Author Discovery* (Let's Get Publishing Book 3). David Gaughran, 2019.

Robertson, Carlyn. "How to Promote Any Book with BookBub Ads." March 3, 2022. https://insights.BookBub.com/promote-any-book-BookBub-ads.

Self Publishing Formula. *Learn Amazon Ads: Use AMS to Find More Readers and Sell More Books.* SPF Books, 2017.

Umstattd, Thomas Jr. "Facebook Advertising for Authors." *Author Media.* March 9, 2022. https://www.authormedia.com/facebook-advertising-for-authors/.

Chapter 65

Contests and best seller lists

Writers love additional ways to get their books in front of audiences, ways to make their books more appealing to readers, and reader- or industry-validation. This translates into *authors like winning writing contests and getting onto best seller lists*. Does this mean you must add these to your to-do list? No. Unless you like the challenge and enjoy having goals to work toward.

If these two things do interest you, however, there are two things to consider before pouring time, effort, and money into them. The first is that not all awards are created equal. The second is that not all best seller lists are created equal.

In other words, it may not matter a hill of beans if you achieved these. Anyone can throw up a website and advertise a contest and collect money for entries, then present a "you're a winner" certificate that means nothing. They might have a contract that gives them permission to publish the entries. Scams come in all forms. So always vet the contests. Writers Beware has an excellent article on contests and awards with tips to spot the predatory ones: https://www.sfwa.org/other-resources/for-authors/writer-beware/contests/. Writer's Digest's *Writer's Market* has a list of reputable contests.

Awards are often used to impress literary agents and publishing house acquisition editors; thus, they aren't as important to indie authors. That said, awards are nice to have, and some readers, industry professionals, or media outlets might be impressed by "award-winning" in your biography or book description. But the contest won has to be a worthwhile one. Contests held by a local chapter of a reputable national writing organization and contests associated with a national conference are generally respected awards.

Contests are also a potential source of valuable feedback, if you receive scores from the judges. Semi-finalists sometimes get feedback from respected editors and literary agents. Do know that contest feedback is highly subjective. One contest judge may love your work, another like it, and the third absolutely loathe it. (This has happened to me and my author friends.)

Placing in a contest, however, may get your work in front of fellow authors and readers and gives you something to share. So there is some marketing value in contests (this, of course, depends on the contest).

Some contests are for published works, and some are for non-published. Some contests are very indie-friendly and some not so much. One conference I know of is very indie-friendly and lets indies enter their published works with no hoops to jump through. Another is more trad pub-minded and only lets "Qualified Indies" enter the published category of their contest. To become a Qualified Indie you must provide proof of at least $5,000 in earnings on that book.

Some awards are based not on you entering and winning a contest but on your fans nominating your book for a reader's choice award of some kind. These are fun because you don't do anything for it but write a great book!

In conclusion, seeking awards isn't the best goal in and of itself—writing the best book is, which, incidentally, might lead to the other. Contests can become expensive and draining emotionally (losing hurts), and could be scams, but you can (sometimes) receive helpful feedback and, possibly, exposure to a new audience from the right contest. And a goal is generally a good thing. So if you have the extra time and money, you might consider finding a *good* contest in your genre and setting a goal to winning it.

———

Another common goal, a different "prize" to win, is getting on a best seller list or achieving a best seller badge on Amazon.

This is where I feel obligated to be, as usual, a weight on the balloon of optimism and say that it's always a good thing to consider if your dream is worth it. This applies greatly to best seller lists, including the famous *New York Times* Best Seller List and the *USA Today* Best Seller List. These lists, especially the *New York Times* Best Seller List, are particular about what they will and won't count (including formats and genres) for their list. The *New York Times* Best Seller List, according to an article on Self-PublishingSchool.com, doesn't accept ebooks published through a single distributor. Meaning, your book in KU can't make the list. The article states: "To achieve bestseller status on the *Times* not only do you have to sell at least 5,000–10,000 copies in one week, but these sales have to be diverse sales." That means wide and in bookstores, chains like Barnes & Noble and Walmart, in multiple countries, etc. It seems that achieving a *New York Times* Best Seller List isn't that likely even for very high-selling indies.

In short, if your dream is to get on the *New York Times* Best Seller List, you should probably go the traditional publishing route.

That said, the *USA Today* Best Seller List and Amazon best seller lists are viable options for indies, the latter especially. It should be noted, however, that the awards themselves don't seem to make that much difference, according to a couple of authors I've heard talk about their experience. Yes, you can add them to your marketing materials and the former to your covers, but the awards don't appear to significantly impact authors' careers. After all, if you can get onto the *USA Today* Best Seller List, you're probably doing pretty well anyway.

According to an article by Nicholas Erik (https://nicholaserik.com/usa-today-bestseller-mini-guide/), to reach the *USA Today* Best Seller List, you need to plan ahead, do a sales promotion, get a BookBub Featured Deal in a large category, set up stacked promotions around that so you're building up sales, run ads (pay-per-click ads, such as on Facebook, Amazon, and BookBub), do newsletter swaps with other authors, and engage your own audience through your newsletter.

Note that this strategy is using a sale, and you doubtless realize the difference between hitting a list with a box set marked down to $0.99 and a single, full-priced novel. Reaching the list is still an achievement, even with a sale, but those two things aren't the same.

But what about Amazon best seller status? This is the easiest to achieve because Amazon has tons of categories, and some are small enough that you can reach #1 fairly easily. I hit #1 in a category once by only selling about 64 copies of a book marked down to $0.99. That wouldn't move the needle in some larger categories. In case you're interested, Kindlepreneur's Publisher Rocket has a feature that allows you to estimate how many books you'd need to sell to rank in each category you query for.

As for Amazon best seller rank, you'll see this on an Amazon ebook page:

Best Sellers Rank: [Rank] in Kindle Store [number of books]
[Rank] in Category #1
[Rank] in Category #2
[Rank] in Category #3

Your book ranks in the Kindle store and in three categories. So, unless you've asked to be included in more categories, you have a chance to rank in three categories and the Kindle store. And, if your book is a new release, you have the option of ranking for #1 New Release in a category. However, do know that Amazon has different lists for free and paid books. People who try to rank by giving away their book are put into a different category than those whose books people are willing to pay money for. In short, Amazon has Kindle store rankings for paid and free books, category rankings, and new release rankings.

If you want to earn a best seller badge, the marketing tactics are pretty much the same as for just selling your books, only scaled up. More ads, perhaps; a sale and stacked promos; a bigger launch, etc. Know, though, that the badge doesn't last. It goes away when your sales fall or another book overtakes yours.

Hitting a best seller list, like winning a contest, is fun and can be a useful goal, but it may not change your career and shouldn't be sought purely for your own validation. It's never wise to get too wrapped up in rank, and checking every day multiple times a day is unhealthy and takes away from writing. I looked at a best seller category recently and noted that book #1 only had about half as many reviews as book #2. I've had readers tell me how much they loved my books, how they'd never connected to a character so much as to the hero of one particular book, but none of those things are connected to rank, and they are much more important to me.

So winning contests, getting on lists, and ranking in stores isn't everything. It can be a fun goal to work toward to help you hone your writing and marketing skills, but it's not an end in itself. It's more of an exercise to help you learn skills to apply to all your books for better long-term career benefit.

References and Resources

Erik, Nicholas. "Mini Guide: How to Hit the USA Today Bestseller List." Accessed March 23, 2022. https://nicholaserik.com/usa-today-bestseller-mini-guide/.

Muniz, Gabe. "How to Get on the New York Times Bestseller List." *Self-Publishing School.* February 4, 2022. https://self-publishingschool.com/get-on-the-new-york-times-bestseller-list/.

Publisher Rocket. https://publisherrocket.com.

Writers Beware/SFWA. "Contests and Awards." https://www.sfwa.org/other-resources/for-authors/writer-beware/contests/.

Writer's Digest's *Writer's Market.* https://writersmarket.com.

Chapter 66

Giveaways and other strategies

On the reader end of contests, giveaways are one method of growing your readership. For a while, authors and small publishers were holding Facebook book launch parties. There would be games, appearances by other authors, and lots of giveaways. I don't see those much anymore. They cost a lot in time and money, and, honestly, most of us were just there for the fun and freebies.

However, other types of contests and giveaways are still being used to some degree. Groups of authors can get together and offer large bundles of books, and in exchange for entering the contest, readers agree to sign up for the author newsletters and, possibly, follow the authors on social media for extra entries. It's recommended by at least one book marketer that you don't offer gift cards (except maybe to Amazon), Kindles, and other prizes because people are more interested in those non-book prizes than in winning your book. Remember that the goal of marketing is to get your book in front of the right readers. If you're going to do a contest, make sure you're appealing to readers likely to eventually buy, read, and enjoy your books.

Rafflecopter, BookSweeps, and KingSumo are three services for doing giveaways. Goodreads also can be used for giveaways.

Rafflecopter has free and paid monthly plans. You can also subscribe for one month and then cancel to get the benefits of the paid services without a long-term commitment.

For BookSweeps, you pay to join a themed promotion to either increase your newsletter list (this is a non-organic method and shouldn't be overused) or gain BookBub followers. People agree to join your mailing list or follow you on BookBub in order to register to win a large bundle of books on a particular theme. They may or may not be interested in finding new authors to buy books from, so do use this, and other such giveaways, sparingly.

KingSumo (AppSumo) has a free and onetime payment level. It's a platform to grow your email list through viral giveaways.

StoryBundle is not a giveaway, but it's a unique option I thought would fit best here. Here's what they say about themselves:

> "StoryBundle is a way for people who love to read to discover quality indie books written by indie authors. You know how it's always hard to find something good to read? StoryBundle hopes to solve that. We take a handful of books—anywhere from six to nine—and group them together to offer as a bundle. Then you, the reader, can take a look at the titles we've chosen and decide how much you'd like to pay. Think of us like a friend that scours independent books for undiscovered gems, then bundles these titles together for one low price that you decide. Yeah, we mean it; you get to set the price that you want to pay!"

Your book is part of a bundle, and the other authors involved are sure to advertise, so there is some marketing reach here. The catch is that some people may be cheap and not pay much for the bundle (but some will be generous), and your books can't be in KU, since entering would violate your exclusivity contract.

Goodreads also allows you to do giveaways of up to 100 print or Kindle ebook copies. Ebook is usually recommended over print due to the extra expense of shipping print copies (and there was an issue with people reselling them). These giveaways are sometimes added to the launch to draw attention to the book. A standard Goodreads contest costs $119, and the premium costs $599. For ebooks, your Goodreads author account and your KDP author account must be linked. When the contest ends, KDP automatically sends the winners the ebook at no extra charge.

I see the occasional indie or trad pub author using these methods, but I don't see them too much and can't say from personal experience how well they work. But now you know about them and can ask around or experiment for yourself!

References and Resources

BookSweeps. "Join a Promotion." Accessed March 23, 2022. https://www.booksweeps.com/authors/join-a-promo.

BookSweeps. "What Is BookSweeps?" Accessed March 23, 2022. https://www.booksweeps.com/overview/.

King Sumo. https://appsumo.com/products/kingsumo/.

Rafflecopter. "Pricing." Accessed March 23, 2022. https://www.rafflecopter.com/pricing.

Rafflecopter. "Tour." Accessed March 23, 2022. https://www.rafflecopter.com/tour.

StoryBundle. Accessed March 23, 2022. https://storybundle.com/faq.

Umstattd, Thomas Jr. "How to Use Goodreads to Promote Your Book." *Author Media*. March 30, 2022. https://www.authormedia.com/how-to-promote-books-goodreads/.

Chapter 67

Concluding getting the word out

Got your book launch and flight path figured out yet? If your brain is a bit overloaded, here's a condensed version of this section to help you sort things out.

Book launch and marketing summary:

Pre-work: Be gaining newsletter subscribers and fans through a reader magnet or other appropriate means (such as blogging or social media).

1. Gain early reviews and launch buzz through ARC readers.
2. Follow good strategies to get honest reviews, including asking for reviews in your book's back matter and thanking those who've left reviews.
3. Consider seeking endorsements, particularly from authors and influencers you already have a connection to and whose names your readers respect.
4. Guest blogging, running your own blog, doing blog tours, and being engaged on social media are all potential sources of new fans, ways to nurture your current fan base, and ways

to waste time and stress you out. Remember your goals and available time.

5. Physical marketing tools such as bookmarks can be very useful for gaining readers or reminding them of your books. They are helpful in situations where someone asks where they can buy your book. Business cards are for networking with industry professionals.

6. Cross-promotion through newsletter swaps and services such as BookFunnel and StoryOrigin can help you reach readers who read in your genre. Joining with authors in group releases and anthologies is a way to share fan bases and reach new readers.

7. Book promotion services such as BookBub, ENT, and Freebooksy can help spread the word about sales and freebies. This can gain new readers and reviews and earn money, though you won't always break even or see a long-term benefit.

8. Running ad campaigns on Amazon, Facebook, and BookBub can be a tremendous marketing tool, can be combined with great craft and packaging to forge a career, or can be a stressful endeavor and waste of money. Using ads effectively is a skill set that requires study and trial and error and is not a magic bullet.

9. Plan your launch ahead of time and don't rush it. Decide on the best strategy for you. Publishing is a game of trial and error, so don't get frustrated if the launch isn't a wild success.

10. Pre-orders are a common tactic to gain sales before the release.

11. Winning contests and attaining best seller status are goals for the driven author. The tactics used to achieve these may help with marketing in the long-run. Contests and best seller status may or may not in themselves actually benefit you otherwise.

12. Giveaways and newsletter building efforts can help increase

your reach but may cost or inflate your newsletter with disinterested fans (or fans only interested in *free* things).

If you can only focus on a few things, focus on building your newsletter subscribers list with good subscribers (those who already like your type of book and so are likely to buy and enjoy yours), do a cover reveal (if fiction), print bookmarks, and get ARC readers. Later, you can run ads, do sales, and try out book promotion services.

Part Ten

Getting the Book Published and Stocked

Chapter 68

Getting the book published and stocked

If you didn't read the Marketing Pre-release section, go back and do that. A lot of the things you'll need to input into your retailer's site are covered there, particularly in the "Branding the Book" chapter. You also need your completed book files from the "Getting Your Book Ready" section.

So this is it. The part where you finally upload your book to retailers and hit publish. It's kind of a scary moment, and an exciting one. So let's get started.

Way back in the beginning of this book, you decided which retailers you were going to distribute through—KDP only, wide, IngramSpark, or an aggregator such as D2D or Smashwords. Because of how many stores there are, and the fact that the process is fairly similar (except for IngramSpark, which is discussed in its own section), I'm only going to walk you through KDP. I will give some comments specific to Apple Books, however.

Take another look at a published book page if you want, because we're about to input the information to make that page yours.

Chapter 69

Retailer account setup

The first thing required is to set up an account on the retailer(s) of your choice. In addition to the typical requests of name, email, password, and physical address, you will need to establish a payment method and fill out a tax interview. You will find the websites of several major retailers provided for you in the References and Resources section. Please know that for Amazon, you are setting up an account through Kindle Direct Publishing. You do not publish through your personal account. I have a few notes about Apple Books at the end of the chapter.

Payment methods

Direct deposit is recommended for the payment method. You can opt for wire transfer or checks, but you must meet a minimum threshold to be sent payment via checks, which is $100 (US). There is no minimum payment for direct deposit. When you set up direct deposit, you will need your bank account information, including bank name and routing number (in short, have a check handy, as the information is on there). If you set up a separate bank account for your writing business, be sure to use that instead of your personal bank account.

Tax interview

You will also need to go through their tax interview process, which they walk you through. You will need a tax identification number: a Social Security Number (SSN), Employer Identification Number (EIN), or Individual Tax Identification Number (ITIN). The EIN is for businesses, so unless you set that up, you will use your SSN. The ITIN is for certain resident or nonresident aliens. It doesn't take long to set up an author account, but the information will be validated with the IRS, and if the tax ID is new, this might cause a delay in processing.

Amazon and other retailers do not withhold taxes for you. You will receive a 1099-MISC from them.

————

Apple Books is more complicated than the other retailers and aggregators, and the verification process takes time. (Reedsy, in their article on uploading to Apple Books, recommends going through an aggregator until you're earning enough from Apple Books to warrant uploading through them.) To publish your ebook to Apple Books, create an iTunes Connect account and an Apple ID (a personal account you might have if you own an Apple device). When your accounts are ready, enter your banking and tax information in Apple Connect.

That done, navigate to https://authors.apple.com/epub-upload and sign in with your Apple Connect account. Your next step depends on your format. If you have Pages, you proceed from there. If you have an epub and you have a Mac, download the iTunes Producer and use it to move through the publishing process. If you have an epub and don't have a Mac, utilize the Publishing Portal. If you have a Word doc or mobi, they offer file conversion or help finding a service to do that.

————

Once you've set up your author account(s) and have saved all your usernames and passwords in a safe place, explore your author dashboard. In KDP, you have Bookshelf (where you manage your titles), Reports, Community (a forum for questions), and Marketing pages. Once you're familiar with your dashboard, you can start setting up your book pages. We'll start with the process for ebooks, then move on to print books.

References and Resources

Amazon Kindle Direct Publishing. https://kdp.amazon.com/en_US/.

Amazon KDP Payments. https://kdp.amazon.com/en_US/help/topic/G200641050.

Apple Books. https://authors.apple.com.

Barnes & Noble. "How to Self-Publish with Us." Accessed March 24, 2022. https://press.barnesandnoble.com/how-it-works.

Draft2Digital. https://www.draft2digital.com.

Google Play. https://play.google.com/books/publish.

IngramSpark. https://myaccount.ingramspark.com/Account/Signup.

IRS. "Taxpayer Identification Numbers (TIN)." https://www.irs.gov/individuals/international-taxpayers/taxpayer-identification-numbers-tin.

Kobo. https://kobowritinglife.zendesk.com/hc/en-us.

Reedsy. "How to Publish (and Sell) on Apple Books in 2022." December 31, 2021. https://blog.reedsy.com/how-to-publish-on-apple-books/.

Smashwords. https://www.smashwords.com/signup/.

Smashwords. "How to Publish and Distribute Ebooks with Smash-words." https://www.smashwords.com/about/how_to_publish_on_smashwords.

Chapter 70

Creating an ebook title

Login to your KDP account (not your personal Amazon store account) and go to your dashboard. Near the top, you will see a "Create" button. Click that. You will be taken to a page of options: Kindle ebook, Paperback, Hardcover, Series page, and Kindle Vella. Choose "Kindle ebook."

You will be taken to your new book's home, so to speak. You will see three tabs: Kindle ebook Details; Kindle ebook Content; and Kindle ebook Pricing. We'll work our way through all three before hitting publish.

KINDLE EBOOK DETAILS

Language: Select the language of your book. For KDP's list of supported languages, see https://kdp.amazon.com/en_US/help/topic/G200673300.

Title and subtitle (optional): Type in the name of your book, and, if it has one, the subtitle.

Series: If this book is part of a series, add that information here. It can be part of the main series or a connected book.

Edition number (optional): If this is not the first edition, put the edition number here.

Author: Put your author name here.

Contributors: Add any additional authors, if applicable.

Description: This is where your book description/blurb goes. Use the formatting tools (italics and bold, for example) to make this readable and nice looking.

Publishing rights: If this is an original work of yours, or a book you inherited the rights to (for instance, your grandfather's memoirs), indicate that you own the rights. If this a public domain work (you didn't create it and it is no longer in copyright) then indicate that.

Keywords: Enter your seven keywords here.

Categories: Choose two categories.

Age and grade range: This field is optional, so unless your book is in the children's category, leave it blank. If you want to list your book in the Children's or Teen & Young Adult categories on Amazon.com or Amazon.co.uk, you must choose at least one Juvenile Category. For Children's categories, you'll need to set the minimum recommended reading age to 0–11 years old. For Teen & Young Adult categories, set the minimum recommended reading age to 13–17 years old. Titles with a Juvenile Category and a minimum recommended age of 12 may be categorized in Children's or Teens, depending on other information about the book. For more information on setting age and grade range, see this KDP Help page: https://kdp.amazon.com/en_US/help/topic/G201506310.

Pre-order: Select whether you want to publish your book "now" (at the end of the setup) or set a pre-order date in the future.

If you choose pre-order, when setup is finished and you click "Publish the Pre-order," a page for the book will show up on Amazon, and people can pre-order your book. Please note the date, time, and **time zone** your final files must be uploaded. The upload deadline is a few days before the book releases. The time zone is GMT, so be careful not to miss the deadline by thinking the deadline is in your time zone or the Pacific time zone, as for the Kindle Countdown Deals. If you miss the deadline, the pre-order will be canceled, you will have to set up a new book, and you will be banned from pre-orders for a year (don't ask me how I know this).

———

Please double-check all information carefully. Certain fields, such as the title and ISBN, cannot be changed once the book is published.

———

Click Save as Draft to stop here or Save and Continue to keep going to the Kindle ebook Content tab.

KINDLE EBOOK CONTENT

Manuscript: Upload your manuscript and choose a DRM setting.

Concerning DRM (Digital Rights Management): There are varying opinions on this, but here is what KDP says:

"DRM (Digital Rights Management) is intended to inhibit unauthorized distribution of the Kindle file of your book. Some authors want to encourage readers to share their work, and choose not to have DRM applied to their book. If you choose DRM, customers will still be able to lend the book to another user for a short period, and can also purchase the book as a gift for another user from the Kindle store. Important: Once you publish your book, you cannot change its DRM setting."

Many recommend choosing no (and I think most do), but that is up to you.

Upload your Kindle ebook cover: Upload the JPEG or TIFF file of your cover.

Kindle ebook preview: Preview your book and check for errors.

Kindle ebook ISBN: Provide your own ISBN or accept their free one. Add your publisher name (your imprint), if using one.

Click Save as Draft to stop there or Save and Continue to keep going to the Kindle ebook Pricing tab.

KINDLE EBOOK PRICING

KDP Select enrollment: Indicate whether or not you want to enroll your ebook in KDP Select.

Territories: Do you have worldwide rights to sell your book? If this is an original work of yours, and you haven't sold the rights to anyone else, then click yes, you have worldwide rights.

Primary marketplace: If you're in the US, choose Amazon.com. If not, choose the appropriate Amazon marketplace.

Pricing, royalties, and distribution: Choose a 35% or 70% royalty and set your price for your main marketplace. KDP will suggest prices for other marketplaces based on current exchange rates. Use those or set your own. Adjust prices to end with the standard 99 cents, if desired.

Book lending: Indicate whether you want to allow customers to lend their copy of your ebook to friends and family for up to fourteen days.

Read the terms and conditions.

Click Save as Draft, Submit for Pre-order, or Publish, as desired.

Repeat for other retailers, if desired.

Chapter 71

Print book setup

To set up your print book, login to your KDP account (not your personal Amazon store account) and go to your dashboard. Near the top, you will see a "Create" button. Click that. You will be taken to a page of options: Kindle ebook, Paperback, Hardcover, Series page, and Kindle Vella. Choose "Paperback." (If you choose to do a hardback, you will simply choose "Hardback" instead.)

As for the Kindle ebook setup, you will see three tabs: Paperback Details; Paperback Content; and Paperback Rights and Pricing. We'll work our way through all three before hitting publish.

PAPERBACK DETAILS

Language: Select the language of your book.

Title and subtitle (optional): Type in the name of your book, and, if it has one, the subtitle.

Series: If this book is part of a series, add that information here. It can be part of the main series or a connected book.

Edition number (optional): If this is not the first edition, put the edition number here.

Author: Put your author name here.

Contributors: Add any additional authors, if applicable.

Description: This is where your book description/blurb goes. Use the formatting tools (italics and bold, for example) to make this readable and nice looking.

Publishing rights: If this is an original work of yours, or a book you inherited the rights to, check that you own the rights. If this a public domain work (you didn't create it and it is no longer in copyright), then check that.

Keywords: Enter your seven keywords here.

Categories: Choose two categories.

Large print: Check the box if your book matches the large print specifications. If not, don't check it.

Adult content: Declare whether the book contains language, situations, or images inappropriate for children under 18 years of age or not.

————

Please double-check all this information carefully. Certain fields, such as the title and ISBN, cannot be changed once the book is published.

————

Click Save as Draft to stop there or Save and Continue to keep going to the Paperback Content tab.

PAPERBACK CONTENT

ISBN: Provide your own ISBN or accept their free one.

Publication date: Leave blank if your book has not been published before. This is not a pre-order, so you don't set the date it publishes. KDP adds the date your book goes live (up for sale).

Print options: Select your paper, ink, and trim size.

Upload your manuscript: This will be your final, formatted, proofread file, preferably a PDF file.

Upload your cover: Upload your print-ready PDF cover file.

Book preview: Launch the previewer to check your book's look and see if any errors were found by KDP. Make sure this is your final, final file. Keep a note of the last typo you fixed and check that it is correct in this uploaded file.

Summary: Contains a summary of your decisions and the print cost of your book (this is the cost to print it, not the sell price). Make a record of your print cost.

Click Save as Draft to stop there or Save and Continue to keep going to the Paperback Rights and Pricing tab.

PAPERBACK RIGHTS AND PRICING

Territories: Do you have worldwide rights to sell your book? If this is an original work of yours, and you haven't sold the rights to anyone else, then click yes, you have worldwide rights.

Primary marketplace: If you're in the US, choose Amazon.com. If not, choose the appropriate Amazon marketplace.

Pricing, royalties, and distribution: Set your price for your main marketplace. KDP will suggest prices for other marketplaces. Use those or set your own. Adjust prices to end with the standard 99 cents, if desired. Choose whether you want to include it in Expanded Distribution or not (you won't click this if you're also using IngramSpark).

Read the terms and conditions, then hit Save as Draft.

If you want to order a physical proof copy, do so now. I recommend this for at least your first book. You can check that the cover is correct, the paper color and cover finish are what you want, and proofread it.

When you're ready (you've checked your proof), click Publish Your Paperback Book. The book will be live in a few hours to a few days.

Repeat the process for IngramSpark, if applicable.

Done?

This is where you celebrate! Or freak out, depending on your personality. Or you can be like Mr. Darcy, who wasn't the type to overflow in mirth, and be quietly joyous. However you process major achievements, do so and then come back for the "after publication" things you need to know.

Chapter 72

Reports, payments, and taxes

You're entering the danger zone now—the reports tab. *How many books have I sold since I checked an hour ago?* This is a struggle during releases and promotions. Okay, everyday.

Reports

Your retailer dashboard has a Reports page where you can see how many copies of your book have sold (or pages read, if in KU). In KDP, you can use the standard Reports tab in your dashboard or use the nice beta version (there's a notice about it at the top of the Reports page).

For the various reporting pages, you can set the parameters to look at sales for different time periods and for different books. This is handy because it allows you to see how your books are doing in comparison to one another, get a feel for if different promotions or marketing tactics are working, and so on.

As tempting as it is, I don't recommend checking your reports more than once a day (if that). Remember that writers write, so choose to write rather than obsess over sales.

If you hang out in online writer groups, especially in 20Book-sto50K® on Facebook, you'll see mentions of Book Report and see pretty graphs showing earnings (many of which will tempt you to despair or envy). You may then look at your KDP dashboard report, and at their beta report, and start to wonder where people are coming up with those pretty graphs. Let me save you the stress. They're using Book Report.

Book Report (https://www.getbookreport.com) is a browser extension that connects to your KDP dashboard and makes your sales data easier to see and analyze. It helps you draw conclusions on which books are working and so forth. It's not a necessity (I don't use it). I mention it only so you'll know it when you see it. They have a free tier, a free trial, and a paid monthly plan. There are other, similar options as well, including ScribeCount (https://www.scribecount.com).

Payments and taxes

So when does the money start rolling in for your masterpiece? For KDP, it's 60 days. Other distributors may vary (some are 45 days), so check your terms. You'll get paid according to the method you set up. As a reminder, don't spend all your earnings right off. Remember to put some aside for taxes and some for future writing expenses.

If you are co-authoring a book and want to know about royalty splitting, references for that are in the anthologies and group release chapter.

Congratulations! Unless you've been skipping chapters, you've made it quite deep into this guide. Thanks for hanging around. We're shifting now to post-publication events and marketing, including getting your work into bookstores.

Chapter 73

Getting the published book out there

The smell of books is still appealing. Most of our marketing efforts so far, though, are more likely to result in ebook sales and KU page reads than print sales. Generally speaking, print is "easier" to sell in person than online. In this section, we'll talk about tactics geared more toward print sales and name recognition than ebook sales. We'll speak of getting into bookstores and libraries, selling at live events, and touch on related topics.

We'll start with ordering your very own copies of your masterpiece: author copies.

Author copies

Once your book goes live, you can order author copies. These are different from the proof copies because these are the same as the ones customers get when purchasing from the store. Remember that proof copies have a line across the cover proclaiming what they are and cannot be resold.

Author copies are resalable and are bought at print cost. You don't earn a royalty on author copies. You can order author copies to put on your own shelf, to give away, to sell in person, and sell direct through your website or a shop like Etsy.

It takes a few weeks to get these in (it seems like KDP is slower about getting authors their copies than customers their copies!). So if you want print copies on the official launch date, you might consider either setting up on IngramSpark and ordering through there early, or doing an early, "soft" (unannounced) launch on KDP of your print book only and ordering author copies. Ebooks and KU reads tend to be the biggest part of a launch, so it's not uncommon for authors to do a soft print launch.

Be sure to keep track of your author copies: how many copies you order, how many you keep for yourself, give away, and sell. Also, record the cost of each book to you—the print cost plus taxes and shipping and handling.

Now that your book is live, and you have copies, what next? How do you get it into bookstores? What other options are there for selling your print book?

Chapter 74

Sell sheet

If you want to pitch your book to libraries, bookstores, and subscription book box companies, you might need a sell sheet, sometimes called a tip sheet. This is a one-page document that gives the bookstore buyer or librarian all the information they need to help them decide whether they want your book. So it's basically like your Amazon retail page, only it's nicely designed, fits on one page of paper, and contains your marketing plans.

What do you put on a sell sheet? It depends somewhat on whether you're writing fiction or nonfiction and if you're also using the sell sheet to promote yourself as a speaker. But here are some things to include:

Sell sheet:

1. A high resolution image of your book cover (use a 300 dpi image rather than the 72 dpi image used for online, as you want it to print well).
2. A book summary.
3. Author bio and, if desired, a professional headshot.
4. Book metadata and distributor: title, author, publisher,

series, ISBN, print page length, publish date, trim size, format, price, distributor.
5. Marketing information: genre, target audience, BISAC category.
6. Strong endorsement(s), reviews, awards, accolades.
7. Contact information: name, email, possibly phone number, website, social media.
8. Marketing plans and publicity.
9. Speaking experience (if applicable).

You might also include key selling points, the book's purpose (or theme), sales data, marketing plans, or design elements that pertain to the book (an illustration for a children's book, for instance). For a nonfiction project, explain why you are an expert on the topic.

You can create a sell sheet in a word processor, but it might be easier to create it in a design program, such as Canva. You can also hire someone to do this. The sell sheet doesn't have to be complex in design, but it should look nice.

Chapter 75

Bookstores and libraries

To sell books in bookstores, you need a book that bookstores can sell.

I hope you caught the double meaning in that and didn't think I was being facetious. Space is valuable in physical stores (just as a book's position in the search results is valuable in online retailers). Traditional publishers have sales teams who work to get their books in stores and positioned for greater notice—they pay extra to have books face outward on the shelves and on the endcaps. Stores don't take just any book; they want books they think will sell. This means that bookstores, especially chains, are unlikely to choose a run-of-the-mill indie book by an unknown author. No offense, but you have to understand what the person on the other end of a deal is thinking. They need to know this is in their best interest. Your ego, your dream, is not their problem.

Can you get into bookstores? Yes. And it depends. What do you mean by "getting into bookstores?" Do you mean every Barnes & Noble in the US has your book? Walmart? Or that the local independent bookstore carries your book? The former two are unlikely for most indie authors. The latter is quite possible.

Practically speaking, there are three ways your books can get into bookstores: bookstore buyers can order the book from a wholesaler catalogue (which you can get into through IngramSpark); customers can specifically request that the store order your book; and you can contract with bookstores to sell your book on consignment, usually at an independent bookstore.

The problem is not making your book available to bookstores to consider (it's in the catalogue) but making it desirable. That's all craft and marketing and so beyond what we're talking about here. Let's look more at the nuts-and-bolts aspect of things.

What kind of bookstores are there and how do they choose books? Are any indie friendly? There are chain stores (like Barnes & Noble), independent bookstores, the racks at the airport, and other kinds of retailers who also carry books (such as Walmart). These have buyers who, according to Books-A-Million's description, "review thousands of books each year for placement in [their] stores. They work closely with publishers and distributors to review all new titles and backlists. Reviewing galleys and marketing materials, along with publisher presentations, allows them to select the books our customers are looking for." So it's tight competition for shelf space.

As for being friendly to indies, it varies. Books-A-Million does not take print-on-demand titles. Barnes & Noble will consider indie titles (you can read more about this here: https://www.barnesandnobleinc.com/publishers-authors/sell-your-book-at-barnes-noble/). Some independent bookstores are happy to support indies, but not all. Stores will likely say on their website how they acquire books.

Let's see what Barnes & Noble says about selling indie books as an example of what a bookstore is likely to want.

They state that "if you have a compelling marketing plan or expect significant media/publicity that will drive customers to book retailers looking for your title, you can email us at sjamison@bn.com." They request you include certain information in the email, including ISBN, name of wholesaler/distributor, and details on marketing/media/publicity. Their buyers will consider the request and reply in 5-6 weeks.

They go on to give a checklist of things your book needs. It must have an ISBN (one you purchased, not a free one), as they use ISBNs to track inventory and sales. Books also need a barcode with the ISBN and price embedded; the price should be printed on the barcode. It needs to be available through a wholesaler and priced competitively. This pricing can be challenging for POD titles, as the print cost is higher than for offset books. They want a description of your marketing plan, publicity, what makes your book unique, etc. I imagine they also want to know that your ebook is available on bn.com and is not exclusive to KDP.

So that's Barnes & Noble. Check the websites of your favorite stores and see what they say about acquiring books. As the market changes and indie publishing grows in acceptance, the situation may improve.

I'd also like to whisper that you can talk to your local store about ordering your book just for itself. A staff member at a local chain store, upon learning I was an author, suggested I contact their headquarters about my book because I was a *local* author. It might be possible to get into a local store as a local author. Your book might be in the local author section and not with your comparable authors, but it's a start.

For independent bookstores, work on a sell sheet that addresses the things Barnes & Noble asks for. Find out who to talk to about buying books and ask if you can send your information to them.

This information is for stores ordering your book to stock on the shelves. Remember that your fans can ask them to order a copy to purchase. So a fan can buy your book from a bookstore even if it's not stocked there.

Also, when considering bookstores, remember that stores typically order from a wholesaler's catalogue. IngramSpark can get you into the catalogue. When you set up with IngramSpark, you choose a suggested retail price and a wholesale discount. You also choose a return option— Return, Return-destroy, No Return. Your choices here make your book more or less appealing to buyers. But remember that books set to "return" can be returned, costing you money. So don't be too keen to get your book into stores unless you *know*, not hope, that it's going to sell. It can cost you money as well as pride if it doesn't.

Convincing buyers to order your book isn't the only way to get it into stores. Some independent bookstores and other local businesses may be willing to take your books on consignment. You retain ownership of the books, and the stores try to sell them for you. They keep a percentage (typically 40-50%, according to Sedwick's book) and handle sales tax. You can talk to local stores, stores near where you grew up, ones at a location associated with your books, or anywhere suitable. You will have to get the books to the store, and possibly take the books back if they don't sell or your consignment agreement ends. Some stores might charge a marketing or setup fee and disclaim responsibility for theft, damage, or lost books. As always, read the contract carefully. And consider the cost of your book, plus shipping and handling, etc. to make sure you're actually making a profit under the terms of the consignment. If you know you're going to sell a lot of books, then you might look into offset printing to reduce the cost of each print unit.

Libraries

Libraries work in a similar manner to bookstores. They can order from the catalogues. Librarians can also take requests from patrons to order books—so remind your fans they can ask the library to carry your books. Many people discover their favorite authors at the local library and go on to purchase their books. Even those who don't have still been touched by them. So getting into libraries is a great thing.

You can also send your sell sheet to the proper librarian to request they carry the book. If you're interested in public speaking, you could ask to host a program for the library. You might be allowed to sell books at the event.

To get your book into bookstores and libraries:

- Put it up on IngramSpark to get into the wholesaler catalogues. Choose your settings wisely.
- Make sure the book adheres to the required technical specifications: ISBN, proper barcode, etc.
- Hone your craft and marketing such that your full priced books sell enough to impress the stores.
- Create a sell sheet and approach the appropriate people at bookstores and libraries to pitch your work.
- Consider asking if independent bookstores and gift shops will carry your book on consignment.

References and Resources

Barnes & Noble. "BN.com and Retail Store Placement for Books." Accessed March 22, 2022. https://www.barnesandnobleinc.com/ publishers-authors/sell-your-book-at-barnes-noble/.

Book-A-Million. "BAM Retail Store Title Submissions." Accessed March 24, 2022. https://m.booksamillion.com/publishers/books.html.

Sedwick, Helen. *Self-Publisher's Legal Handbook*. Ten Gallon Press, 2017.

Chapter 76

Subscription book boxes

Some book lovers enjoy a curated collection of books shipped to their door and so use a subscription book box service. For a set price each month, or quarter, these companies send their subscribers a book of the month, often with goodies of some kind (from tea to trinkets to signed bookplates and bookmarks). But how do authors get involved in this process?

This is a tricky question, as it depends on the individuals running the book boxes. Some may accept queries from indie authors, some may only choose traditionally published books. I did some searching online for book box subscriptions companies. None of the ones I looked at had a place for authors to inquire about having their books included in the box, and it looked as if their featured books were all traditionally published. But this doesn't mean that you, as an indie, can't get into one. You just have to spend time looking for the right one. And, you may hate to hear it, but you need to know the right people.

So get your sell sheet ready and hunt up subscription boxes for your genre and target audience, and listen out for book box owners at conferences and in author groups. When you're searching, try specific categories of books. Some boxes target a particular genre, such as YA fantasy, noblebright fantasy, or mystery. When you find likely companies, use the contact form or email address given to send a query with the information from your sell sheet.

Because most companies only want books that have proven themselves to be good sellers, consider waiting until your book has earned its place in the market to put it forward for book boxes and even for bookstores. Having a lot of quality reviews, a good sales record, and a loyal fan base you can introduce to the book box (helping the company expand its reach won't hurt their consideration of your book) will be a huge help to you. Remember that the company wants to know what you can do for them.

My experience with book subscription boxes is limited to one company which has a noblebright fantasy theme. Companies may vary, but this one paid 50% of the retail price of the book plus shipping. Whatever was left (if anything), was the author's to keep. This means the print cost of your book determines whether you make a profit, take a loss, or simply get extra exposure and bragging rights. I also needed bookplates, which were not paid for. I paid to get those printed and shipped. (A bookplate is a sticker or card of some type signed by the author that a reader can stick into the print book.)

As with any option where your print books are sold by someone else, you may not make much money, but a subscription book box is great for exposure, building credibility, and can lead to readers buying your other books.

You can even create a subscription box on your own or through a company such as Cratejoy (https://www.cratejoy.com/sell/marketplace/). Please note that I have no personal experience with this company and thus cannot comment on the quality of their service.

Chapter 77

Live events

Have you seen the episode of *The Andy Griffith Show* where Helen writes a children's book and has to choose between being a famous author traveling around doing book signings and staying with Andy and the children in Mayberry? If you did, take heart, it's very unlikely, whether you are traditionally published or indie, that you will be called upon to travel far and wide for your writing career. Yes, it does happen, but likely only for the big, big names. The cost of travel for a book tour is too high for publishers to do this for authors they aren't certain are going to bring in a lot of fans. And for most authors, there's not going to be a lot of fans showing up at events far and wide. Or near. We know that, but we still do events anyway . . . authors are a very hopeful lot.

What about me as an indie author? Should I participate in live events?

It depends on what you want. It can increase name recognition among fans and other authors and build relationships with bookstore owners. It might sell books and lead to happy, devoted fans. Or it might not. It *will* force you to work on your presentation of your author self and your books. You will need to tell person after person about them, after all (assuming the event actually draws a crowd, which isn't guaranteed).

Some things to consider when deciding on a particular in-person event are your time; money to get a space/attend/buy stock/get a good display/etc.; how much stock you must sell to break even; taxes; whether your target audience is likely to be there; and your own selling skills. Any event is going to require your time. You might also need help getting books into the store and want company for the event. You might have to pay for the event, and you will need to purchase stock and create a compelling display. You might also want bookmarks or other swag. You will need to collect sales tax and remit that properly wherever you go. You'll also want to consider how likely it is that people will show up to the event and whether they are in your target audience. Do you have enough product for people to buy to make it worth your while? The more books you have, the more seriously people will take you and the more opportunities you have to interest people. Are you comfortable talking about your book and addressing strangers? If not, then go to in-person events! The experience will be painful but a good one. Practice beforehand and enjoy it as much as you can.

What in-person events are there? What is a book signing like?

In-person events include book tours, book signings, launch parties, speaking engagements, craft fairs, Renaissance faires, conferences, and conventions, among others.

A book signing is when an author sets up a table or booth some-where to sell and sign copies of his or her book. This can be at a local bookstore, library, school, writer's conference, or elsewhere.

It varies by venue, but you usually have a table or part of a table to yourself and have to create a display of your book(s) in that space. It's important to find out beforehand how much room you have and plan accordingly. You might want a plain setup, or a pretty tablecloth and dish of candy, or a fancy themed setup. You'll want some way to display the books so people can see the covers; marketing materials; and ways to transact business (cash or card reader). You can sit or stand (standing is recommended) at your table and greet people who stop by. You tell them about your book and answer questions. You may or may not sell anything. You usually get to chat with the other authors during lulls. But each event is different, and I've only been to small, simple affairs.

Many libraries have open houses where they invite "local" authors to sign books. These "local" authors often come from several hours away. I've done several library open houses, at three different libraries, and while it's somewhat fun and a good networking opportunity, it's seldom profitable and can be disappointing when you sit for hours and sell very little. People don't go to libraries to spend money, after all. It is a good start, though, if you want to get into doing live events, as creating a good table setup and getting the hang of talking to people about your book takes practice. These tend to be free or low cost, making them less of a risk as well.

If you've been invited to a speaking engagement, you will likely have the opportunity to sell books at the "back of the room." People will already know who you are, which is a huge help. Some speakers actually write books mostly for these "back of the room" sales.

Launch parties celebrate the launch of the book and may have a theme matching the book. It can be part fun and celebration with friends and family, and part business with books available for sale. If you have the time, money, space, and party planning expertise, this could be a fun and profitable way to celebrate.

Writing conferences and conventions are other opportunities to sell your book in person—as an attendee or vendor. Conferences often have tables where attendees can set up to sell their books at no extra charge. Sometimes you can attend as a vendor only to sell books and merchandise; there is a cost for this. Homeschool conventions, Renaissance faires, comic conventions, and others may allow you to purchase a space to sell books. Some of these are very strict about setup, requiring a booth, decor, costumes, and possibly even "appropriate" speech patterns (talk like a pirate or merchant from the Middle Ages, for instance). From what I've heard, conventions and faires can be great places to sell books (especially if you were already going to them before you became an author and so understand the people there). Some may want you to have liability insurance or to be self-insured.

Speakers at conferences tend to have good book sales because the attendees "know" and trust them, or want to support them. Some conferences have a store to handle sales, some don't, and in those cases, it would be helpful to have someone with you to handle sales. It's difficult to work on transactions, sign copies, and listen to people who are trying to talk to you, without messing something up.

A book tour is essentially a string of book signings, where the author or a group of authors travel to different locations and set up in bookstores or other venues with the expectation that readers will come buy their books. As an indie author, you have to foot the bill for this and set it up yourself with the bookstore or wherever you are going. As always, be careful of scams, as some companies will offer to set you up with a tour, promise fans and fame, and flatter you with what a great book you have (always beware the flatterer), but may not be able to deliver.

Logistics of live events

For any live event, you'll need to consider the logistics. If you're going to a bookstore for a signing, will they order copies of your book for the store that you then sign? That's a risk for them because they don't know if the books will sell, and if the books don't, they might return them through IngramSpark, and you'll be charged. If you bring the stock to sell, the bookstore isn't out-of-pocket, but you have to lug around the books and handle the money and sales taxes yourself. You also need to ask yourself why anyone would come to buy your books at the venue you choose. How will they find out about it? And how are you benefiting the bookstore you set up in? They will want to know what's in it for them. Are you going to bring in customers who will buy books from them? Or only family and friends who want to support you but may not be planning on spending any money? Will you need help setting up your display, carrying books, handling transactions, etc.? Someone to watch your booth while you go to the bathroom? (You can ask other authors or event staff for this last bit.)

Live events can be places of great shame: some people are so creative with their displays, with brilliantly organized, aesthetically appealing, marketing-savvy displays, while some of us are just happy to have shown up with a spare pen and change. But we made it! What you need for your display depends on the type of event you're going to and what you want. A simple signing at a local bookstore requires very little. A booth at a summer library event in a large city, or at a Renaissance faire, may require a lot.

Here's a general list of good things to bring to a live event:

1. Your books. The amount needed varies by venue. I'm sorry I can't give a solid number! Probably no more than twenty total copies at a small event. Genres sell differently; the number of event guests varies, so you might ask an author who's been to the event before or the event coordinator what is normal.
2. Pens to sign your book. Each author has their own favorite pen for this. Figure out beforehand what works and bring spares. Also figure out how you will sign books—just your name or with some message?
3. A notepad for customers to write their name on so you can be sure you spell it correctly.
4. Payment methods: cash and a card reader. Most authors don't take checks. If you plan on using a card reader, get your products set up in it beforehand and make sure you will have Wi-Fi or cell phone data to use it (though some may work in an offline mode).
5. Bookplates. This is for fans who already have your print book. It depends on the type of bookplate, but you might need a different style of pen for this. I ended up using a Sharpie Ultra Fine marker for my sticker bookplates.
6. Display stands, boxes, etc. to display and organize your books. You can purchase book stands (like those used in stores) or use boxes or crates. You can use picture frame holders to display single books as well.
7. Tablecloth. You might need a nice tablecloth to cover the white, plastic tables you'll be at for some events.

8. Bookmarks. You'll also want bookmarks so people can take home a reminder of your book.
9. Business cards. These are for professional contacts (not random strangers at your table).
10. Water or a snack for yourself. Some provide this, but you might need to bring your own.
11. Price information. Price tags, a card with information, or a poster. It varies. But do have your prices clearly stated.
12. A QR code directing readers to your ebooks and audiobooks. This can be on your bookmarks or a separate card or sign. This is great for those who prefer these formats, as they can purchase them immediately.
13. Your elevator pitch and other marketing copy.
14. A booth buddy.
15. Comfortable shoes. It's recommended that you stand beside your table instead of sit behind it, as you want to appear inviting.

You might also consider a dolly or cart for your books and supplies, eye-catching signs (perhaps vinyl to last well, or a poster in a thin picture frame), and a book- and event-appropriate costume to make you stand out or serve as a conversation starter.

Personally, I think live events can be good experiences. But do weigh your time and budget into your decision. Can you afford to spend two hours of drive time to hang out at a three-hour event and make only $50, if that? Some events cost money for the space. You have to buy stock and, if you choose, table decor and other items. I recommend starting at free, local events.

Chapter 78

Selling direct and selling merchandise

Selling direct is something I've been hearing about increasingly lately. Authors are wanting to decrease their dependency on retailers and earn more profit, and so are starting to sell books directly. This usually means through their website, using a website plug-in or a storefront (such as Shopify) to handle the monetary transaction, and a book delivery service to deliver the book.

In addition to connecting directly with customers, selling direct gives you more control over price—you can charge over $9.99 for a large box set without being penalized with a 35% royalty as you would on KDP—and you can use coupons. You also get the money from the sale almost instantly rather than waiting the 45 or 60 days for stores to pay you.

What can you sell direct? You can sell ebooks (if they are not in KU), print books, audiobooks, signed print copies, and other merchandise.

If you have character art or a great cover background (no title) to serve as artwork, you can partner with companies to sell print-on-demand merchandise, including stickers, mugs, totes, t-shirts, and whatever else strikes your fancy. If you do this, be sure you have the rights to use the artwork in this manner. Check with your designer to be sure. You might have to pay extra for this right.

Selling ebooks and print books directly

This is not difficult to do, but it will take a little research, time, and a few "how-to" articles or videos to get accounts set up and the book delivery service connected to the storefront. Usually, you set up a page on your website showing the products for sale. Depending on whether you have a plug-in and how money is collected, the visitor might stay on your site or be transferred to the storefront of the company handling the monetary transaction to then complete the transaction. Storefronts I've come across include Shopify, Payhip, PayPal, and Square, but there are others. WooCommerce is a WordPress plug-in to handle this sort of thing. Some storefronts charge a small fee per transaction (you don't pay anything unless you actually sell products), while others charge a monthly fee (you pay regardless of whether you earn any money from sales). Some may or may not collect sales tax for you. If not, you will need to handle that yourself. Note that you have a storefront through the company (I have a Payhip storefront) as well as on your website. So you can have the same products on your website, on the storefront of the company that handles your transactions, and on Etsy too! Yes, don't forget you can set up on Etsy as well.

Once the financial transaction is complete, your product will need to be delivered. BookFunnel is a popular service to deliver ebook and audiobook files to customers. They also handle customer service issues, which could potentially save you a lot of time. Many authors already have BookFunnel, so it's convenient, and the ebook file delivery is free. Audiobook delivery is in beta and will eventually cost. You will need to connect the storefront to BookFunnel so that BookFunnel automatically sends customers an informational email to tell them how to get their product. (If you'd like to see how this works, you can check out my Payhip store here: https://payhip.com/EJKitchensAuthor. You can use the coupon code LJZBY8PBCK for 25% off all products.)

If you're selling print books, you can keep a stock of books at home and fulfill orders as they come in. You can sign the books and add book-marks or character art, if you like. I once ordered a couple of books through an author's website and was happy to find the personal touch of a signature in each book. Running to the post office can be a hassle, however, but you can print shipping labels at home and have the packages picked up. Another, less personal option, is to use a service such as Lulu to fulfill the print order for you, such that you never see the book.

As for other merchandise, authors are connecting with designers and print-on-demand companies to create products, including shirts, totes, stickers, and mugs. Redbubble, Zazzle, Printify, and Printful are some print-on-demand companies. There's a lot to consider before jumping into this, though, so you'll have to do your own research. Again, you must make sure you have the rights to use any images for this type of commercial use.

And if someone contacts *you* about creating merchandise connected to your story world, congratulations! Just remember that your characters and settings are *your* intellectual property. Anyone wanting to make and sell products revolving around your IP should get a license from you. You can handle this however you want. You don't have to charge. Just be aware that you have a say on the use of your IP. *USA Today* bestselling author Elisa Kova has a web page devoted to addressing this issue. The link is below if you'd like to see how she handles it.

An issue we haven't discussed for selling direct is actually getting people to buy direct. Readers are used to buying from a particular store, have subscriptions, have a payment method set up, and are comfortable with getting ebooks on their devices through them. Convincing them to buy somewhere else may be difficult. Offering books for sale on your website before they release in stores, offering them at a discount, or offering exclusive box sets or stories are a few ways to encourage readers to buy direct.

Finally, selling direct is something for the savvy indie to keep an eye on. It's a great way to connect with readers without losing money to retailers (though there is a small fee involved in the financial transaction). But it does take a little research and work to set up and effort to get readers to buy direct.

References and Resources

BookFunnel. "Deliver Your Ebook and Audiobook Sales." Accessed March 24, 2022. https://authors.BookFunnel.com/help/delivery-actions/.

Kova, Elise. "Licensed Merchandise." Accessed March 24, 2022. https://elisekova.com/interested-in-licencing/.

Penn, Joanna. "How to Sell Ebooks and Audiobooks Direct with Payhip and BookFunnel." *The Creative Penn.* February 19, 2021. https://www.thecreativepenn.com/2021/02/19/sell-ebooks-and-audio-books-direct-with-Payhip-and-BookFunnel/.

Six Figure Authors Podcast. "SFA 017 – Selling Ebooks Direct, Growing Your Newsletter with Bonus Content, and Benefits of In-Person Events with Damon Courtney from BookFunnel." July 19, 2019. https://6figureauthors.com/podcast/selling-ebooks-direct-grow-ing-your-newsletter-with-bonus-content-BookFunnel/.

Six Figure Authors Podcast. "SFA 115 – Making More Money Selling Your Books Direct." January 13, 2022. https://6figureauthors.com/podcast/making-more-money-selling-your-books-direct-katie-cross/.

Six Figure Authors Podcast. "SFA 126 – More Tips for Selling Direct with Katie Cross." March 31, 2022. https://6figureauthors.com/podcast/more-tips-for-selling-direct-with-katie-cross/.

USPS. "Print Click-N-Ship Online Postage." Accessed March 24, 2022. https://www.usps.com/ship/online-shipping.htm.

Chapter 79

Concluding getting the book published and stocked

Most of us grew up going to libraries and bookstores to get our fiction-fill or our questions answered. The draw of print books is still strong. Getting into the larger bookstores isn't easy for an indie, but it's not exactly a guarantee for traditional authors either. But take heart, there are ways to get into some of them, as well as independent bookstores and libraries, and to sell to the public at author events and conventions. And in addition to selling print copies of your work directly to readers, you can also sell ebooks, audiobooks, and merchandise directly through your website.

There are so many opportunities for the indie author! And things are constantly changing, so we never know what will be available—or gone—soon.

This is it for getting your book published. I'll briefly discuss other uses of your IP and formats not covered earlier (including audiobooks and Kindle Vella), then I have a few concluding remarks about being a published author and planning for the future.

Part Eleven

Beyond Ebook and Print

Chapter 80

Beyond ebook and print

One of the amazing things about writing a story or nonfiction piece is that we can use that same intellectual property in a number of ways! For instance, you can use it for ebook, paperback, hardback, audiobook, translations, plays, movies, courses, and study guides. To name a few. In this section (the last before "The End"), we'll talk briefly about the two major writing formats we only glossed over earlier (audiobooks and serials) and other ways to use your intellectual property: plays, screenplays, translations, and foreign rights.

Chapter 81

Audiobooks

Listen up, people! Sorry, couldn't resist. But we are going deeper into audiobooks in this chapter. As a reminder, audiobooks are digital files of your books produced by narrators. When I say *produced*, I mean the narrators not only voice the books but handle the production and sound engineering aspects—all the technical stuff of getting the files ready to be uploaded. They are incredible, hardworking professionals, and they are often referred to as Producers. (Some narrators partner with sound engineers to handle that part of the process, but many do it themselves.)

Audiobooks can be purchased through Audible, Amazon, iTunes, and many other retailers, sold direct through your website, and checked out through libraries (online). Some readers like to purchase the audiobook and ebook together and listen while they read (using Whispersync in Audible). Audiobooks are beloved by those with vision impairments and those who enjoy listening while working around the house, commuting, or exercising. I once had a busy mom thank me for getting audiobooks of my stories made!

How do you get your work produced as an audiobook? How do you get it into stores? How much does it cost? Great questions, and we'll discuss these and more in this chapter. We'll begin with the basics.

The basic process of audiobook production looks like this: find a narrator, hire said narrator, listen to and approve produced audiobook files, upload files to the distributor of your choice, and publish. At this point, you may be wondering if Amazon distributes audiobooks, since they seem to do everything else in the self-publishing industry. And the answer is . . . yes! But not exactly. They own one of the biggest audiobook distributors, ACX. ACX and Findaway Voices are the most commonly used distributors and the two I am familiar with, so I will limit my discussion to them. There are, however, other distributors, and The Alliance of Independent Authors recommends these additional options: Author's Republic, Kobo Writing Life, Lantern (formerly ListenUp Audio), PublishDrive, and Soundwise. You can read more about them here: https://selfpublishingadvice.org/audiobook-publishing-alternatives-to-acx/. ACX, Findaway, and Author's Republic will also connect authors and narrators, thus serving as a place for audiobook creation as well as distribution.

When it comes to audiobook production, your three biggest decisions (after whether or not your book should be made into an audiobook) are your distributor, your narrator, and your budget. These are all tangled together, particularly your budget and your choice of narrator, so let's start by discussing those two, then moving on to distributors.

HOW TO PRODUCE AN AUDIOBOOK: COST AND NARRATORS

From a financial perspective, there are four ways to have audiobooks produced: narrate it yourself, go through Royalty Share, pay upfront with Pay for Production, or sell your audiobook rights to a company to produce it (like traditional publishing, only for audiobooks). Let's briefly look at each method.

Narrate the audiobook yourself

You purchase the necessary equipment, train yourself in voice narration and sound engineering, set up a studio in your home or rent the use of one, narrate the book, do all the sound engineering to bring it up to quality and to match the necessary technical specifications, then distribute it through ACX or Findaway Voices, or the distributor of your choice. You own all the rights to the audiobook.

If you can do all of this and produce a quality audiobook, you're amazing! But if you don't have the background in this and have heard all the people who preach doing it for "free" and so are contemplating it, remember to consider your listeners and make sure they are getting a quality product. That doesn't mean spending money you don't have to gild the lily with a super expensive narrator, but it might mean saving up to spend money on a quality narrator or going through the Royalty Share option. Most of the people who recommend recording yourself are in the nonfiction world. Narrating nonfiction is very different to narrating fiction as it doesn't require different character voices. Ask if the time, effort, and money for equipment to do this yourself is worth it when you could be writing another book instead.

Pay for Production

You can pay upfront for the narrator to produce the audiobook and so own all the rights. Narrators charge a certain amount Per Finished Hour to narrate your book. This can be a very expensive option ($1,000 and up, often) but is generally preferred by those who can afford it. It ensures the narrator is properly compensated and gives the author freedom with how they sell or give away the audiobook.

If you own the book, you can put it up on ACX exclusive (40% royalty) or non-exclusive (25% royalty) to be distributed to Audible, Amazon, and iTunes. If you choose non-exclusive, you can also put it up elsewhere through Findaway or another distributor. You can sell it direct through your website, using a storefront like Payhip to handle the transactions and taxes and using BookFunnel to deliver the files. You can put it up for free on YouTube to try to gain new "readers" there.

Some narrators will want all the agreed upon payment before delivering the final files, but some are willing to work out a payment plan. The cost of Pay for Production can be steep and brings no guarantee of being paid back ever or quickly but is preferred by narrators and gives you more flexibility in what you do with the audiobook. Some authors try to release their audiobook at the same time as their book release, but others choose to wait until sales can fund audiobook production or until all the audiobooks in a series can be produced together. Some authors might try crowdfunding the audiobook version.

————

Let's delve into the cost of Pay for Production. When you pay upfront, you pay by the Per Finished Hour (PFH). So you pay the number of hours in the finished project times the narrator PFH rate. If the audiobook is ten hours long and the narrator's rate is $200 PFH, you would pay $2,000.

To calculate the number of finished hours for an audiobook, ACX recommends dividing the total word count by 9,300, as most performers narrate about 9,300 words per hour. Thus a 90,000-word novel, narrated at the average rate, would be about ten hours (rounding up some). Narrator PFH varies greatly, from $75 at the inexpensive range to much higher ($250 PFH or more, for instance, is common). For simplicity, a 90,000-word novel at $200 PFH would cost $2,000.

How many copies sold would it take to earn back your investment? That depends in part on your royalty rate (which, generally, varies from 20% to 40%, but we'll go into that in the distributor section.)

Royalties of what, you may ask? What will be the retail price of your audiobook? I can tell you like mysteries . . .

In all seriousness, this is something of a misty horizon that only the winds of publication can clear, at least for ACX. It does not let you set the price yourself. Each retailer your audiobook is sent to will decide on the retail price (hence you only know once it's been published). If you distribute through Findaway Voices, you can set your own price, though Audible, Amazon, and iTunes may only take that as a suggestion.

Pricing is largely based on audiobook length, so longer audiobooks are priced higher. There are also different prices for retailers and libraries (with libraries being charged two to three times the retail price). Findaway Voices has an interactive tool that can help you set a good price for each (this tool requires an uploaded audiobook to judge project length, however). You can also search out audiobooks in your genre of comparable length and see what they are priced. Remember that pricing gets really murky where credits and memberships are concerned, so retail prices are for outright purchases only.

ACX does provide a price range, based on audiobook length, for Audible's pricing. It runs as follows:

- under 1 hour: under $7
- 1 - 3 hours: $7 - $10
- 3 - 5 hours: $10 - $20
- 5 - 10 hours: $15 - $25
- 10 - 20 hours: $20 - $30
- over 20 hours: $25 - $35

I have two roughly 60,000-word audiobooks that retail for $19.95 each, and a 120,000-word one that retails for $24.95. Those are distributed through ACX. I have another distributed through ACX for Audible and Amazon and through Findaway Voices for elsewhere. It's 90,000 words long. Findaway suggests a retail list price of $11.50 and a library Cost Per Checkout price of $25.99. Audible gave it a price of $19.95.

This gives you an idea of how much an audiobook retails for, but what does paying yourself back for a Pay for Production audiobook actually look like? It depends on many things, royalty rate and purchase type included (à la carte or subscription credit, for instance). We'll talk more about this in the distribution section, but I'd like to go over a few numbers here to dispel the misconception I had starting out (that I'd earn $8 for every $20 audiobook sold and soon pay myself back.).

Without further ado, here's a very simplified example assuming a 40% royalty, the most you'll receive, and all copies sold through ACX. For your 90,000-word novel that cost $2,000, if it was priced at $20 and you earned $8 from each sale, you would need to sell 250 copies to break even—*if* the copies were bought à la carte (*à la carte* means someone buys it outright). And that's a big *if.* There are many pricing models, and based on my study of ACX's confusing reports, this is what earnings on a $20 audiobook actually look like (generally): $8 per à la carte unit, $4 per membership credit, and $3 per "other." Half of my sales are membership credit, one quarter à la carte, and the remaining quarter "other." If this holds true for other authors, the math, then, to equal $2,000 (just to break even) looks like this, with n being the number of copies needed to break even.

$8(0.25n) + $4(0.5n) + $3(0.25n) = 2,000 —> n= 421 copies

That's for the 40% royalty rate; for the 25% rate, you need to sell 674 copies. This number does not account for returned audiobooks.

As you can see, audiobook earnings are not as cut-and-dried as you'd think from the touted 40% royalty rates, making Pay for Production more of an investment than most realize. Which is why many go with the next method we'll discuss: Royalty Share.

———

Royalty Share, Royalty Share Plus, and Voices Share

Royalty Share (ACX) is when a narrator agrees to produce your audiobook with no upfront charge and in return earn half royalties (you each get 20% of the retail price). Royalty Share Plus (ACX) is when the narrator produces the audiobook at a reduced rate with the agreement that they will also receive half of the royalties. They might ask for an upfront payment of half their normal PFH rate. With both of these, you must be exclusive to ACX for seven years (your audiobook will only sell through Audible, Amazon, and iTunes), though there is a buyout option. Voices Share comes from more narrator-friendly Findaway. Authors pay half the narrator's PFH rate and share 20% of their royalties with the narrator for ten years, leaving them with 60% (20% goes to Findaway, but these are retailer's royalties, not royalties from the retail price). Voices Plus would look like this: If an audiobook retails for $10 and the retailer has a royalty rate of 50%, the royalty is $5. The narrator would receive $1 (20% of $5), Findaway would receive $1, and you would receive $3. The audiobook can only be distributed through Findaway during the ten-year term so they can manage the royalty sharing, but the audiobook is still wide. There is also a buyout option.

Narrators generally prefer Royalty Share Plus or Voices Share because they know they will get something for their work. This is also a way for authors to get a better quality, more experienced narrator at a lower upfront cost.

The Royalty Share option may sound perfect, but you must consider your narrator—will the audiobook earn enough for the narrator to be decently paid for their labor? Is the quality of a narrator willing to work for nothing but future royalties up to scratch? They might be fantastic, or they might not. If you're not experienced with audiobooks, get someone who listens to them frequently and who has a keen ear to help you choose a quality narrator. A poor narrator can ruin a great book. Reviewers can be harsh or give you lots of returns. Also, if you go this route and you use ACX, you must be exclusive with ACX, meaning your audiobook will only be available through Audible, iTunes, and ACX. Audible is the major player in the audiobook world, but it is not the only player.

Sell your audiobook rights to a company to produce it

There are companies that function like traditional publishers for audiobooks. They obtain the rights from you to produce the audiobooks; they pay for production, and then pay you a royalty.

Podium Audio, Tantor, and Oasis Family Media are a few of these. I suspect you need really good sales for them to take on your books. Podium Audio says on their Author Inquiries page, "We do not take unsolicited submissions of unpublished manuscripts, and we do not offer production-for-hire services. However, if you have already published your book on Amazon (or another publishing platform) we will take a look at your listing and be in touch if we are interested in partnering."

HOW TO PRODUCE AN AUDIOBOOK: AUDIOBOOK DISTRIBUTORS

As mentioned earlier, there are two commonly used audiobook distributors: ACX and Findaway Voices. We'll look at both in-depth here.

ACX

ACX (Audiobook Creation Exchange) is a marketplace for professional narrators, authors, publishers, and rights holders to connect and create audiobooks. It is owned by Amazon. Completed audiobooks can be uploaded to ACX for distribution, or authors can search for and find narrators through the site to create audiobooks. ACX will distribute audiobooks to Audible, Amazon, and iTunes. They are currently only open to residents of the US and UK and those who have a US or UK Tax Identification Number. ACX has a royalty rate of between 20% and 40%, depending on whether the audiobook is exclusive to ACX (40%) or not (25%). If the audiobook is exclusive but was produced using Royalty Share, the 40% royalty is split between the author and narrator, 20% to each. ACX sets the price for the audiobook; you do not.

Something else to mentioned is the ACX Bounty Program. This is essentially a referral program. ACX provides a special referral link to your audiobook, and you can include that wherever you promote your book: in your newsletter, social media, or website. If someone uses that link to make their first purchase as a *new* Audible member, then you receive a "bounty." If you own full rights to your audiobook (you paid upfront for it), you earn $75 each time your referral link is used to make the first purchase by a new Audible member. If you used the Royalty Share program, you receive $50 and your narrator receives $25. You earn the Bounty when the Audible member has been a member for 61 days (and thus proves themselves to be a genuine member, not someone gaming the system on your behalf).

ACX's royalty reports, unfortunately, are distressingly complicated, unclear, and part of the contention between authors and ACX (that and their return policy). The net sales are confusing, which is significant since they are what the royalties are ultimately based on, as most customers don't pay the retail list price. A royalty report would include these items:

ALC: audiobooks purchased by those who are not AudibleListener members. These are à la carte purchases.

AL: audiobook units purchased by AudibleListener members using their membership credits.

ALOP: audiobooks purchased by AudibleListener members but not using their membership credits.

Qualified Returns: audiobooks returned within 7 days of fulfillment.

Bounty: bonus payment earned when a qualifying book is the first purchase by a new AudibleListener member.

In your sales report, you earn royalties based on net sales in those categories. However, AL, ALOP and ALC purchases all yield different net sales (you might see different values for à la carte purchases for the same audiobook, for instance), which often don't reflect the retail price. This makes understanding your ACX earnings a nightmare. Let me illustrate with my audiobook *Midnight for a Curse*. The most common single unit ALC net sales from the last few reports was $19.95; for AL, $10.37; for ALOP, $7.49. After studying reports and scouring stores for prices, this is what I inferred: The $7.49 ALOP net sales appears to be the cost of adding the audiobook to the purchase of the ebook as sold on Amazon; the $10.37 AL net sales are for the Audible Listener credits; and the ALC net sales of $19.95 is the cost of the book à la carte from Audible (you can buy it from Audible for $19.95 or from Amazon for $17.46, so the ALC can vary). But this is me guessing, using the reports that make sense. I've seen reports with an ALC of $7.49 (maybe they put the audiobook on sale?) and an ALOP of $13.96; and, most confusing, are the ones with the net sales of $1, $2, or $3 where I received no royalties. I say all this to illustrate that I rarely earn a royalty based on the full price of $19.95 (only for some ALC sales, which account for less than one-fourth of my sales). As we've already discussed, you won't be earning $8 per $20 audiobook sold as often as you might initially think (or $4 if you used Royalty Share). Given that half of my sales are AL, $4 is a much more common royalty.

ACX does offer promo codes for free copies of your audiobook (25 for the US and 25 for the UK), for you to give away in hopes of gaining reviews and reaching new readers.

Let's move on to Findaway Voices now.

Findaway Voices

Findaway Voices is an audiobook distributor and is connected to Findaway Voices Marketplace, an audiobook creation platform. It's a wide platform and does not require exclusivity. They distribute to Audible, Amazon, iTunes, and many additional stores, including Walmart, Kobo, Chirp, and library provider OverDrive. You can upload a finished audiobook to them to be distributed to retailers, or you can find and work with a narrator through the marketplace, as with ACX. You can pay the narrator upfront or pursue their Voices Share option. Authors get an 80% share of the *retailer's royalty*, set the price themselves (though some retailers will choose their own list price), and can participate in promotions (you can put it on sale!). You can get promo codes to use through the Author's Direct app to give it away for review, or, if you own all the rights, you can put it up on a storefront and give away coupons for it.

Let's look more in-depth at Findaway's royalties. Findaway takes a 20% fee for their work, leaving authors with 80%, but this is not like selling through KDP, where you get a royalty based on the *retail price*. Findaway is a middleman, essentially, who has bargained with retailers on your behalf. These bargains set forth the royalty rate that you receive from that partner and that Findaway takes their cut from. This is the *retailer's royalty* and might be between 32% and 50% of the retail price. For an example of pricing, if the audiobook is priced at $10 and paid for à la carte, and the distribution partner gives a 50% royalty, leaving a royalty of $5 to be divided between you and Findaway, you can get 80% of the $5: $4. If the retailer puts your audiobook on sale, you still get the same royalty; they take the cut from the sale, not you. This is the à la carte business model for retailers.

Additionally, there's the credit subscription model, two unlimited subscription models (Combined Portions and Pool Subscriptions), and two library models (One-copy, One-use; and Cost Per Checkout). In the credit subscription model, customers pay with a credit, and you earn a royalty based on the audiobook list price as for an à la carte purchase. However, certain partners (including Apple, Amazon, and Audible) will set their own price, affecting your payment. For the unlimited subscription models (like Netflix for audiobooks), royalty amounts tend to be lower than for other retail models, and are based on the amount of the audiobook listened to, but you are reaching a huge new audience who can try out your book without the barrier of making a purchase. For the two library models, One-copy, One-use is similar to the à la carte model, with the library buying one copy and only allowing one patron at a time to listen to it. Yes, you only get paid once no matter how many times the audiobook is listened to, which is why Findaway recommends you set the library list price two to three times higher than the retail price. In the Cost Per Checkout model, the library pays a small amount each time a patron borrows your audiobook.

I don't have enough data from Findaway to tell you much here, except that most of my sales have been to libraries (that particular audiobook is distributed to Audible and Amazon through ACX, and elsewhere through Findaway, so this is not surprising).

Once you've considered your choice of distributor and your budget (your PFH rate or that you will do Royalty Share, Royalty Share Plus, or Voices Plus), it will be time to search for a narrator.

HOW TO FIND AND WORK WITH A NARRATOR

Finding a narrator and finding the *right* narrator for your audiobook aren't the same thing. Here's a few tips for choosing and working with narrators, as well as suggestions for where to find them. Findaway can suggest narrators for you.

How to find a narrator:

- Check the audiobooks of your comparable authors and see who their narrators are. Listen to the samples and see if you like them. Read the reviews.
- Make a note of any narrators you enjoy from books you've listened to.
- Search the profiles of narrators on marketplaces such as ACX, Findaway, and Author's Republic.
- Search hiring services such as Fiverr and Upwork.
- Ask around author groups for recommendations.

If you go through a marketplace, you can search narrator profiles and listen to samples to find a favorite, or you can post your title information in the marketplace, along with what you want in a narrator (gender, age, accents, style, and so on), marketing strategies, and a short sample of your book (an audition script), for narrators to find. Interested narrators will submit their auditions to you, and you can choose from among them. You and the narrator will agree on terms (Pay for Production and PFH rate, Royalty Share or Royalty Share Plus, and timeline). Once you've reached an agreement, you'll send the narrator an electronic copy of your work that they can print out and mark up, and any notes on pronunciations, character voices, and so forth. Then the narrator will produce the audiobook chapter by chapter. You will listen to each chapter, making suggestions as needed. Once you approve the finished audiobook and pay the narrator, the distributor will do a quality control check on it, then release it. You can set or request a specific release date.

If you find a narrator outside a marketplace, consider asking if they wish to work through one of the marketplaces. Working through ACX or Findaway offers a bit of a safety net and may be preferred by the narrator.

I recommend finding several narrators whom you like, then contacting them to inquire about their availability, price, and timeframe. Ask them to do an audition (this is really important!). Then choose from there, taking a few other considerations into account as well.

Here are things to consider when choosing a narrator:

- Quality of their audition and other samples.
- Cost.
- Availability.
- Audience expectations—a male narrator, a female narrator, dual narration? Young or more mature? Accent? Genres have their own expectations for narrators just like they do

for covers and tropes. Be familiar with these and take them into account.

- Popularity. Some listeners follow narrators like some readers follow authors, so choosing a popular narrator may be beneficial in gaining listeners. It might mean your narrator is more expensive, however.
- Experience. How many audiobooks have they produced? How do these rate? Are they in your genre?
- Will you work well together? How will they react to needed changes?
- Future availability, if you're doing a series.

———

Audiobooks require a square cover, and you can ask your cover designer to design one to match your book cover. It's usually a reasonable add-on fee. As for marketing, many find that marketing their ebooks (growing your newsletter, gaining reviews, ads, promoting sales) helps boost audiobook sales. Chirp, which is associated with BookBub, has a newsletter to announce audiobook sales (the audiobook must be available on Chirp). Audio Thicket (associated with book promotion site Freebooksy) also has an audiobook promotion service. You can use your promo codes to gain reviews and reach new readers. There are Facebook groups devoted to connecting listeners to authors with review copies (these have variable review rates, however), review websites, and a Goodreads group as well. Audiobook marketing is still young, with new avenues in development. We'll see what develops for this popular format.

Audiobooks are a growing market and are beloved—and deeply appreciated—by many.

Audiobooks summary:

- Audiobooks need a distributor. Options include ACX, Findaway, Author's Republic, and others.

- They can be paid for upfront through Pay for Production or through Royalty Share, which requires no upfront cost, only a royalty split.
- Pay for Production cost is determined by the number of finished hours for an audiobook times the narrator's PFH rate.
- PFH rates range from $75 up, with $250 or more being common.

References and Resources

ACX. "Bounty Referral Program." https://www.acx.com/help/bounty-referral-program/UEF9JUCH9AZEKA4.

ACX. "How Long Will My Narrated Book Be?" https://help.acx.com/s/article/how-long-will-my-narrated-audiobook-be.

ACX. "How Much Will My Audiobook Sell for in Stores?" https://help.acx.com/s/article/how-much-will-my-audiobook-sell-for-in-stores.

ACX. "The Basics." https://www.acx.com/help/general/200474410.

ALLi. "Audiblegate Campaign: Fair Deal for Rights Holders." Accessed March 21, 2022. https://www.allianceindependentauthors.org/audible-campaign/.

Authors Republic. https://www.authorsrepublic.com.

Chesson, Dave. "Audiobook Narrators: A List of Our Recommendations." *Kindlepreneur.* March 24, 2022. https://kindlepreneur.com/audiobook-narrators/.

Cross, Colleen. "The Truth Behind Audible Subscription Earnings." *Self-Publishing Advice.* February 20, 2021. https://selfpublishingadvice.org/the-truth-behind-audible-subscription-earnings/.

Doppler, John. "Audiobook Publishing Alternatives to ACX: A Comparison." *Self-Publishing Advice.* April 8, 2021. https://selfpublishingadvice.org/audiobook-publishing-alternatives-to-acx/.

Findaway Voices. https://findawayvoices.com.

Findaway Voices Blog. "How to Calculate Your Audiobook Royalties." May 17, 2018. https://blog.findawayvoices.com/how-to-calculate-your-audiobook-royalties/.

Findaway Voices Blog. "Marketplace Is Open for Authors." February 14, 2022. https://blog.findawayvoices.com/marketplace-is-open/.

Hamilton, Jason. "How To Make An Audiobook: Publishing on ACX and Audiobook Marketing." *Kindlepreneur.* April 6, 2022. https://kindlepreneur.com/how-to-make-an-audiobook/.

Chapter 82

Kindle Vella

Ever since Charles Dickens released *The Pickwick Papers* in nineteen installments over a twenty-month period, stories published as serials have had a place in the world of story telling. Sites such as Wattpad, Kindle Vella, Radish Fiction, Webnovel, and others carry on this tradition. Bite-sized serial fiction has become quite popular in international markets, such as China, South Korea, and Japan, and is gaining notice in the US. It's little wonder, then, that Amazon created and is pushing its own platform for bite-sized serial stories: Kindle Vella. Is it something to try? Some authors swear by serials, or at least their experience on Wattpad, others have abandoned them, and some have never tried them.

If they are something you already indulge in, then you might consider it. If not, before you run out to try earning extra money on them (such as from Vella), or building a fan base (such as on Wattpad), remember that writing a serial is *not* the same as chopping up a novel into small pieces. There is an art to writing serials, just as there is for writing short stories and epics. They are also not a way to essentially blog your book bit by bit to keep you accountable. On Vella, people are paying for each "episode" of your story published, so it must be professional.

If writing a serial is an art you want to learn, then go forth and create excellent works for these platforms. If not, don't get caught up in the hype or feel you have to try it to be an author. Also, for free platforms, consider whether readers looking for free material will be willing to pay for your books later. And for paid platforms, if the pay is worth your time?

Since it's always good to keep up with what customer-savvy Amazon does, let's look into publishing with Kindle Vella. I should also note that Vella is mobile-centric, so the idea is that people are reading short pieces on their phone through the Kindle app.

Publishing on Kindle Vella

Publishing on Kindle Vella is straightforward and doesn't even require a formatted book. It's more like publishing a blog post in many ways. You can upload a docx or doc file, or type your work directly into the online editor.

You reach your Vella dashboard through your Amazon KDP dashboard. You'll then be taken to "Your Kindle Vella Library." Click "Start a story." This will take you to a "Tell us about your story" page, where you'll fill in information on your story: whether it's complete or ongoing, the story title, author name, story description, story image, categories, and story tags (which are like keywords).

The story image is the equivalent of a cover image, only it's without a title or author name (so just an eye-catching image). Vella recommends that this be a square (1600 x 1600 pixels, 72 DPI minimum; JPEG or TIFF), rather than the vertical rectangle of an ebook cover. However, it shows up as a circle in the store, so keep that in mind. You can easily search online for "Kindle Vella covers" and buy a cheap pre-made or ask your favorite cover designer to make one (be sure they understand what a Vella image is, as it's not a regular book cover). The story image is for the entire story, thus each episode does not need its own image. Story images are typically $100 or less.

Your Kindle Vella story is published as episodes (typically between 600-5,000 words long), with the first three episodes available to readers for free. After that, readers buy tokens, which they can then use to "unlock" episodes. Tokens are purchased in bundles. Currently, the pricing structure is 200 tokens for $1.99; 525 for $4.99; 1,100 for $9.99; 1,700 for $14.99.

The number of tokens required to unlock an episode varies by episode length. One hundred words of length requires one token. So a 3,025 word story would be unlocked for 30 tokens. Amazon offers 200 tokens for free to get readers started.

Authors earn 50% of the revenue from token redemption. However, not every token is worth the same. There's a bulk discount effect on tokens bought in the large bundles, which Amazon takes into account when paying royalties (example below). In addition, there's a small fee, like a credit card fee, associated with the purchase of tokens, which is deducted from the revenue that is shared. Authors are also eligible for a bonus based on customer activity: redemption of free and paid tokens, Faves, and Follows (discussed later).

———

Here's how royalty earnings per episode are calculated:

(Number of Tokens to unlock episode) x (Tokens bundle price/# Tokens in bundle - taxes and fees) x (50% rev share) = Earnings per episode

For example, let's look at a 2,000 word episode, which would cost 20 tokens, when the tokens are purchased in a 200 Tokens bundle versus a 1,700 Tokens bundle. Taxes or fees are not included.

Episode purchased with 200 Tokens bundle:
20 Tokens x ($1.99/200 Tokens - 0) x 50% = $0.0995

Tokens are $0.00995 each in the 200 Tokens bundle. A 2,000 word episode is worth about ten cents.

Episode purchased with 1,700 Tokens bundle:
20 Tokens x ($14.99/1,700 Tokens - 0) x 50% = $0.0882

Tokens are $0.00882 each in the 1,700 Token bundle. A 2,000-word story is worth about nine cents.

This means that you might make $0.25 for every reader who bought a 5,000-word episode at the 200-Token tier. If your story had, say, 25 episodes of the same length, that's $6.25 per reader who finishes the story.

If a reader purchased that 5,000-word episode from a 1,700 Token bundle, you would earn $0.22 for that episode. Assuming a story of 25 episodes of the same length, that's $5.50 for the complete story.

This would be a final story word count of 125,000 words, which, as an ebook, you'd likely price at $4.99, giving a royalty of $3.43 at a 70% royalty rate with $0.09 delivery fee. As for a KU comparison, my 120,000-word novel *To Catch a Magic Thief* has a Kindle Edition Normalized Page Count (KENPC) of 603. Using an estimate of $0.004 per page, that's $2.41.

If a reader purchased all the episodes of your serialized story, then you'd actually get more per story through this platform (at least in this example). But there's no guarantee a reader will read through. If they're purchasing an ebook, you get the money upfront. In addition to a higher profit, there is also the audience factor. You might be reaching a different audience here, who might go on to buy your full-length works (or not). It might be worth it to release a story this way, then remove it and bundle it into an ebook as a full novel (assuming the story structure works both ways). However, remember that the content for Vella needs to be polished and publication ready. Also consider how your main readership (if you're publishing full-length ebooks and print books) will react if the stories they are waiting for are delayed to be sent through Kindle Vella. It might be worth a try, or not, depending on your goals, preferred story style, audience, and time.

Kindle Vella is an interactive platform. While readers can leave reviews and give star ratings on Amazon, they can interact with stories and individual episodes by choosing to "Follow" stories they enjoy so they will be notified as each new episode is released. They can "Fave" the story they enjoyed most that week, giving it a "crown." Readers can also give a "Thumbs Up" to episodes they enjoyed reading. Authors can "connect" with readers by leaving author notes for each story.

KDP recommends that you release frequently and tell readers when to expect new episodes (such as every Friday and Monday). You cannot chop up a story already published to sell as a serial or sell one available for free elsewhere. You can publish on Kindle Vella, then later unpublish and compile your story into a book. You can publish the serial on other sites dedicated to serials so long as they are behind a paywall. In short, you can only publish original content not available for free elsewhere. This original content can be a completely new story world, or material related to your current series. This could be a great way to give your readers more of a story world or additional material about their favorite characters without writing a new book.

Summary of Kindle Vella:

- Serials are bite-sized stories and an art unto themselves, not chopped up novels.
- Amazon has a new platform for serials called Kindle Vella, which can be reached through the KDP dashboard.
- Kindle Vella publishes stories in episodes (600-5,000 words long) that readers unlock with tokens.
- Tokens are bought in bundles of different sizes, yielding tokens of different values.
- You earn a 50% royalty of the token value times tokens used.
- Kindle Vella requires a square story image with no text.
- Word documents are unloaded to Kindle Vella or the episode is written directly in the online editor.

References and Resources

Amazon KDP. "Kindle Vella - Publish an Episode." Accessed April 5, 2022. https://kdp.amazon.com/en_US/help/topic/GQXRPEL7X6FLCRRH.

Amazon KDP. "Kindle Vella - Reader Experience." Accessed April 5, 2022. https://kdp.amazon.com/en_US/help/topic/G6F5YEPRLMKR3PV7.

Amazon KDP. "Kindle Vella - Royalties, Reporting, and Payments." Accessed April 5, 2022. https://kdp.amazon.com/en_US/help/topic/G5TFR9WSHB46ZKFN.

Amazon KDP. "Kindle Vella - Start a Story." Accessed April 5, 2022. https://kdp.amazon.com/en_US/help/topic/GKWM7L5U6ESNFT5X#storydetails.

Chesson, Dave. "Wattpad Review: Is Wattpad Really Worth It?" *Kindlepreneur.* January 3, 2022. https://kindlepreneur.com/wattpad-review/.

Hamilton, Jason. "Kindle Vella: Description, Features, and Tips for Authors." *Kindlepreneur.* Accessed March 25, 2022. https://kindlepreneur.com/kindle-vella/.

Radish Fiction. https://www.radishfiction.com.

Wattpad. https://www.wattpad.com.

Webnovel. https://www.webnovel.com.

Chapter 83

Plays and screenplays

Turning your novel into visual formats, such as plays and screenplays, are other popular uses of your intellectual property. It's beyond the scope of this guide (and my expertise!) to discuss them in depth, but since many, if not most, of us have dreamed of having our books turned into movies or TV shows, I did want to mention a few things involving the film industry and share some references on screenwriting and the business of being "in the movies."

Getting your book turned into a movie generally doesn't turn out to be the dream authors imagine. From the conference speakers I've heard, it's a long, difficult road. You know how many stories are lost in their adaptations, with the movie and books seeming like separate things entirely. Depending on if your greatest love is the money and fame or the story itself, this can really hurt. There is also the pain of having your story optioned but never produced. (I'm not sure I would mind this, though, since I get paid anyway!)

But wait, what's an option and how do you get paid without your movie being turned into a book? An option is when a production company or studio reserves the right to make your story into a film, TV movie (Movie of the Week), or TV show. This is only for a specific length of time, such as a year to eighteen months. The standard option also includes the possibility of two renewable one-year options.

They are essentially paying you to hold on to your film/TV rights (not sell them to anyone else) for a specified length of time while they try to secure the funds for the adaptation and get a scriptwriter (this could be, but isn't likely to be you). They may renew your option, let it lapse, or, possibly, actually produce the movie. In this case, you will get the purchase sale money. It's much more common to get an option, or multiple ones, than a "green light" to have the work produced.

You will likely need a literary agent or lawyer with expertise in this area or a film agent.

References and Resources

Act One. "Hollywood Writing Program." https://actoneprogram.com/online-writing-program/.

Baehr, Ted. *How to Succeed in Hollywood (Without Losing Your Soul): A Field Guide for Christian Screenwriters, Actors, Producers, Directors, and More.* WND Books, 2011.

Bloom, Alex. "7 Steps For Adapting Your Novel Into A Screenplay." *The Creative Penn.* December 13, 2017. https://www.thecreativepenn.com/2017/12/13/adapting-novel-screenplay/.

Rosen, Fred. "Selling Your Book's Movie and TV Rights: What You Need to Know." *Writer's Digest.* September 25, 2012. https://www.writersdigest.com/whats-new/selling-your-books-movie-and-tv-rights-what-you-need-to-know.

Snyder, Blake. *Save The Cat! The Last Book on Screenwriting You'll Ever Need.* Michael Wiese Productions, 2005.

Chapter 84

Translations and foreign rights

Translations and foreign rights are a great use of your intellectual property and a way to share your work with others.

Foreign rights are the right to publish your book in its original language in countries other than the original country of publication. In other words, for a book published in English in the US, the right to sell it in English in Germany or Japan or the UK would be a foreign right.

Translation rights are the right to publish in languages other than the book's original language. Creating a French edition of a novel that was originally published in English would be a use of translation rights.

Using your foreign rights is actually quite easy as retailers have international stores. When you check in the KDP dashboard that you have worldwide rights to your book and can sell in all territories, you are using your foreign rights. If the box is checked, KDP will make the book available in English in their foreign marketplaces. I have sold books in Canada, the UK, India, Mexico, Germany, Australia, Japan, and other countries this way. Amazon even recommends setting up an Author Central account in its overseas Kindle stores to further your international presence. These accounts would be in English since the books are in English.

However, this is only selling through Amazon's stores, which don't dominate the overseas market. If you want more control and to reach other stores, you can consider getting a foreign rights agent, similar to a literary agent for traditional publishing. You can also contact foreign publishers yourself via email, or you might meet them at an international book fair, such as the Frankfurt Book Fair, London Book Fair, and Book Expo America in New York City.

Two resources for locating foreign agents and international publishers are The International Literary Market Place (https://www.literarymarketplace.com/lmp/us/index_us.asp) and IPR License (https://frankfurtrights.com).

When contacting a foreign rights agent or publisher, you will want a sell sheet with a summary of the book, reviews, endorsements, sales figures, author biography, and links to your website and Amazon author page.

For translations, you would need the book translated, of course. A foreign publisher might do this or you can have it done yourself. This—assuming it is done well—will be costly, so take that into consideration.

If you plan to pursue foreign rights or translation rights, know that it requires a lot of research and consideration, not to mention legal savvy, as you'd be signing contracts. You should also ask if your book works well in the international market, as some are more universal than others. And if you do this, be sure to adjust your territories with your retailer accordingly.

References and Resources

IPR License. https://frankfurtrights.com.

Knight, Matt. "Selling Foreign Rights – It is easier than you think!" *Sidebar Saturdays.* November 11, 2017. https://www.sidebarsaturdays.com/2017/11/11/httpswp-mep7vddb-x3/.

Orna Ross and Helen Sedwick. "Selling Your Books Internationally." *Jane Friedman.* February 6, 2019. https://www.janefriedman.com/selling-books-internationally/.

Six Figure Authors Podcast. "SFA 081 - Selling Foreign Rights and Pitching at Book Fairs with Judith Anderle." March 11, 2021. https://6figureauthors.com/podcast/selling-foreign-rights-and-pitching-at-book-fairs/.

The International Literary Market Place. https://www.literarymarketplace.com/lmp/us/index_us.asp.

Chapter 85

Concluding beyond ebook and print

There are many exciting uses for your intellectual property and many formats to write in. Audiobooks and serials are gaining in popularity with readers and authors. Companies such as ACX and Findaway Voices make it relatively easy to find and work with narrators to produce and sell audiobooks. Kindle Vella offers an intriguing new format to KDP authors for serialized fiction. Translations and foreign rights are ways to expand your audience overseas.

Reaching new readers, serving those who need audiobook versions, and diversifying your income through an extensive use of your IP is something to consider.

Now, it's time to wrap up.

Part Twelve

The End

Chapter 86

The End

You've made it to The End of your manuscript, the end of the publishing process, the end of this book, but what now? What is being a published author like?

Most of the time, life is no different, but then sometimes . . . sometimes you get emails from fans who love your books. People you know or vaguely recognize will come up to you to talk about your book (in a quiet or an enthusiastic manner) or to talk about the books they want to write or that you should write. Your friends will introduce you as an author, and your new acquaintances may or may not be impressed. You'll be able to connect with certain people through a shared love of writing, which is truly wonderful. You'll be asked for advice on writing or publishing by your friends for themselves and for their friends. After a few years, you might get asked to speak at events. You may also get bad reviews and disappointed or angry fans. You may have coffee with someone from your town whose brother gifted her a jump drive he found at an airport exactly one year from the date you lost a jump drive somewhere at or between Dallas, TX, and Birmingham, AL, and who just happens to have aspirations of being a writer. You never know what being an author will entail. But it's a wonderful gift, red ink and all.

I would like to leave you with three pieces of advice.

First, remember your goals for writing and your purpose. I write because God gave me a talent for it and a passion for it. To not write would be disobedient to his design for my life. I also want to create quality stories readers will enjoy and come away the better for them. I want to teach and help people through my nonfiction. I want to earn money from my labor and enjoy the relationships I've formed in the writing community.

Write down your goals, your author brand, and your purpose to help you stay on track when things are hard or when you just need stability and focus.

And remember that to be a writer means you write. Writing great books, and more great books, generally comes before marketing and social media. And consequently, the more great books you have, the more marketing you can do. So don't get hung up on your first book by trying to make it a best seller, a replacement for your day job, and the next Hollywood blockbuster. Keep writing and growing.

Second, learn how to deal with fans well. Be nice to and patient with the critical and mean ones. Learn how to accept the admiration of the starstruck, who think it's amazing that they've met an author (even if you know how few copies you've sold compared to the authors this person is likely thinking of), and to talk about your books with those who've actually read them. And if you write fantasy, you'd better get your world building straight, because you will meet people who love to talk about that sort of thing and who will ask about any parts of your books that didn't make sense to them.

Remember that people read a lot of books; don't expect them, even your super fans, to remember all the details of your book. You are just one of many favorite authors to them. They read quickly and so may not remember things with the clarity you do. Though some may remember your books better than you do!

There will be several comments and questions you'll get regularly as an author. If attention or self-promotion bothers you, come up with "canned" responses ahead of time to help yourself out. You also need to decide if and how you want to help aspiring writers. Don't be afraid to say no to requests. You might also need to burst some bubbles about publishing a book being a simple matter of sending it to an English teacher to "edit" and then putting it up on Amazon for instant fame and fortune.

Here are some comments and questions to prepare for:

- What do you write?
- Where can I find your book? Is it in the local bookstore?
- How did you become an author?
- When did you start writing?
- What's your author name? My [sister/aunt/kindergarten teacher/whoever] loves to read. I'll tell them about your books.
- You're an author? I'd like to read your books. [Having bookmarks with your website or Amazon author page is helpful here.]
- I've always wanted to write a book but [insert excuse here].
- How do you finish your books? I've never managed that.
- Where do you get your ideas?
- I have this book idea. Want to help me write it?
- You should write this idea. [Expounds on idea.]
- You shouldn't write fantasy if you're a Christian. [Be kind and know your theology.]
- My friend is writing a book. [Continue with request for help.]
- Will you sign my book?
- It's so cool I know an author!
- Are indie authors "real" authors?
- You write fantasy with magic! I play Dungeons and Dragons and would love to talk about your magic system.
- You're an author! You must be rich. [Cue laughter by said author.]
- How many copies have you sold?

In truth, when you get into the indie author world, depending on your personality, of course, being an author starts to lose its shine. You know *lots* of authors now, and you know they do laundry just like everyone else. They aren't a rare breed anymore; most aren't household names, so it can be hard to accept whatever stardom you receive. Rather than trying to disillusion people, consider acting like a gracious royal instead. If meeting an author makes people feel special, accept the role of the "royal" with poise and grace, for their sake. I don't mean you're to brag or look down on anyone because you're an author. You're simply not going on about how authors are just people because you're embarrassed by praise or attention. That's not what this is about. This is about *them* feeling special. If you tear yourself or the profession down in an attempt to be humble, you rob them of the feeling that someone special is paying them attention. (If you're busy being "humble," the focus is on you, which isn't really being humble. There are a lot of bad notions of what being humble is, so I thought I'd throw that in.)

Third, learn how to deal with reviews. I've mentioned this before, but I'll go into more depth here. This is a hard thing for most of us. Our books are our babies. We don't want people disparaging them or us, and bad reviews can feel like a personal insult. Sometimes our fans don't like our latest projects, or stop liking us altogether. This goes with the territory. Bad reviews aren't fun, but if you want to be a professional author, you gotta learn to take them. Actually, some bad reviews are so ridiculous they're kinda amusing, but some really hurt. Not everyone is the right reader for your books, and that's fine. Some may disagree with your worldview or have very wrong expectations for your book and are mad when it doesn't live up to them. Let readers have their opinions. Bad reviews, in isolation, likely won't hurt your book much, if at all. The things some complain about may be what another reader wants, and that bad review might induce them to buy the book for that aspect or convince them to find out for themselves which reviewers—the lovers or the haters—are right.

Some authors never read their reviews to avoid getting distracted by the hurtful and the positive ones. Some obsess over them to an unhealthy degree. They get hurt, angry, despondent, and may even let a few bad reviews wreck their confidence, causing them to lose sight of the positive ones. If you read your reviews, read them carefully and dispassionately. Be grateful for the positive ones and cautious with the negative ones. Ask what there is to learn from them. Reviews shouldn't be treated like an ego boost but a way to learn what your readers want and don't want. Did many of them rave about a certain secondary character? Maybe consider giving that character a bigger role in the rest of the series, or a novel of his/her own. Did they complain about the few "bad" words you used? Maybe they lauded your humor, something you hadn't thought much about, or considered to be a strength. You might also discover some flaw in your writing you need to work on—that's useful too. Your reviews, coupled with sales, might let you know that a book or series just isn't resonating with your readers. This might be something you can fix (maybe you're targeting the wrong readers or need to work on an aspect of your craft) or you may need to consider moving on to a different series.

Use your reviews to help you figure out who your readers are and aren't, and what they do and don't want. You want to make your readers happy. Whether that "happy" is a novel that wrenches their hearts and leaves them crying or one that makes them laugh until their sides hurt, our job as entertainers is to make them happy. Honest reviews are a way to learn how to do our job better, providing we approach it wisely and humbly.

This knowing what to take and what to leave in reviews and critiques of any kind is a tough skill to acquire. It's important to have a few *honest* friends, who are knowledgeable in writing or at least in judging books, who know your books and who are in your audience, to help you sort through them. At least until you figure out how to do this yourself.

You have to know who you are as a writer too. I write adventure-romance stories set in fantasy worlds. One agent I really respect rejected a manuscript of mine with a mix of praise and censure, the censure being that the female main character's POV "devolved into a romance." Looking at his other comments, it became clear he wanted an epic fantasy, but that's not what the novel was meant to be. I could have taken his advice to heart and ripped up the novel and forced it into something else, or abandoned it. But I talked to a few wise friends who knew my books and were in my target audience. They assured me what I had was what *my* readers wanted. It simply wasn't what this agent wanted. I published the book myself, and my readers were happy with it. So you don't need to take every piece of feedback to heart.

In short, remember who you are as a writer, stay focused on your goals, learn to enjoy your interactions with the admiring—or not-so-admiring—public, and keep writing.

This is the part where, as a writer of fairy tales, I get to say "and they lived happily ever after [and published many wonderful books]. The End."

————

If you would like a compiled list of all the resources and references listed in this book, plus additional author resources, visit my website at https://www. ejkitchens.com/author-resources.

Acknowledgments

It's impossible to express how much I owe to the many, many authors, literary agents, podcasters, book marketers, and others who have knowingly or unknowingly helped me over the years through the generous sharing of their knowledge and experience. I am very grateful for these "mentors." And for my family and friends who've patiently listened to me talk on and on about indie publishing, who've encouraged me, and who've read my books. A very special thanks to my sister Julie, who inspired this book! Also to my beta readers: David, Megan, Michala, Lauricia, Ann, Brittany, Ted, Emily, Laura, and Diane. To my fantastic editor, Jasmine, and my talented cover designer, Megan, who made the work presentable.

And a huge round of applause for my readers, those kind souls and kindred spirits I get to share my worlds and characters with! *Soli Deo gloria.*

About the Author

E.J. KITCHENS loves tales of romance, adventure, and happily-ever-afters and strives to write such tales herself. When she's not thinking about dashing heroes or how awesome bacteria are—she's a biologist, after all—she's enjoying the beautiful outdoors or talking about classic books and black-and-white movies. She is a member of Realm Makers and lives in Alabama. While she mostly writes fantasy, she also enjoys editing and writing about writing.

May she beg a favor of you? You've already kindly read her book; would you also leave a review? Those gold stars can power more than fictional worlds: they encourage, inspire, and help authors through hurdles so we can seek out the people looking for books like ours to read. It's a daunting quest, and without you, fearless reader, it would fail. Would you join it?

To learn more about E.J. Kitchens and her books, visit her website and sign up for her newsletter: www.ejkitchens.com.

Also by E.J. Kitchens

THE MAGIC COLLECTORS: Of Magic and Mirrors

THE ROSE AND THE WAND*

TO CATCH A MAGIC THIEF*

THE MAGIC COLLECTORS: Of Magic Made

WROUGHT OF SILVER AND RAVENS, book 1

WROUGHT OF SERPENT AND SNOW, book 2

THE MAGIC COLLECTORS: Realm and Wand

THE KING'S SPELL, book 1

THE KING'S ENCHANTRESS, book 2

CURSE KEEPER, CURSE BREAKER

MIDNIGHT FOR A CURSE*

CURSED FOR KEEPS*

THE STAR CLOCK CHRONICLES

Beginning with "Dawn Bringer"

SHORTER WORKS AND nonfiction

"Caught on Film" (Mistry and Wilder series)

"A Spell's End" (ENCIRCLED)

"How to Hide a Prince" (TALES OF EVER AFTER)

"The Seventh Crown"

PEN TO PRINT: A BEGINNER'S GUIDE TO SELF-PUBLISHING

*Also available as an audiobook

Notes

Notes

Notes